A LIFE OF CONTRASTS

A LIFE
OF
CONTRASTS

THE AUTOBIOGRAPHY OF
DIANA MITFORD MOSLEY

Times
BOOKS

First published in Great Britain in 1977 by Hamish Hamilton, Ltd.

Library of Congress Cataloging in Publication Data

Mosley, Diana, Lady, 1910-
A life of contrasts.

Includes index.
1. Mosley, Diana, Lady, 1910-
2. England—Biography. 3. Mosley, Oswald,
Sir, bart., 1896- I. Title.
CT788.M66A35 1978 941.082′092′4 [B] 77-93053
ISBN 0-8129-0758-2

CONTENTS

(Illustrations follow page 152)

A LIFE OF CONTRASTS

1

Grandfathers and Grandmother

NEITHER OF MY grandfathers had a conventional Victorian family upbringing. Algernon Bertram Mitford, youngest of three sons, was born in 1837, and not long afterwards his mother, Lady Georgina Ashburnham, ran away from his father, Henry Mitford, and went to live with Francis Molyneux whom she subsequently married.

Bertram was sent to Eton at the age of eight. He had been there some years when his first cousin and exact contemporary Algernon Charles Swinburne joined him. He mentions this in his *Memories*, adding that the aureole of golden hair ascribed to the poet as a boy was really ordinary red. One detects a certain irritation in his references to Swinburne, probably because of the fame of his remarkable cousin and also because of his doubtful reputation and eccentric behaviour. Grandfather was very conventional.

After school and Oxford Bertram Mitford joined the Diplomatic service and served in Russia and the Far East. He fell in love with Japan, which when he was there en poste was just emerging from its centuries-old isolation; he saw a medieval Japan hardly changed since the days of Lady Murasaki which was thenceforward quickly to disappear. A notable linguist who could speak both Chinese and Japanese, he translated a number of Japanese legends and stories; his *Tales of Old Japan* was a success and was reprinted several times.

When he was thirty-seven he married Lady Clementine Ogilvy; they had nine children. Their eldest son was killed in the First World War, and when Grandfather died in 1916 my father inherited.

Grandmother idolized her husband and his children revered him. It so happens that everything he did and everything he admired is now completely out of fashion, beginning with Batsford, in Gloucestershire, where he built a large 'Tudor' house. His garden, once famous, is just the opposite of what most people now think a garden should be; drifts of daffodils in the grass are considered gaudy, blue cedars beyond the pale though they are still planted in the suburbs of Paris, a favoured setting for municipal playing fields.

The style of his memoirs is equally unfashionable; there is nothing about his states of mind, or his wife and children or the mother who ran away. As to Houston Stewart Chamberlain, whom he so greatly reverenced, to say that he is out of fashion would be understatement; he is abhorred as one of the most pernicious and wrong-minded thinkers ever to put pen to paper. His long books were lovingly translated one after another by Grandfather, who made the journey to Bayreuth not only for the music but also in order to see Chamberlain who married Wagner's daughter Eva. He became friends with the whole family. Winifred Wagner told me that Grandfather's photograph always stood on Siegfried Wagner's writing table.

He was devoted to King Edward VII and helped him with the garden at Sandringham. The King once visited Batsford and upset my puritanical Grandmother by asking for Mrs. Keppel to be invited. About sixty years later Kitty Ritson told me: 'Mother and I were to have gone to Batsford for the King's visit, but at the last moment Mother said that I must be left behind. When I asked why, she said it was because a *great friend* of the King's was to be there,' an explanation which puzzled Kitty at the time.

In old age Grandfather became almost stone deaf; he occupied himself with gardening, playing patience and reading Nietzsche, immured in a silent world. He had spent his fortune on Batsford so that when he died a great deal had to be sold; as a family we were always short of money.

Grandfather Bowles was a very different person. Born in 1843 he was the illegitimate son of an early Victorian cabinet minister, Milner Gibson. Except that her name was Susan Bowles, nobody knows who his mother was. Tom Bowles's father brought him up with his own numerous family; fortunately Mrs. Milner Gibson loved Tom. Because of his illegitimacy he was sent to school in France, and he kept certain French habits of the eighteen fifties to the end of his life. He insisted upon a *déjeuner* at 11.30; this meant that he always lunched alone and made him an inconvenient guest when he stayed with us. At dinner he was convivial.

When he was twenty-five he founded a magazine, *Vanity Fair*, now remembered for the Spy and Ape cartoons of notabilities. It was scurrilous and witty, and as well as a little fortune it made him countless enemies.

Like my other grandfather he married a Scotch girl, Jessica, daughter of Major General C. G. Evans-Gordon. She died at the age of thirty-five leaving him with four young children. He had a passion for the sea and held a master mariner's certificate; after the death of his wife he spent months at sea in a sailing yacht with his four children, the youngest aged three. The little girls were always dressed in sailor clothes and he put his boys into the Navy.

For many years he was Conservative M.P. for King's Lynn. An expert on sea law and sea power, *Punch* caricatured him as an old salt with a wooden leg. He was clever, sarcastic and opinionated; the enemies he had made with *Vanity Fair* never forgave him his jokes; he was not given office.

I can remember both grandfathers, but Grandmother Redesdale I knew well for I was grown up when she died. A merry, rosy, immensely fat old lady, deeply interested in her children and grandchildren and their governesses and nurses and households, she spent most of the year at Redesdale Cottage near the Scotch border. In the winter she came south and visited us and various cousins, but she was based on London where she stayed at some huge and fairly cheap hotel. Farve said: 'Mother spends her time in the hall of the Charing Cross Hotel receiving the guests.'

With her many chins, pink complexion and dimples she looked innocent and babyish. Every new baby in our family when it first opened its blue eyes was said by Nanny to be 'very like the Dowager', though the truth was the other way about.

I am now several years older than Grandmother was when we moved into Batsford and she went up to Redesdale in accordance with the old English custom whereby when a man dies his widow has a sort of minor suttee imposed upon her and has to leave her home immediately to make way for the new generation; if she is lucky the granny is invited for a few days once a year, just to see how her daughter-in-law has changed everything. It is impossible to imagine Grandmother rushing about as we do, motoring herself all over Europe alone like Pam; or swimming and sun-bathing; or, like Debo, shooting; impossible to imagine her giving a passing thought to fashion. In the nineteen-sixties when very short skirts were the fashion Nancy said: 'Now we shall have to choose whether to be dowdy or ridiculous.'

'Which will you choose?' I asked.

'Oh, ridiculous of course,' she replied.

Bertrand Russell was Grandmother's first cousin, their mothers, daughters of Lord Stanley of Alderley, having been sisters. Grandfather Redesdale's first cousin, as I have said, was Swinburne; their mothers too were sisters. We were proud of these two cousins, each in his own way a rebel of genius and neither approved of by our elders, and from a far distance a little reflected glory seemed to fall upon us. A much nearer relation, however, was Susan Bowles; yet although we once tried to discover something about her it was already too late, she was swallowed up in the mists of time.

Grandmother Redesdale told us that when she was first married, one night at the opera Grandfather whispered: 'My mother is in the stage box.' Grandmother could dimly see an old lady with white hair. They never met; divorce in those days was an insurmountable barrier. This great-grandmother was born in 1805; when she died in 1882 she had been married to Francis Molyneux for forty years. Some say that he, and not Henry Mitford, was our great-grandfather. Nobody knows, and presumably nobody cares.

The question marks remain. In any case, even if 'everything' were known about one's forebears, for the most part it would only be a list of names. All the same, their genes partly make us what we are. Physically I resemble Grandfather Redesdale and like him I am deaf, but my grandparents are no more responsible for me than are my grandchildren:

> Catherine
> Jasper
> Valentine
> Sebastian

Daphne
Patrick
Marina
Alexander
Patrick

to whom I dedicate this book.

2

'. . . She Can't Live Long'

WHEN I WAS born, on an afternoon in June 1910, my mother
cried. She was to have seven children, six of them girls, and
she wanted only boys. I was the fourth child, and in my case
it was particularly annoying because had I been a boy the
family would have been nicely balanced: two of each.

We had a nurse called the unkind Nanny, who left when I
was four months old because it had been discovered that she was
in the habit of knocking Nancy's head against a wooden bedpost,
on purpose, for a punishment. When she first saw me, aged
an hour or so, the unkind Nanny said: 'She's too beautiful; she
can't live long.' Modesty does not forbid me to repeat her
words, for anyone who has ever seen a new-born baby knows
very well how plain, not to say repulsive, I must have seemed to
a normal person. Nancy once described a new-born baby as
'a howling orange in a black wig', while François Mauriac
wrote of his own infant son: 'Bébé n'est qu'un paquet de chair
hurlant et malodorant.' The Nanny's observation was reported
to me by my siblings when I was old enough to understand,
and it made a great difference to my childhood. Perhaps she
really knew that I should not live long. When life became
unendurable, when all the others in concert were teasing, I
could sometimes stop them by a reminder: 'You know I can't
live long. You'll be sorry.'

The painter Henry Lamb once told me he thought it great
good luck to be born in an inconspicuous place in the family;
my place was inconspicuous. Tom was one year older, Pam
two and Nancy five. They were all more noticed than I was,
particularly Nancy, the eldest, and Tom because he was a
boy. 'Oh, it's quite different for Tom; he's a boy'; these words
were often heard in our nursery. Lamb's theory was that a
child should grow untrammelled by the excessive attentions
of its elders. Anxieties about such things as exams, a future

career, or even physical development communicate themselves
in a crippling way to the child from its over-loving or possessive
parents, he thought. This certainly never happened to me; my
very existence was of interest only to Nanny and to Tom, who
was almost my twin.

The unkind Nanny left, and Nanny came. All my first
memories are of her. I can remember the warm, creaking pram
hood, raising my head from the comfortable pillow and seeing
Nanny in her black straw bonnet with a black velvet bow and
her dear, beloved face. She used to manœuvre the pram on to
the pavement at Mr. Turner's shop and collect her *Daily
Chronicle*. We lived in Victoria Road and went twice a day to
Kensington Gardens.

Nanny was a Liberal and on her day off she went to the
Congregational Church. For her church we collected farthings
for lepers, and silver paper; she told us to be careful not to
let it get smudged with chocolate because dirty silver paper
was no use to the lepers.

After tea I used to sit for a little while on her lap. She paid
no attention to me but went on talking to Ida our nursery-
maid. Then she put me down in a hurry saying: 'Come along
now, you children, hurry up and get dressed.' We were changed
into clean frocks and taken down to the drawing-room to see
Muv. An hour later Nanny fetched us, it was bed time. I said
my prayers to her: God bless Mother and Father, sisters and
brother, Nanny and Ada and Ida, and make Diana a good girl
amen. If she was not too busy she sang a hymn; we preferred her
hymns to our Church of England ones. The favourites were
'There were ninety and nine' and 'Shall we gather at the
river?'

On Sundays we were taken to the children's service at
St. Mary Abbots. It was quite short, and one was given a
stamp with a picture of a Bible story on it. By thus invoking
the common human passion for collecting, the clergyman made
sure of his congregation; a blank space in the stamp book was
not to be thought of.

When I was four the war began and we were all—including
Tom—given wooden frames and scratchy wool and taught to
make long tube-like mufflers for the soldiers. My father joined
his regiment, the Northumberland Fusiliers, and disappeared

to 'the front'. Aged twenty-two he had fought in the Boer
War; he had been badly wounded and went through life with
only one lung. My mother gave birth to another daughter,
and called her Unity Valkyrie.

We used to spend August with Grandfather Bowles at
Bournhill Cottage, a house by the Solent. Dressed in striped
bathing gowns we dipped in the cold sea and were given a
petit beurre when we came out. Nanny dried me on a rough
towel while I ate the biscuit; it got sand on it from my salty,
numb fingers. We played for hours under the pines, on the jetty
and near the sea with our cousins Dick and Dooley Bailey,
and after tea Caddick, my grandfather's butler, came down to
bathe; he wore a bathing cap to keep his hair neat.

One night we were woken and bundled out of the house in
a hurry and hustled on to the lawn. Bournhill Cottage was on
fire. My grandfather could be seen throwing everything he
could lay hands on out of the windows, and Caddick also dashed
to and fro carrying his silver. We were sitting huddled on the
lawn wrapped in blankets, with jerseys over our nightgowns;
we were told on no account to move.

'Good morning, Mr. Caddick,' called Tom as Caddick
hurried by, but he got no answer.

After a while even Grandfather stopped rescuing his possessions, and we all sat together and watched the house burn down
to the ground. Some marines who saw the blaze from their
ship came ashore and tried to help, but it was too late; they
found the cellar undamaged, and drank Grandfather's wine
instead. The balconies were made of wood in a criss-cross
pattern; they looked like a set piece in a firework display as they
flared and glowed against the dark sky before crashing down.
I watched in a dream—then suddenly: Teddy! I had left him in
my cot. 'Teddy, Teddy,' I shrieked, 'save him! I must get Teddy!
Somebody! Get Teddy!' But it was too late, nobody could get
to the night nursery now. I minded his loss terribly. That the
house was burnt meant nothing, but I thought I should never,
ever sleep again without him.

At dawn we were taken to Eaglehurst, the next house along
the coast, for a seemingly endless day. Tom and I had sometimes
been to tea there with the Marconi children, but at the time
of the fire the inventor and his family were away. I was put

to bed on a sofa in Muv's room; no Teddy and no Nanny. Misery engulfed me.

Next day we went back to Victoria Road. Farve had come home unexpectedly on leave; he was told by the cook that Bournhill Cottage was burnt down, but she had no idea whether we were all alive, she said. At that moment we appeared, bulging out of a cab, with our buckets and spades but without our indoor toys. I heard Muv say: 'Yes, everyone is safe, and the dogs, such luck, it was Nancy and Pam who woke up, their room was full of smoke.'

Nancy and Pam had a bedroom over the boiler room. When she was put to bed Pam said she smelt burning. 'Don't be silly,' said the nursery-maid. Now she was proved right, and it was the nursery-maid who was silly. Pam was often right but seldom listened to. They got me another bear, but it was a hideous yellow plush, nothing like Teddy's worn brown velvet body.

Until he went off to the war Farve worked in an office in London as manager of a woman's weekly paper belonging to my grandfather called *The Lady*. Grandfather was not in the least interested in *The Lady* except financially; he had a magazine called *The Candid Quarterly* in which he criticized the government and all his energy went into that. When my parents married they had not one penny between them, so Farve was given this extremely unsuitable job and my mother an allowance. The job was unsuitable because Farve hated London, loathed being indoors and abominated the printed word; however, he did his best, and as a substitute for outdoor sport he got a mongoose and hunted the rats in *The Lady* office with it.

In the summer Victoria Road was let and we lived at a cottage near High Wycombe, in what was then almost the country. Farve had a bloodhound he used to hunt us children with, and a brown and white mongrel smooth-haired terrier which I called Luncheon Tom and loved more than anything else in the world except Nanny. At Old Mill Cottage we had a horse, and a cart called 'the float'. Muv used to drive us all over the place, but we had to get out and walk up hills because we were so heavy. The float had enormous thin wheels which crunched on the road as we bowled along.

With Nanny and Ida we went for walks; they only took the upright pram and often Pam was in it because she had infantile paralysis, so I had to trudge, and very hot and tired I used to get. Tom and I generally went hand in hand, and he never stopped talking. I loved to listen to him; he was the cleverest person I knew except Nancy, and she did lessons with a governess and was too grand to bother with us. There were two walks; one was in a vast field called the Rye, the other along the valley to the Hoop and Spade Factory. This was a long low building from which came the shriek of many saws and the smell of sawdust. Hundreds of hoops and spades were stacked in view of the road. We liked to stop and listen to the saws, but I dared not go inside, though Tom did. The sound of the saws was frightening; I was timid and unadventurous.

On my birthday they made me a wreath of pinks; it was always a hot day and we had tea in the garden. I hardly ever remember my birthday not being fine; all the same I regretted being born in June. If only I could have had my birthday a couple of months sooner, when Edward VII was alive! 'You've only lived in one reign. We've all lived in *two* reigns,' the others used to remind me. 'Baby! Only *one* reign.' It seemed so unfair that a few weeks could have made this enormous difference.

When we were in London Pam, Tom and I went to Miss Vacani's dancing class once a week. We were always put in the second row, where the less talented pupils struggled along as best they could to keep up with the stars in front. The most brilliant of the latter was Cela Keppel, who not only danced perfectly but looked beautiful; her hair was yellow, not tow coloured like ours. Miss Vacani called her out in front to face us. 'Now, Cecilia, show the class how it should be done.' I was very content to watch Cela, and quite dreaded: 'Now! All together again, one, two, three,' but Tom took his lessons more seriously. 'Miss Vacani, Miss Vacani,' he called in his loud, insistent voice. 'Miss *Vacani! Look!* Am I doing it right?'

Once when Farve was on leave in Paris Muv visited him there, and she came back with yards and yards of the pale blue cloth from which French officers' uniforms were made. Nancy, Pam and I had winter coats made out of it. These coats—first my own, then Pam's and Nancy's handed down—lasted me six winters from when I was five to when I was ten. I knew we were poor; there was no help for it.

The war had made us poorer. Farve's army pay was less than he had earned at the office, and Grandfather wrote to Muv and said that owing to increased taxation he was finding things rather difficult, and had decided to economize by reducing her allowance. I know this because she thought it funny and told us about it long after; at the time it must have seemed far from comic, for she had five children. She let both Old Mill Cottage and Victoria Road and we went to live at Malcolm House, a square box near the church at Batsford belonging to Grandfather Redesdale.

3

Batsford

Muv hated Malcolm House, but we loved it. For the
first time we were living in the real country. One day during
that summer I saw a vision. At least I said I had seen one, and
the others believed me and made me describe it so often that
I hardly know now whether it was a dream or whether I saw
it with my mind's eye. It was the conventional sort of vision
where heaven opens and angels appear in a golden light. Nancy,
Pam and Tom flew to Muv to complain, 'Oh Muv, it's *so* unfair,
Diana's seen a *vision*.' They were in despair about it.

My sixth birthday was spent at Malcolm House, and not
long afterwards Grandmother, meeting Pam and me in the
garden at Batsford said: 'Come, I will take you to visit Grandfather.' We knew Grandfather had been ill for some weeks;
he was supposed to have caught a chill while fishing at Swinbrook. He was seventy-nine, a soigné old gentleman with
silvery hair and moustache and brilliant blue eyes. We were
not in the least prepared for what we were to see.

Grandmother took us upstairs and along a corridor, and
opening a door gently she pushed us before her into a vast
bedroom. The blinds were down, and in the dim light, sitting
bolt upright in bed, was a terrifying apparition. Could it be
Grandfather? A thin, bright yellow face; a shock of white hair
standing on end? I do not remember what he said to us; I
could not take my eyes off his face. The visit was soon over
but it filled my mind for many days.

He died in August. Pam, Tom and I crept into the churchyard and looked into the newly-dug grave. The gardeners had
lined it with flowers, so that one saw only a sort of vast box
of blossom and not a scrap of earth. I had never before seen a
grave, and as I always believed that everything that happened
to us was the unvarying norm, for years when I heard of a
death I pictured a grave lined with flowers. We each had two

new cotton dresses, a mauve and a grey, as mourning for Grandfather, and on the day of his funeral the bell tolled in our very ears because the garden of Malcolm House was next to the churchyard.

A couple of months later we moved into Batsford, and my grandmother went away to live at Redesdale. Because of the war, and our poverty, we only used a few rooms; the rest of the house was in dust sheets.

A family of children came to live with us there to get away from wartime London; they were neighbours in Victoria Road, the Normans. Sibell and Mark and Pam and Tom and I were all bosom friends; we seldom quarrelled. There was also a smaller girl, Mary, and a baby boy. Sibell was always in tearing spirits; she was much bolder than we were, and we loved dashing about in and out of the unused rooms, and the feeling of being far away from the grown-ups.

When I was seven another child, Jessica, was born. Nanny was busy, and I had started lessons in the schoolroom. Our governess, Miss Mirams, used to say: 'Now, Diana, try and remember that you are the least important person in the room.'

Sibell and Mark's parents came down to see them quite often. They amazed me in several ways. One day after luncheon they were drinking coffee with Muv on the terrace when Mary went up to her mother and deliberately knocked the cup out of her hand. I held my breath but Lady Florence only said: 'Oh darling, was that an accident?'

Even more abnormal, I went into Farve's business room with Sibell one evening before dinner to say goodnight, and there was Mr. Norman sitting in an armchair, reading. He put down his book and talked to us for a few minutes. As we went up to bed I said to Sibell: 'Does your father often read?'

'Oh yes,' she replied.

'I've never heard of a *man* reading,' I said.

'Oh haven't you,' said Sibell. 'Lots of Fa's friends read.'

Until that moment I had always imagined reading was for women and children only, though I knew that men wrote. Even my grandfathers had published several books apiece, and at that very time there were vague murmurings, which reached us, among the uncles and aunts and Farve about Sir Edmund Gosse, who had written an 'insolent' (so they said) preface to

Grandfather Redesdale's third volume of memoirs; Gosse was getting this book ready to be published posthumously. The insolence consisted in a hint that Grandfather found no intellectual companionship within his numerous family, which was of course perfectly true.

Muv's brother, Uncle George, pleased Farve with an epitaph supposed to be suitable for this literary enemy:

> Here lies Gosse,
> No great loss.

Uncle George made this couplet rhyme, while Farve pronounced loss to rhyme with horse, as we all did, which rather spoilt the joke.

Farve was now back from 'the front'; he was Assistant Provost Marshal at Oxford, and lived in rooms at Christ Church. We used to visit him there; he had installed a pianola; Muv laughed but we thought it made the most heavenly sounds. Farve put some rainbow trout in Mercury, and generally made himself at home in Tom Quad.

When he came to Batsford we played hide and seek all over the house. All the lights were put out except in the library where Muv sat with the youngest children. There were five staircases up and down which we thundered, but during the silent moments I nearly died of fright, straining my ears to hear a creaking board, somebody creeping quite near. Then there came the sound of footsteps thumping down the corridor, a distant scuffle and scream and Farve's triumphant roar when he caught someone.

Meals in the dining-room were an ordeal when he was at home and had it not been for prestige reasons I would have preferred to stay upstairs with Nanny. However quietly one sat, however far away from him, he saw in an instant if a drop or a crumb was spilt. He thought spilling a disgusting and unnecessary fault, and did not realize how difficult big knives and forks can be for small hands to manage. When, despite one's efforts, something was spilt he roared with rage. At the end of his life, forty years after the days I am describing, he was still the same. Once we were lunching at a London hotel in a vast restaurant; he was nearly blind; yet several tables away he spied a little boy: 'Look at that degraded child throwing its food over the good table cloth,' said Farve.

A rather brutal saying of our elders was: 'Those who ask don't get; those who don't ask don't want.' We wanted nearly everything; the question was how to get it if one might not ask. Tom thought of a way round; he called it 'my artful scheme of happiness'. He looked long and lovingly at the desired object, and when this had been noticed he began to speak. '*Oh, what* a lovely box; I don't think I've ever seen such a *lovely* little box in all my life. Oh how I wish I could find one like it! Do you think I *ever* could? *Oh* (to the owner) you *are* lucky!' He made his voice positively sag with desire. It nearly always ended in his being given whatever it might be he craved. Tom was seven when he invented his artful scheme of happiness.

Miss Mirams thought our way of talking sounded affected.

'He mustn't talk like that when he's at school,' she told Muv. 'What mustn't he say?' asked Muv. 'Well, for instance, "how *amusing*". Boys never say "how *amusing*",' said Miss Mirams.

There was a nursery rule, made by Muv, that we were not to be forced to eat what we did not like or want. I was intensely thankful for this; I was seldom hungry and many nursery foods stuck in my gullet I disliked them so much. Pam and I were both 'fussy', but Nancy and Tom had good appetites and often ate our food as well as their own. They were more than welcome to it.

'Isn't Pam *wonderful*,' Tom said once when, after the long journey up to Redesdale, the exhausted Pam could not swallow anything, 'the way she refuses food.'

One day Muv came into the schoolroom and said: 'Children, Mrs. Hammersley is coming to stay, she will arrive tonight. While she is here you are not to practice.'

'Why not?'

'Because she is very musical.'

I was pleased to be let off my scales, and puzzled by the reason for it. How could somebody be so musical that she could not bear to hear the piano played?

At this time Unity, now three years old, had a familiar, 'Madam', whom she blamed for anything naughty she might have done. One of her sins was drawing with a pencil on the wallpaper near her cot. When Nanny began to scold, Unity's eyes became huge. 'But, Nanny, Madam did it! I *saw* her do it!'

Mrs. Hammersley was greatly interested in Madam. She took Bobo on her lap and said: 'Tell me, Unity, what is Madam *like?*'

Unity gazed at Mrs. Hammersley. 'She's got black hair, and a black dress, and a white shawl,' she replied, describing what she saw.

'Oh,' cried Mrs. Hammersley. 'Am *I* Madam?'

Unity did not answer.

While we were at Batsford Farve lent a cottage in the village to his aunt, who usually lived at Dieppe. She had chosen Dieppe because it was cheap, and because it had a casino; she was an inveterate gambler. I had seen her once before, and it is probably my earliest recollection. We were at a children's party in London, and Aunt Natty took me on one of her knees while on the other sat a tiny girl with red hair, blue eyes and thin white hands. 'Two Dianas,' said Aunt Natty. I looked up at her Brobdignagian face under its black lace cap, and at the other little girl, and wished she would put me down. Now here she was, at Batsford, still larger than life. At this time we loved her more than all our other uncles and aunts put together.

She was quite different from Grandmother, except that they were both stout and stately and like most old ladies in those days both wore uniform. Grandmother wore a widow's veil thrown back over a bonnet and a voluminous black gown, and Aunt Natty a lace cap and a tent-like robe and a cape. Great-granny was still alive; she also of course wore uniform. She set off her black with a blue satin ribbon. 'Now, Blanche, you are *not* to copy this,' she said to her daughter, but Aunt Natty copied it at once. Her cloak's lining was edged with blue. After Grandfather's death, Grandmother would not have dreamed of wearing a coloured ribbon; only a little white relieved the black.

Aunt Natty came to tea with us every day and told us stories, or rather serials, for she always promised to go on the following day. Most of the stories were about herself and her brothers and sisters when they were children. In one of them she and Grandmother had new coats which they disliked: navy serge with brass buttons. The Prince Consort died, and they went to Great-granny. 'Mother, shouldn't we wear mourning for the Prince?' Great-granny considered for a moment and then ordered the gold buttons to be cut off and black ones sewn on instead.

Aunt Natty's cottage was joined on to the electric light house. There was a steep bank the other side of the road at the back, and here, when there was snow, Tom and I used to take our toboggans. The run got faster and faster the more we used it, and at last I came down head first such a bat that I crashed through the door of the electric light house and was picked up unconscious among the dust and the glass accumulators. While I was in bed with concussion Aunt Natty came every day to the night nursery to tell me stories.

Her own grandchild was the other Diana—Diana Churchill. She often spoke of her. One day she showed me a little brooch with pearls and an emerald on it. 'I offered this to the other Diana,' she told me.

'How *lucky*.'

'She didn't want it. She said Granny Blanche, I'd rather have a Kodak.' She pronounced her name, Blanche, with a short a, as in Granny.

This episode amazed me. How could anyone refuse 'jewellery'? We all longed to possess something precious. There were so many of us that even my clothes were not my own; I was just their tenant on their way from Pam to Unity, at least in theory, though it was not always thought worth while to keep them for four whole years. I longed for something to belong only to me, and perhaps for this reason they gave me Dicky, the nursery bird. 'You can call Dicky yours if you like, darling,' Nanny said.

'Oh, but *that's* no good; he must *be* mine. Muv, can Dicky be mine?'

'Yes. I'm sure he can,' said Muv.

After that, when we had one of our conversations about what we possessed of our very own, I was able to say: 'Well, Dicky's mine, and he must be very valuable.'

When I was grown up I never allowed my boys to have

a caged bird in their nursery; I agreed with Blake that it would put heaven in a rage. Yet Dicky was loved, and he seemed happy.

He was a goldfinch; he went with us everywhere, with a green baize cover over his cage in the train. When we were very small we also took our pony in the carriage with us; Muv, Farve, Nanny, Ada, Nancy, Pam, Tom, me, Dicky, Brownie and Luncheon Tom, all in a third class carriage. Brownie was an extremely tiny Shetland pony. I think it was saintly of Farve to travel with us children; possibly it only happened once, and that is why we never forgot it.

In the business room at Batsford there was a little object which I craved so much that one day Farve gave it to me. 'You must take great care of it,' he said. It was a pink jade goldfish, Japanese.

Grandfather had been one of the first Europeans to live in Japan as a young diplomatist. He went there again when he was old with Prince Arthur of Connaught to take the Order of the Garter to the Mikado. He saw that the country had changed from the thirteenth century to the twentieth century during his lifetime. 'Tell us how it was in the old days,' said the ladies at Court. Grandfather's wild garden, where one came upon surprises like the Buddha preaching to bronze deer among the bamboos, was of Japanese inspiration. Indoors and out there were hundreds of Japanese objects he had collected.

I clutched the fish in my hand because I could not bear to be parted from it. At night it stood on a table near my bed, so that when my eyes opened I saw it and felt happy. One day the inevitable happened. I dropped it on a stone floor and it broke: its lovely twisted tail snapped off. Farve knew. 'You've broken the goldfish,' he said. To my despair at having destroyed the beautiful thing was added the knowledge that I had made him sorry he had given it to a child of seven. Occasionally throughout my life in a museum or an exhibition I have seen fishes that resembled Farve's gift to me when I was 'a silly little baby' as the others called me; I cannot look at them without a pang.

Aunt Natty had a Scotch terrier at Batsford. She told us how she had brought him over from Dieppe hidden under her cloak, so that he should not have to be parted from her and put into quarantine. Just as she was walking through the

Customs he wriggled. 'Madam,' said the Customs man, 'have you got a dog under your arm?'

'Certainly not,' said Aunt Natty.

'Well, Madam, then what's that there moving, then?'

'So I flung open the other side of my cloak and said: "Cannot you believe the word of an Englishwoman?" and I walked through.'

Evidently the Customs man was too awed to stop her as she sailed by him. My parents disapproved of this story. 'Oh *Natty,* how *could* you?' said Muv.

Aunt Natty could, and did, do anything and everything she pleased. She was the first unprincipled grown-up who came our way. She often said 'I love privilege', the sort of remark that Grandmother and Muv, though so different in other respects, both thought outrageous. She never wrote letters, but every morning gave Hooper, our groom, a sheaf of telegrams to be sent from Moreton-in-Marsh. We often found him in despair outside the post office. 'Can't read Lady Blanche's writing,' he said. Nor could we, and nor could the post mistress; she had a puzzle writing which looked almost Chinese.

She never dressed till lunchtime, but used to throw a cape over her flowing nightgown and walk about the village in what we considered a strange déshabillé. Once she invited Tom and me into the cottage to drink chocolate. '*Not* cocoa, there's nothing more disgusting than cocoa,' she told us. She was not dressed.

'Ah, you are looking at my feet!' she said.

'Oh no, Aunt Natty, we're not,' said Tom and I; but we were. Her legs were bare, and although one could only see her fat ankles, and her feet in bedroom slippers, it seemed very curious to us for in those days one never saw a grown-up's legs except in stockings.

We all knew that as soon as the war was over Batsford was going to be sold because we were too poor to live there. We hoped the war would go on forever. The last summer there, when I was eight, a huge garden fête was held, in aid of the wounded soldiers. Nancy decided that we would act a play, and charge sixpence for tickets. I cannot remember the plot of this play, but when the curtain went up Nancy and one of the village boys were on the stage, dressed as a farmer's wife and a farmer. The boy had the first line, it was: 'Phew, wife, the heat is tremendous.' Nancy's partner pronounced this as Few, woife, and he gave every subsequent syllable exactly equal value, so that it sounded utterly unlike somebody talking in real life. The rest of us were the farmer's wife's children, which Nancy relished.

A cousin of Muv's, Georgie Gordon, kindly offered to rehearse us, and we worked hard for several weeks in the ballroom where it was quiet. Two days before the fête we were to have our dress rehearsal. We had great fun dressing up, and Muv was the audience. All through the play Georgie, who prompted, was very busy indeed; and at the end, after a rather worrying silence, Muv spoke:

'I'm very sorry, children, but I'm afraid you can't do your play.'

'Can't do our play, Muv? *Why* can't we?'

'Well, really, you see I'm afraid it's too *bad.*'

We were dumbfounded. Georgie found wonderful excuses to save our faces, and our play died.

Aunt Natty gave the pearl and emerald brooch which had been rejected by my namesake to be raffled at this fête, and there were many stalls and side-shows. We made hundreds of pounds for the wounded soldiers, a fortune.

Although the Batsford fête was the biggest we ever had, in after years there were often fêtes on the lawn at Asthall. Every single time, Muv was seized with panic just before the opening when she looked at the stalls; she thought they were too bare. She would rush into the house and bring out anything she happened to see. We soon learnt to hide our possessions when a fête loomed up. At Batsford, the White Elephant stall would have been a treasure house to any Orientalist; Farve managed to buy one of Grandfather's Japanese buddhas for sixpence, but by the time he had realized what was happening the stall was nearly empty. At Asthall Muv once disposed of two of Jessica's most beloved toys, a cat and a rabbit called Nimmy and Shu-Shu. Poor Decca was in deep despair; next day we got new toys and went from cottage to cottage until we found the person who had bought them; luckily she was willing to exchange, their fur was almost rubbed off by Decca's love, and their purchaser preferred the new ones.

Batsford was sold to Sir Gilbert Wills. We were very sad to leave, but fortunately Farve liked Sir Gilbert and often went back to stay for shooting. Farve never felt neutral about anyone; he saw people as black or white without nuance. 'Such a clever cove,' he would say of somebody he was fond of. Often he liked a man but hated his wife. 'A meaningless bit of meat,' he called one such disliked lady.

When we left Batsford some of the furniture, pictures and books were sold too. Farve was a one-book man, he had read *White Fang* by Jack London; he thought it perfect but this did not make him decide to read any more books. Tom, who was ten years old at the time of the sale, was what Farve called 'a literary cove'. He and Nancy and I were omnivorous readers, Nancy particularly so. Her enthusiasms were contagious, and when I heard her say: 'My favourite book is *King Solomon's Mines*' or '*The Chaplet of Pearls*', I always looked inside the book, just to see. When I found it too difficult I went back to *Mrs Tiggy Winkle*, or *Herr Baby*, resolving to try again next year.

Farve allowed Tom to decide which books to sell—some had to go, because the Batsford library was bigger than the Asthall one. Am I dreaming this? I think not; I can hear Tom's loud treble voice: 'Oh *no*, Farve, you can't sell *that*.'

Towards the end of the war I was often doubled up with pain. I was laid on a sheeted table in one of the visitors' rooms and my appendix was removed. I awoke from the anaesthetic in a huge red brocade bed and everybody brought me presents. The others had been sent away to our Farrer cousins for my operation: Pam, convinced that the prophesy 'she can't live long' was about to be fulfilled, spent her all on a paintbox for me. I suppose nowadays the surgeon would insist upon a clinic. Personally I prefer a brocade bed and beautiful unhygienic surroundings which (if one cares about such things) hasten recovery.

4

Asthall

FARVE HAD SOME land in Oxfordshire, and when Batsford was sold he planned to build a house near the coverts on the hill above Swinbrook. For the present we were to live at Asthall, an old manor house near a church, built of aged, gabled stone with leaded windows. Farve bought it; it was beside his farms and near the river Windrush, but he did not care for it; he wanted to live with the pheasants on the hill. He loved pheasants, and spent hours watching the baby chicks with Steele, the keeper, leaning on his thumb-stick and saying little. His greatest joy was to look out of his window in the early morning and see cock pheasants strutting on the lawn. Of course he also loved shooting—not the garden pheasants, they were sacred—and his other passion at this time was fishing.

I was nine years old when we went to live at Asthall. It had a long hall panelled in old oak, with a fire at each end. Over one fire-place hung a portrait of François I by Clouet. There were doors to the garden and windows on each side, yet we sat comfortably near the fire sheltered by Chinese screens. Muv's drawing-room had only French furniture; Louis XVI commodes and secrétaire, and white chairs covered in old needlework. There was a water colour by Richmond of our great-grandmother with her sons, Grandfather and his elder brothers wearing muslin skirts and blue ribbons, their hair in long yellow ringlets, and a Louis XVI gilt-bronze clock and barometer which are now mine; I bought them years later in one of Farve's numerous sales.

In the dining-room there were portraits including one of our great-great grandfather William Mitford, the historian of Greece; and one of Farve, almost unrecognizable. He had been persuaded to have his portrait painted and chose a Belgian camouflage expert for the job. A stranger to vanity, Farve thought it a wonderful likeness and a splendid work of art. Muv, like all her contemporaries, was painted by Laszlo; she was at the height of her beauty. This picture is now at Chatsworth.

The books were housed in a converted barn in the garden, and four extra bedrooms were build above. This library was all the world to Tom and me at Asthall, partly for the beautiful leather-bound books which we could read as much as we liked provided we put them back where they belonged, and also because it was some way from the house and we could be there undisturbed. There were comfortable sofas and a grand piano. Already when he was ten Tom could play divinely and I was perfectly content to sit and listen to him. When he was away at school I missed him dreadfully. For one thing, he could do no wrong in Farve's eyes; a proposition which would have enraged him coming from one of us was considered reasonably if expounded by Tom, who in many ways seemed the more adult of the two.

During the term Pam, who had quite recovered from her polio, and I went once a week to a dancing class at Hatherop Castle. We sat up together in the outside dickey at the back of a little Morris Cowley, dressed in trench coats belonging to Farve over our dancing frocks. In spite of the coats we arrived completely numbed and paralysed with cold; even our governess, who sat by Turner in front, was frozen, but we were blue and trembling. When the class was over, on went the trench coats and we climbed into the dickey and drove home through the bitter night. Strangely enough, we looked forward to these outings.

When we had been at Asthall a few months Muv went up to Victoria Road where her last child was born. Nancy got the telegram; she ran upstairs with it and saw me standing at the end of the corridor talking to a housemaid. 'Annie! We are seven!' Then, to the question in Annie's face: 'Another girl.'

'Oh, Miss Nancy, *what* a disappointment,' said dear old Annie, almost in tears. It was this incident that led Nancy to tell Debo in after years: 'Everybody cried when you were born.' Mabel, our parlourmaid, was at Victoria Road; she used to say, 'I knew what it was the moment I saw his lordship's face.'

I thought the baby, which was a complete surprise to me, quite perfect from the very first moment.

Nancy became cleverer and funnier every day. We used to sit together and scream with laughter, which naturally irritated everybody. Before long a grown-up would come along and remind one of some duty: 'Have you fed your chickens?' 'Have you done your practice?' Nancy had by now been wise enough to abandon these activities, but I kept chickens, pigs and even calves in a supreme effort to make money.

Rather like Farve and his pheasants, which were cherished only to die, I did not mind when these creatures were sold to the butcher. It was what they were *for*. On the other hand, when our pets died—usually violent deaths—we cried for days; the most terrible of all these occasions was when my guinea pig was killed by Nancy's border terrier.

Every day except Sunday we went out riding with Captain Collison, the agent. The kennels, garage and stables could be reached by a short cut across the churchyard, and although we were never allowed to ride on Sundays we used the church-yard path even more than usual then, because of fetching dogs for coursing. Farve had a lurcher and every Sunday between October and March Uncle Tommy came to luncheon with his whippet and we all went out coursing.

We were cursed by Farve if we did not keep in line; one struggled and hopped along through turnips or kale or over the prickly stubble. When a hare got up there were cries of 'Loo after it!'; the lurcher and whippet were slipped and they streaked after the hare, which doubled and twisted and usually got away. Sometimes it was caught; the first one went into Farve's hare pocket, and subsequent ones were given to us to carry. Uncle Tommy and Farve used to say: 'Wasn't that a beautiful sight?' and stand for a while leaning on their thumb-sticks while the dogs got their breath, then on we would go to look for another hare.

What became of the hares we caught out coursing I do not know. They were never eaten in our household, though Farve often said regretfully how delicious jugged hare could be. Muv's father was a food crank, and she followed his rule for herself and for us by observing the food laws laid down by Moses. Until I was married I was not allowed to eat bacon, ham, lobster, pigeon, rabbit, hare or mackerel, or any of the other meats forbidden to the ancient Israelites. Farve insisted on having bacon and sausages with his eggs at breakfast, but we might not partake. As a result we positively craved for them, and Tom's first letters from school were full of nothing but sausages. 'Oh Muv, it's so unfair. If Tom can have sausage why can't we?'

'Tom's a boy.'

Muv never came coursing with us, or shooting, or hunting, or even hacking. Farve no longer cared for riding, which was a great sorrow to Hooper. 'If only we could get her ladyship up on a horse,' he said to us once, 'perhaps his lordship would play the man.'

We thought this wonderfully funny, because Farve *was* man to us, and nobody, not even his brothers, came anywhere near him in manliness.

Uncle Tommy lived at Swinbrook Mill Cottage; we adored him. He was a sailor, and after the war he became a farmer. His methods, and theories out of books, were scoffed at by the village labourers and the local farmers, or at least greeted with great shakings of the head. Forty years on, I asked him: 'When you tried those experiments with grass and the Swinbrook farmers were so sceptical, were they right, or were you?' 'I was,' he said. He had sayings that he used over and over again. 'Nothing perfect!' 'The best of everything for everybody' and 'Be it this or be it that'.

In common with many people of their generation, Farve's and his brothers' conversation abounded in French expressions and idioms. As a small child I did not always understand what they meant. Thinking that they interfered in what did not concern them, Farve always called bishops 'les touche à tout', and until I was twelve or so I thought touche à tout was French for bishop. He was not anti-clerical, it was their presence in the House of Lords he disliked.

In the summer holidays Farve's old tutor, M. Cuvelier, came to stay. He was a French master at Eton and lived in Slough. He had gone to Batsford in the eighties to teach the family, and I think the fact that they did their first lessons in French may account for the great difficulty Farve always found in spelling English; words which are the same in both

2

languages are nearly always spelt differently. Farve disliked putting pen to paper: when he was obliged to he had the Concise Oxford Dictionary at his elbow.

We called M. Cuvelier 'Monsieur', but Farve and his brothers called him 'Douze Temps'. This was because when they were boys he used to tell them about his adventures as a soldier in the Franco-Prussian War; loading a rifle was done in twelve movements which he mimed for them. 'Un! deux! t-r-o-i-s!' (very slowly) and so on. At one point he had to tear or pull something with his teeth, which fascinated us.

Douze Temps' presence always put Farve in the sunniest of moods, and he and my uncles became boys again before our astonished eyes. Farve, who was twice his size, used to pretend to be a wounded soldier to be carried across the Rhine on Douze Temps' back: this had been one of the sagas. There were cries of 'Mais non, mais non, mon cher, voyons! C'est ridicule! Ah, non!' in the old cracked voice and shouts of laughter from Farve and from us.

When Monsieur was at Asthall we heard tales of Farve's childhood. He had a violent temper as a boy, and once when he had been locked in his room he made the poker red-hot in the fire, intending to kill his father and Douze Temps when they should come to release him. It was M. Cuvelier's speed and agility in snatching away the brandished poker which saved them from being, at least, badly burned. Farve was so naughty that it was considered unfair to his elder brother Uncle Clem to send them to Eton together; he went to Radley, where he was bored to death and learnt nothing.

According to Farve, Uncle Jack was Grandfather's favourite child: 'Brave as a lion and clever as a monkey.' Farve's guns were his holiest possession. The thought of anyone touching them, let alone borrowing them, made one's blood run cold; of course no one would have dared. Probably Grandfather did not feel so strongly about his guns as Farve, but all the same he was a strict parent of whom his children were very much in awe. According to Farve, le petit Jicksy went to Grandfather's business room one day in February, when the shooting season was over, and asked if he might borrow a gun to shoot pigeons. Permission was given, for nothing was ever refused him. That night it snowed, and six weeks later, when the thaw came, the gun was found lying beneath a cedar, ruined by rust. But Grandfather did not mind a bit, because of le petit Jicksy being as brave as a lion and clever as a monkey; 'Don't think of it again, dear boy,' he was supposed to have said.

Possibly this story might not electrify others to the extent it did us. The notion that one of us children could leave one of Farve's guns lying out in the snow was simply too terrifying to think about.

We also understood perfectly how brave George Washington had been when he did not tell a lie. Farve was not a gardener like Grandfather but he always planted one or two small things to look at from his window. Between the paving stones he put Virginia stocks—'My interster seeds' he called them. On the grass bank he had an anenome—only one, so far as I know— which was the apple of his eye. 'Come and see my fulgens,' he used to say when a red dot appeared in the expanse of green. 'It's out.' If some rash child had picked the anemone it would have more than equalled any cherry tree.

Since various legends about Farve's fierceness have grown up it may be worth saying that not only did he make us scream with laughter at his lovely jokes but that he was very affectionate. Certainly he had a quick temper, and would often rage, but we were never punished. The worst that ever happened was to be sent early to bed. A reviewer of Harold Acton's biography of Nancy, judging from a badly-reproduced snapshot, wrote that Farve's face was suffused with the scarlet of passion and that he must have been 'a very frightening man indeed'. In fact there was no red, or even pink, in Farve's face; his skin was a pale uniform beige; it never altered with his moods. Set in the beige were brilliant blue eyes. Muv took him to see her old friend, the artist Helleu, in Paris during the war; he said he was khaki from head to foot 'only the eyes are not khaki'.

'When your parents were young,' Farve's cousin Kitty Ritson told me ages later, 'they were so beautiful they were like gods walking upon earth.'

After Bournhill Cottage burnt down we had no seaside of our own to go to; Nanny took us once a year to lodgings at Bexhill. The house belonged to a friend of hers, also a Congregationalist and very interested in missions to Africa.

The sitting-room we used was hung with spears and shields among the pampas grass, and sometimes one met a negro on the stairs.

While we were at Bexhill we used to go on a bus to St. Leonards to see Nanny's sister. They were twins, and very much alike; when I was small it made me uneasy to be with Nanny's sister unless Nanny was there too, because I got the sensation that Nanny had changed. That she might ever change was my worst nightmare; even a new bonnet took a great deal of getting used to. Pam, Tom and I had terrible nightmares; we bored one another with them in the mornings. Pam's were about steam rollers. More than once I dreamt that Nanny had grown very tall and thin and brittle; she was like Augustus in *Struwelpeter*. She wore a tight belt round her tiny waist, in my dream, and all of a sudden she snapped in two.

When we went to Bexhill these dreams were several years away; we loved our visits to Nanny's sister, who lived over a hardware shop kept by her husband; she had two clever daughters who passed their exams and became head-mistresses.

One of the things we looked forward to at Bexhill was the food; particularly the cream, out of cardboard tubs. 'Bought cream' was so much more delicious than the ordinary cow's cream we got at home.

Our school-room life was humdrum, but the holidays were perfect. Tom came home, and we dashed about to dancing parties in the Christmas holidays, tennis parties in the summer. We had been brought up to despise 'games', sport was all my father cared for; golf, and cricket, were considered beyond the pale. Tennis, however, Tom and I played, though not at all well; we did it because it led to endless parties. Our cousins Dick and Dooley Bailey lived fifteen miles away; there was constant coming and going between Asthall and Stow-on-the-Wold. They were much better at games than we were; Dick chose to be a dry-bob at Eton, while Tom thankfully gave up cricket and took to the river.

I was so pleasure-loving and got so excited at the thought of some particularly glamorous party that often when the great day came I had to go to bed with a high temperature. Muv sent for Dr. Cheatle. He prescribed three days in bed; when he first came to us he sometimes gave medicine, but chancing to see a row of unopened bottles in Nanny's cupboard he laughed and ceased to make suggestions which involved swallowing anything. Muv believed the good body would cure itself; she only got Dr. Cheatle just in case one had been struck by dire disease.

When I was dressed for a party I looked in the glass and disliked what I saw.

'I can't go,' I used to say to Nanny, '*everything's* wrong.'

'Never mind, darling,' Nanny always had the same answer. 'It doesn't matter. *Nobody's* going to look at *you*.'

Tom invited friends to stay. 'Would you like to hear me play?' he began, as soon as a friend arrived. They went straight to the library, followed by me, and Tom played to us. Even when he was at his private school he played to his guests; he must have picked them with care, for it is not every ten-year-old boy who would want to sit indoors all day listening to classical music. Jim Lees-Milne was the friend I preferred. He hated games just as much as we did, and when Tom had finished playing we used to talk. Jim made us read Byron, Shelley, Keats, and Coleridge, and we agreed that when we were grown up we would scorn material things and live on a handful of grapes near the sea in Greece.

Since the days of the children's service and the stamps, church-going had altered its aspect. We were made to go to church every Sunday; this was one of the firmest family rules. We tried to put off going until evensong—after all, the world might come to an end at lunchtime, and then one would feel a fool to have wasted the morning in church. This argument played constantly in my mind; it was the best reason for procrastination.

There was a choice of services—matins at Swinbrook with Farve, who liked us to go with him, or evensong at Asthall with Muv. Farve never set foot in Asthall church, although it was ten yards from our house. The living was not in his gift, and he took no interest whatever in Asthall affairs although most of the village belonged to him.

Mr. Ward, the clergyman, generally used to scold his tiny congregation in his sermon; it was most unfair, but they got the scolding due to the rest of the village for laxity about

church attendance. He read his sermons, and propped the sheets
of paper on a brass lectern attached to the pulpit. One could
see light through the last two sheets, and by this one knew when
the hour of delivery was at hand.

Mrs. Ward was a tremendous singer; she could fill the
church with her powerful contralto, which made us scream with
laughter. Of course the screams were stifled, but we shook
and heaved with the effort. Once Mr. Ward preached against
profance persons who ran and shouted with their dogs through
God's holy acre. This was meant for us, because the churchyard
path was our short cut to the stables. Farve was amused when
we told him, but did not mend his ways.

Until I was eleven I hated going to church; it almost spoilt
Sunday for me. Then, under the influence of an Anglo-Catholic
governess, I became for about a year a subject of religious
mania. A service a week was not half enough for me; I considered that one should go to church every single day, or, better
still several times a day. Hours spent anywhere but in church,
or praying in my room, were so many wasted hours.

I was terribly concerned about Muv and Farve, and what
might happen to their immortal souls. True, they went to
church on Sundays; but did they *believe?* Uncle George said
that Muv went to church as a patriotic duty; if this were true
it would be fatal.

The thought of converting Muv occupied me for months.
She must be made to believe in transubstantiation, original
sin, the immaculate conception as well as the virgin birth, and
the real presence. She must be persuaded to turn to the east
and curtsy at the right moment during the creed.

Miss Price taught us the New Testament, the lives of the
saints, the history of the early church and the meaning of the
sacraments. Our only geography was a study of the Holy Land;
and the journeys of St. Paul which we traced and coloured with
different inks. She stayed with us four terms, about the limit
of time any governess could abide us for. Then she packed up
her shrine—crucifix, brass candlesticks, brass vases always
kept bright and full of flowers—and went away. After she left
I drifted back into a mild agnosticism, but I shall always be
grateful to Miss Price because she made me understand, from
the inside as it were, what religion can mean to a person.

When I was eleven Muv took us to Dieppe for the Easter
holidays; she rented Aunt Natty's house and we had a French
cook. For the first time in my life I realized how delicious food
could be. I doted on Dieppe. A few years afterwards I went
back there and found a quite ordinary sea-side town; it was
nothing like the fairyland of my memory. Just before we left
for home a frightful thing happened: Bill Hozier, Aunt Natty's
only son, shot himself. Muv got the telegram, and she had to
break the news. Bill Hozier was an inveterate, penniless
gambler; his debts had been paid several times by his brother-
in-law Winston Churchill, and now he was in debt again and
decided to end his life. We knew something sad had happened
but were not told exactly what it was; we cannot have understood much about it, for my memories of Dieppe are of
unclouded happiness.

Aunt Natty stayed with us quite often at Asthall, and when
a few years later she died I was very sad. If one could summon
the departed from the shades, she would be among the first I
should choose.

Three or four times a year we motored over to Stratford for
the Shakespeare plays in the nice, hideous old theatre before
the fire. We got there so early that we sat gazing at the safety
curtain for at least half an hour; on it were the words; For
Thine Especial Safety, and round the ceiling something about
the poet's pen, which gave to airy nothings a local habitation
and a name.

We knew the actors and actresses by heart, and were quite
accustomed to one of the merry wives of Windsor turning into
Desdemona overnight, but I was always shocked by what
seemed to me their extreme old age. It was not quite easy to
see good old Baliol Holloway as the ne'er lust-wearied Antony,
or his elderly leading lady as a *lass* unparalleled. Nancy and I
so often began to shake with silent laughter that Muv forbade
us to sit together. On the other hand we thought them quite
suitable as the Macbeths. It was the same thing with Shaw's
St. Joan. Sybil Thorndike, in grey wrinkled stockings, with
ancient, knobbly knees and affected moaning and bleating—
'I hear my V O I C E S'—was too far removed from my idea
of Joan of Arc. Yet not long ago, when she died aged ninety, I
read eulogies of her in the part, for which she was chosen by

Shaw himself. As a child I was either deficient in imagination or else saw things too plainly in my mind's eye.

Some of our governesses were cleverer than others; none of them was exactly a Hobbes. Counting French govs we had in the holidays there were about fifteen in all. By modern standards our curriculum had disastrous gaps. Nobody thought of giving us lessons in sex, for example, now considered an essential subject. I wish its importance had been discovered sooner; it would have made our childhood hilarious, to see Miss Smith or Miss Leach at the blackboard conscientiously showing us what we must do. Modern state schools recently appealed for volunteers to teach school leavers to read. What can they have been at, for a whole decade at school? They should try to fit in a reading lesson occasionally between the sex classes, for as Goethe said: '*Kannst du lesen, so sollst du verstehen,*'* though obviously sex is more fun than anything as humdrum as reading.

Early in June the cry of 'The mayfly's up' set Farve in excitement and the business room in a buzz. For weeks he had been oiling his lines and looking through his flies; he had also fished, with a wet fly. I often went with him. According to Farve, if one trod on a twig, or sneezed, even a hundred yards from the bank, every trout heard it and swam away for miles, even perhaps to a stretch of river belonging to somebody else. I hardly breathed during our fishing expeditions; I loved being with him, and considered it an honour to be allowed to go.

During the may-fly season there were carefully chosen men guests at Asthall. Meals were irregular, and there were all the things I liked best—asparagus, tiny peas and beans, mayonnaise, cold soufflé, trout en gelée.

At night, when Pam and I were in bed, Farve and his friends were still on the lawn at half past ten and after when it got too dark to fish. We could hear them talking and laughing, and the whirr of the reels as they pulled their lines out to dry.

Farve was as happy when he was fishing as he was nervous and short-tempered when he had a shoot. On shooting mornings we kept well out of his way. We could hear him from the schoolroom window: 'Where's that infernal feller Forester?' 'I'm here,' said a mild voice. Major Forester had been doing

* If you can read, you should be able to understand.

up his bootlace behind one of the cars; he never came again. People did not want to be cursed when they were on pleasure bent.

I was sorry about this because I was deeply (though of course secretly) in love with Lady Victoria Forester. She had slightly protruding front teeth, and I used to sit by the hour pressing my teeth with my thumb in the vain hope of growing more like her.

Once when I was standing with him waiting for driven partridges Farve's loader, for some reason, was not his favourite, Turner. The man was slow. Farve took both guns and laid them reverently on the stubble; then he picked up the loader and shook him. It was done in deathly silence, Farve never spoke out shooting for fear of turning the birds.

We were all very cross with him about this episode and put him in coventry for two days, but when he was obviously not minding we relented, and spoke to him again.

Our family was divided between those who longed to go to school and those who dreaded the very idea of it. Farve thought that boys must go but girls must not. Nancy was for school; she thirsted for learning. She was allowed to go to Hatherop where a dozen girls did their lessons together; it was a compromise. She was there when I had my religious mania.

The thought of being sent away from home was enough to give me a temperature. If Nancy wanted to afflict me with a really unkind tease she well knew what to say. 'Last night after you had gone to bed I was talking you over with Muv and Farve;' my blood ran cold; however often she said this, and although I half knew that Muv and Farve would not talk me over with Nancy, a terrible sinking of the stomach made me feel sick. 'We were saying how good it would be for you to go to school.'

'Did Muv and Farve say it would be good for me?'

'Yes. We agreed that you might not be so stupid and babyish if you went to school.'

Sometimes the anxiety induced by one of these conversations was so painful that I summoned up courage to ask Muv if they really were thinking of school for me. 'School, darling? Oh I don't think so. But you mustn't be rude to Miss Edwards you know,' she might add, taking advantage.

This dislike of schools is something I have never grown out of; for one thing I cannot abide the zoo-like smell.

The pupils at Hatherop had been Girl Guides, with the headmistress as their Captain. When she came home Nancy managed to persuade Muv to allow her to perpetrate a devilish scheme, which combined the advantages of achieving an all-time high as a tease for me with gratification of her will to power and being considered praiseworthy by everybody, parents, uncles and aunts included.

She announced it one day at tea. 'I am going to form a company of guides; I am going to be the Captain and you and Pam can be patrol leaders; you will have to call me "Captain",' she said.

'I won't be a Girl Guide,' I said firmly.

To my surprise, because I could not believe she was to be allowed to get away with this, Muv supported Nancy.

'You'll join, won't you, Palmer,' Muv said to Pam, who replied listlessly, 'Yes, I suppose so.'

I felt I might begin to cry at any minute; if only we had had warning of what was afoot I could easily have persuaded Pam to be on my side, and then Nancy's tease would have been out of the question. It was simply that Pam did not see as promptly as I did what a pest being a Girl Guide was going to be.

'Well, I shan't,' I said.

'Dana, I'm afraid you must,' said Muv. 'You see, we can't expect the village girls to join if you children aren't in it.'

'Oh but why *should* I, I shall *hate* it, Muv, it's so *stupid*, and anyway Nancy won't be a proper captain, she'll only be pretending.' But it was no good. Muv said I must join, she promised me one thing, however: if I still hated it at the end of a year I could give it up. A year seemed an eternity, but there was nothing to be done, and I became a very sulky and unwilling Girl Guide.

It turned out to be all I had feared, and more. Ten of the village girls were told they had got to join, and Pam and I picked sides for our patrols (No damned merit went into the choice of the patrol leaders). We were all fitted out in stiff blue drill dresses, black stockings and shoes and hard round felt hats. Nancy, as captain, had a different and rather becoming hat turned up at one side with a cockade. We stumped about at the end of the garden, trying to light damp things with three matches and run a hundred yards in twenty seconds. Nancy tried to make us salute her with three uplifted fingers, and shake hands with our left hands, but this we refused to do. She studied a Girl Guide magazine in order to discover further humiliations to inflict upon us; she even threatened to get a flag and make us salute that. Sometimes we had competitions which Nancy would announce with assumed éclat for the following week:

'You are to collect all the most useful things you can think of and put them in your pockets, and the best collection will win a prize,' she said. 'Only in your pockets mind, you mustn't carry anything because a guide must always have her hands free—unless of course she is a standard-bearer or something like that,' she added.

The following Saturday the guides turned up with their dresses sagging in all directions. A guide uniform is a positive nest of pockets, and full advantage had been taken. I had not been able to think of anything very useful to put in mine, except money, which was not allowed. My collection was meagre—a box of matches; a small bandage made out of a strip from an old sheet, provided by Nanny; a magnifying glass, and a pen-knife with a corkscrew and an attachment for prising stones out of horses' feet.

The village girls produced marvels. One of them took a quite huge bottle out of one of her pockets, and stood it beside an assortment of bootlaces, chocolate, sticking plaster, Beechams pills, a notebook, pencils, lint and bandages. Between us we had enough bandages to stock a hospital; it was the one thing we had all thought of.

Muv was the judge. 'What's in the bottle?' she asked.

'Fluid, m'lady.'

'Fluid? Yes, I see. What sort of fluid?'

'*Fluid*,' said the girl, turning very red and shy.

At last the year was up; I counted the final weeks with mounting rapture. When the great day came I went to Muv. 'I've done what you said and been in the guides for a year. I can leave now, can't I?'

A storm broke about me. '*Leave?* Just when it is doing the

village girls so much good, and they are all enjoying it so much? Of course you can't leave. It would set a very bad example. They'll all want to leave if you leave.'

The tears welled up, but I managed to say: 'But you *said* I could! You promised that if I still hated it at the end of the year I could give it up! Well, I *do* still hate it, more than ever. And why should the village girls want to stop if they all enjoy it so much?' But it was no good; I was commanded to continue being a guide. Even Farve was against me: 'So selfish,' he said.

After a few more months, however, the Swinbrook and Asthall troop of guides petered out. Nancy lost interest; she was never there on a Saturday for one thing: she was gadding. The whole episode was an injustice of my childhood. It came about because Muv wanted to fill the gap until Nancy came out, while Nancy was enchanted to have such a solid, non-stop, reliable tease on hand.

Thinking about it all years later I wondered why so much emphasis was put on bandages, tourniquets, broken limbs. In the lanes round Asthall there was small chance that one would come across people with broken bones, and if one did, a telephone call to Dr. Cheatle would ensue. Nobody in his senses would allow one to minister to his injuries. I said to Kitty Mersey, who had also been a Girl Guide in her childhood, 'I wonder they didn't teach us something useful; to cook, for example.' She replied: 'Oh, they did teach us. Boiled cod.'

In spite of the guides, Nancy and I became great friends. During the winter, except on hunting days, we used to sit together aching with boredom. At least in theory we ached, because Nancy wanted to be in London, and though I hated London I saw her point—we wanted people, our friends; the animals were no longer enough. She was as clever and funny as ever, and sometimes wrote stories which I thought supreme. One was about a Lady Caraway somebody or other who could not marry the man she loved because his name was Seed. She had to arrange for him to be given a peerage.

Mrs. Hammersley came to stay from time to time. She knew clever, unattainable people—'My *friend*, Logan Pearsall Smith', 'My *friends*, the Huxleys'. We envied her. She talked in her deep, hollow voice about books, writers, painters; also about travels.

'I am going to *Rome*,' she told us once.

'Oh, isn't Mrs. Hammersley lucky! She's going to *roam*,' said Unity. 'Where are you going to roam *to*?' she asked.

Once a term we all descended upon Eton in a troop, to visit Tom. I could never make out whether he liked us coming or not. We quickly tired of the playing fields, so he obligingly let his bed down from the wall and we took turns lying on it in his tiny room, which was almost filled with piano. It was a concession of his tutor's that he might put a piano in his room. At that time Tom wanted to be a professional musician; he played the flute in the school orchestra, and the organ in chapel, but the piano was his instrument.

There is something infinitely exhausting about the air of Eton which affects even the casual visitor. After a good rest, and a certain amount of bickering during which Tom kept his usual Olympian calm, we went to have tea at the Cock Pit. We knew dozens of Eton boys, and the Cock Pit was a pivot of school life.

Tom's housemaster was called Mr. Dobbs. 'He's Irish,' said Tom. 'His address is Castle Dobbs, Dobbstown, County Dobbs, Ireland.'

Once a year we were taken to a dentist in Queen Anne Street by Farve. The only reason I can imagine why Farve came was that he liked the dentist and enjoyed his company. When we arrived at Paddington Farve hailed a cab and got into it; as one clambered after him: 'Child! Mind the good shoes!' he cried gaily. Farve's London suits and shoes were always called *good* by him, though his tailor suffered from being forced to put hare pockets inside the jackets. 'A cove must have a hare pocket,' said Farve.

In the waiting room he stood and looked out of the window while we nervously turned over the leaves of an old *Punch* without taking in the jokes. Once one was safely in the dentist's chair Farve's affability knew no bounds. He and the dentist chatted about this and that; our teeth were not among the chosen subjects.

After a quick look the dentist applied the drill, but even then his attention was divided; he would glance for a moment at his victim, then away again to Farve. Gazing through tear-filled eyes at the chimney-pots on the houses opposite I promised myself never, ever, to go to a dentist again once I was grown up.

'How did it go?' asked Muv when we got back to Asthall, worn out by the terrible day.

'Torture.'

'Nonsense, dear child,' said Farve.

It was this dentist, so unaccountably popular with him, who pulled all Farve's teeth out, and made him the false teeth which according to Nancy he wore out at the rate of two sets a year by grinding them in his rages.

When I was fourteen the Asthall schoolmistress, who played the organ in church, left the village. Mr. Ward asked me to take her place, and after that I no longer minded going to church. 'Sorry, Farve, I can't come to Swinbrook. I've got to play the organ here,' I was able to say.

The organ was at the back of the church to one side; a small mirror reflected Mr. Ward and his doings. A village boy pumped. He was very dreamy, but I knew the services so intimately from the days of my mania that I found it easy to prompt him. Unless he worked the wooden handle up and down no sound came.

I gave the note to Mr. Ward. 'Oh Lord, make haste to help us,' he intoned. Then a chord, and 'Oh God, make speed to save us', Mrs. Ward's ringing contralto boomed. During the sermon I turned the pages of my music, deciding on a voluntary; anything, even 'Swanee' and 'Ramona', was suitable provided it was played slowly enough to sound holy.

There was a third church on Farve's land, Widford. It was away in the fields by the river; no road led to it and there was only one service a year—harvest festival. It was tiny and old— 'restored in 1100' said Farve; there were box pews: 'a cove could have a deck of poker during the sermon,' as he observed one day when Grandmother was at Asthall. '*Dowdie*, darling,' she said disapprovingly, tucking in her chin, in her *pas devant les enfants* voice. Covered in sawdust there were bits of Roman mosaic pavement; Widford had been a temple before it became a church.

All round us there were remains of great antiquity. On the

hill above Asthall there stood a Saxon barrow, it was like a
giant flower pot containing a group of trees. Uncle George
asked Farve if he could open the barrow.

'We shall find warriors lying there,' he told us, 'with great
golden spears and shields.'

After a long and patient dig, sifting every spadeful of earth,
a few oddments came to light; needles, for example. The
barrow must have been a woman's burial place, the experts
said. While he had his men Uncle George dug up a bit of the
Roman road and found the handle of a spoon, formed by a
greyhound chasing a hare. He gave everything to the Ash-
molean, and took his wife to see his treasure. 'Only *that* little
heap?' she said, disappointed.

A problem that occasionally worried us was, how should we
manage to keep alive when we were grown up? The question
was raised at meal-times. 'I hope you children realize you've
got to earn your own living,' Farve would say, and my tears
welled up at the thought; 'you won't get anything from *me*,'
he would go on, 'I've got nothing to leave you,' and Muv, more
serious, 'But of course not, girls don't expect it.'

We all hated this conversation, but I had an idea what I
might do; I still thought I could live with my friends in the
Isles of Greece.

We had our friends and cousins to stay in the holidays;
Rosemary and Clementine Mitford, the daughters of Uncle
Clem who had been killed in the war, often came. Rosemary
was my best friend, and Clementine at the age of eight was the
most beautiful human being I have ever seen in my life. There
were also Dick and Dooley Bailey, Diana and Randolph
Churchill, Cecilia Keppel, Sibell and Mark Norman. We went
away to stay with all these children. On our return home, full
of what I had seen and heard, I looked in vain for an audience.
Nanny slightly disapproved of one's ever going away on any
pretext; Muv was not much interested. 'Oh did you, darling,' or
'Oh was it, h'm' was about as much as one could hope for, and
she stretched her arms and yawned. She might add: 'I'm sure
Chartwell's lovely; Clementine is so clever;' it was no use
hoping for more than that.

She also had certain prejudices: for example, she did not
care for rich people. She realized, of course, that some people

could not help being rich, but she looked upon it as a quite serious disadvantage.

Tom and I loved staying at Chartwell; Diana and Randolph became our bosom friends. Cousin Clementine was beautiful and kind, Cousin Winston a perennial wonder. We hung on his words at mealtimes, and at the end of dinner he occasionally sang 'Soldiers of the Queen' and other ballads of his youth, beating time as he did so with his shapely white hand before getting up and going off for a game of six-pack bezique followed by hours of work on his book. When we first resumed relations with these cousins they used to say: 'What's the use of a W.C. without a seat?' But by the time we visited Chartwell he was back in Parliament, and Chancellor of the Exchequer in Baldwin's government. A fellow-guest at Chartwell, our cousin Edward Stanley, was asked one night at dinner by Cousin Winston whether he was a Liberal, in the old tradition of the Stanley family.

'No,' said Edward.

'Why not?'

Edward said he could not belong to a party led by Lloyd George. Thereupon Cousin Winston launched into such a superb paean glorifying his old friend and former leader as completely to convert at least one of his listeners.

Someone who was in and out of Chartwell in those days was Brendan Bracken, an extraordinary looking young man with an almost negroid cast of countenance, thick red hair and black teeth. He never stayed long for he was not liked by his hostess. Randolph loved his company, though they bickered. Diana said: 'There's a rumour that Mr. Bracken is papa's *son!*' with shrill giggles, and Randolph added: 'Mummy won't call him Brendan because she's so afraid he might call her Clemmie.'

An American we knew also disliked Brendan. 'Everything about the man is phoney,' he said; 'even his hair which looks like a wig, is his own.'

It does not take children very long to become attached to a house; we loved Asthall, though Farve did not. He still spoke of his intention to build; on the site of his choice there was a rather unattractive farm house called South Lawn. One day, to our sorrow, some people came to 'look over the house'. The schoolroom door opened and they peeped in. 'This is the schoolroom,' said Mabel. We stood up, and they quickly shut the door again. Muv, who had also grown fond of Asthall, was not happy about Farve's plan for selling it. She insisted that if it were sold we must have a London house; Nancy and Pam were both grown up now, and during the summer they were busy in London. Pictures of Asthall appeared in *Country Life*; we could not recognize it from the descriptions of the agents. An elm tree beyond the tennis courts became 'an ancient rookery' and one of the water meadows 'a natural polo ground'. For a while, the sale hung fire.

Now that the hated guiding was over we returned to our old habit of bicycling to Burford on Saturday for shopping. In the weeks before Christmas we bought presents for each other at Packers, the stationers; for our parents we had generally made some horror in the schoolroom, a beaded tray cloth or embroidered anti-macassar. We wrapped up the presents in good time, and gave them on Christmas morning between opening our stockings and church. Nancy once despised my present so much that she threw it straight on the fire. Strangely enough I did not mind a bit; I knew it was a hopeless present and admired her courage in demonstrating her displeasure. Muv, on the other hand, loyally put our gifts in her room and pretended to love them.

On Christmas night we had a fancy-dress dinner. With our aunts and uncles we opened the dressing-up chest and did what we could with the contents. One was not allowed to buy anything or prepare in advance; it was a test of resourcefulness and imagination. Tom and I worried a good deal over our disguises, but Nancy and Pam did not. Nancy always made herself either irresistibly comic or exquisitely beautiful; Pam, no sooner were her animals fed, flew to the box and got out a shapeless purple gown and necklace of wooden beads. In this she appeared, Christmas after Christmas, as the Lady Rowena from *Ivanhoe*.

When everybody was ready Farve took a flashlight photograph. The responsibility of this made him cross; we stood waiting, half shrieking at each other's wonderful aspect, half trembling at Farve's visibly mounting rage. Uncle Jack was always last. 'Jicksy, Jicksy, the boy's late as usual, JICKSY,' he roared up the stairs. 'Coming, dear boy,' said Uncle Jack mildly, and Farve laughed in spite of himself at the strange apparition.

After dinner we played 'commerce' for money prizes. Farve ruled the card table with the utmost strictness; chatter was discouraged. 'Don't talk—how can anybody think with you making that infernal row—take your degraded elbows off the table, child—your turn, dear boy,' he kept up a steady barracking.

I looked forward to Christmas for weeks, but it hardly ever passed off quite smoothly. One of the trouble makers was the decorations. At Batsford the gardeners made swags of bay and hung them all round the stone hall; at Asthall we did it ourselves, putting sprigs of holly here and there; two above each picture. Months later Farve would spy a strange bulge in the canvas; it was the holly, which had fallen down behind and was spitefully working its way through. 'Look what you children have done to the good picture! I *will* not have holly in this house.'

All of us children, except possibly Tom, were afraid of the dark and of ghosts, yet we could not resist the books that doubled our night terrors: *Ghost Stories of an Antiquary, Dracula, The Turn of the Screw*. Asthall was very old; the panelling gave mysterious cracks, and outside our bedrooms was the churchyard where owls hooted in the yews. We sometimes wondered whether Farve, like us, believed the house to be haunted; and we thought that, just possibly, it was one of the reasons he was so determined to leave.

Inevitably, Asthall found a buyer and we had to go. It was the end of my childhood; I was now sixteen, and had lately grown about a foot and could no longer be teased, as formerly, for being small and puny. While Builder Redesdale, as Nancy called Farve, did his worst at South Lawn, we all went to Paris to economize.

Farve's finances were a great mystery to us, and have remained so. He almost always thought he was ruined and the workhouse loomed large in his conversation, yet at the same time he would every now and then begin to build again. He invested in gambles, but I have no idea what sums were involved because money was a taboo subject in families like ours and our parents would as soon have spoken about sex to

us as money. An invention he put money in made us all laugh
so much when he described it that he went off in dudgeon to
his business room, and one heard the strains of his favourite
soprano singing a Puccini aria. The idea was that wirelesses
were ugly (as indeed they were; just as bad as televisions
now, they spoilt a corner of any room), and that they were
to be made beautiful by being encased in papier maché in
lovely designs, a jewelled casket for example, or a Spanish
galleon, or a Buddha which, according to Farve, could take
his place 'among the old famille rose'. Needless to say, these
objects were infinitely more hideous than even the nastiest
of wirelesses. Muv dreaded the jewelled casket, but she never
had to put up with one because the whole venture ended in the
law courts. Farve was sued for slander by the South American
casket maker for allegedly saying he was not the marquis he
pretended to be. We all went to hear the case, which was
decided in Farve's favour. Diana Churchill came with us and
whispered to me: 'It's so unfair. Cousin David was *bound* to
win, just because he looks like God the Father.'

5

Paris

FARVE LIKED PARIS in very small doses; he was not a town lover, but at least in London he had the consolation of the Marlborough Club and the House of Lords. He worked hard in committees, and sometimes of late the strains of Puccini and Kreisler on the business room gramophone had been stilled, and one found him poring over a Blue Book.

Nancy wrote him letters from Paris addressed 'Builder Redesdale, The Buildings, South Lawn, Burford, Oxfordshire'. The old name of South Lawn was taboo; he wanted his house to be called Swinbrook, although it was a mile from the village, but Nancy never hesitated to tease him.

Muv's friends the Helleus had found us a cheap hotel to live in quite near them, in the avenue Victor Hugo. Helleu had done quantities of dry-point etchings of Muv when she was young and he admired her very much; he also admired Farve, and us children, and never stopped saying so, which was wonderfully unexpected and stimulating. Nanny's repeated words: 'Nobody's going to look at *you*, darling' did not correspond with reality when Helleu was about.

Madame Helleu had been asked to find a day-school for me nearby, and I was taken to the Cours Fénelon in the rue de la Pompe. Muv and I had an interview with the headmistress. She asked when I had last been vaccinated? I had never been vaccinated, even as a baby; vaccination was one of Muv's deepest aversions, along with white bread and pork. 'Ah!' said the headmistress. 'Then I regret she cannot come to the Cours Fénelon until you have it done.' 'I am sorry,' said Muv. 'She cannot be vaccinated.' There was a long pause while my fate was in the balance. Then, 'Oh, tant pis,' said the headmistress, and I was accepted.

I learned more at the Cours Fénelon in six months than I had learned at Asthall in six years. A dozen or so girls, of whom I was one, went every morning for preparation, presided over by an elderly governess, Mlle Foucauld. In the afternoons were the Cours proper, at which we were lectured to and questioned by bearded professors from the Sorbonne. Half-way through the morning's lessons there was a break of twenty minutes and we ran down to the yard. 'Ne dégringolez pas les escaliers!' called Mlle Foucauld, who was always trying to make us behave like young ladies.

When we got to the yard they picked sides and we played a ball game, throwing the ball from team to team. If you dropped the ball when it came your way your team lost a point. At first there was great competition to have me, because tallness was an advantage, and then being English, and dressed in such countrified clothes, made them confident that I must be une sportive. They soon learned their mistake; every time I was supposed to catch it the ball dropped dismally to the ground. There was a chorus of those sort of throaty groans which French children of both sexes make when they wish to mark disappointment or disapproval. The only other foreigner, a Peruvian girl, and I were relegated to the worst place. I did not mind; it was a recognized thing in our family that we were abnormally hopeless at games.

When the break was up we climbed the stairs, more slowly than we had come down but all talking at once. 'Taisez-vous, taisez-vous mes enfants,' said Mlle Foucauld.

After the fresh air in the yard our classroom smelt really terrific. It faced south on to the rue de la Pompe, and on the 15th of October Mlle Foucauld spent the whole morning with a hammer and nails, nailing sausages of red stuff round the window frames. Once the sausages were in position the windows could not be opened again until they were ripped off the following spring. The autumn of 1926 must have been particularly hot, for the sun blazed in day after day and the smell got worse and worse as we sat and sweated in the hermetically sealed room. The Peruvian girl was a garlic eater, which did not improve matters.

In the afternoon we sat in the big lecture room grouped round Mlle Foucauld. She was so anxious for us to shine that sometimes she would 'souffler' the answer to some hard conundrum put by one of the bearded men. I used to scan her face out of the corner of my eye, and strain my ears; she hardly ever let one down. 'Très bien, Mademoiselle Meetfor,' was the reward, which pleased her just as much as it did me.

Most of the girls did lessons in their own homes in the mornings and only came to the rue de la Pompe after luncheon. They were usually accompanied by their governesses, who sat by them during the Cours, though some of them came with a footman. Towards the end of the afternoon when one crossed the vestibule a few of these men would be sitting among the boots, umbrellas and overcoats, waiting for their charges.

I was allowed to go back to our hotel, les Villas St. Honoré d'Eylau, by myself; it was very near. When I arrived I joined the others and Nanny for tea. There was almost always a drama about the desert rats. These were the only creatures we had been allowed to bring to Paris with us; one couldn't keep pigs and chickens in an hotel, and dogs and cats would have been liable to quarantine when we got back to England. The rats were adorable; they were pale yellow with lustrous black eyes. Of course they could not be made to languish permanently in their cages, and when they were out they always behaved badly. Once they bored a hole in the carpet in the corner of our hotel sitting-room and disappeared. We took it in turns for hours, having meals on the shift system, to kneel by this hole making loving sounds to coax them to come out again. We were terrified of what the hotel servants might do if the rats re-emerged when we were not there. Annie and Nellie at home never cared for our pets, and we felt that French housemaids might show their dislike in a practical way. We were also rather afraid of Muv, who did not want us turned out of the hotel, and Nanny was getting tired of the desert rats. 'Put them away, darling, do; hurry up; I shall tell your mother of you.'

Lord Crewe was the English ambassador, and his granddaughter Middy O'Neill was one of Nancy's greatest friends. Nancy and Pam were often invited to the embassy, and they also had a number of new French acquaintances who invited them to parties. Sometimes I was allowed to go too. I had a friend, Mary Clive, whose father was Military Attaché. I went to luncheon with them at their old house on the other side of the river. I was just beginning to notice what houses were like; General Clive was pleased when I admired it. 'You see the plan,' he said. 'Like all old Paris houses it is built between courtyard and garden.'

Although they lived in a rather ordinary block of flats, the Helleus' drawing-room was perfect. It was white, the Louis XVI chairs and sofa were covered in white or pale grey silk, the curtains were white and on the walls were carved gilt wood eighteenth-century frames, empty. Helleu said if you were not rich enough to possess the pictures you wished for it was best to have frames and use your imagination. The drawing-room was his studio.

At Christmas we all went back to our new London house, 26 Rutland Gate. The economical Paris visit was over, but I was to return to the Cours Fénelon after the holidays. Muv had put all her favourite furniture from Asthall into Rutland Gate and it looked charming. Pam and I had a bedroom overlooking the Ennismore Gardens churchyard, and Farve had a dark business room on the ground floor; he had been allowed to choose the stuff for his curtains. It was a frightful sort of sham tapestry covered in dingy leaves and berries. 'Oh, Farve, how *ugly*,' we said; but he imagined he saw birds and squirrels peeping out of the foliage, and this made him feel nearer the coverts at home.

The drawing-room was as bright as Farve's room was gloomy. The curtains were pale blue taffeta, the sofas covered in flowery pink chintz, and the French furniture had been put there. On the wall hung my favourite among our pictures, a handsome young man with powdered hair in a blue velvet coat by Perronneau, in a splendid carved gilt frame.

Muv was pleased with her new house and never went to see how the Buildings were getting on. Farve spent a good deal of his time at Swinbrook; his dream was taking shape there. Not only a house, but garages, cottages and greenhouses were going up, and he had added a squash court to be built a little distance away in the garden. We were each to have a bedroom to ourselves. 'The best of everything for everybody,' said Uncle Tommy when he came up to see us in London. Uncle Tommy was now married; he had left the Mill Cottage and gone away to live at Westwell.

I went for a visit to Chartwell. 'Papa, guess who is older, our Diana or Diana M.?' said Randolph one evening. They had all agreed that I looked almost grown up, which it was my dearest wish to be. Cousin Winston looked from one to the other. '*Our* Diana,' he said. 'Oh, *Papa*, nobody thinks so but you!' said Randolph. In fact, Diana C. was a year older than I was. Eddie Marsh thought having two Dianas was muddling and said I had better be called Artemis instead.

Churchill was devoted to his children, especially to Randolph, but until they were almost grown up a little of their company went a long way. 'Papa says he won't be bunged up with brats,' Randolph used to say. This was never resented, but was taken for granted by us all. The Churchill children did not mind being called brats, which in their family had become almost a term of endearment. When, some years later, Randolph referred in their hearing to my step-children Vivien and Nicky as 'Tom's brats' he was never forgiven by them.

We had now ceased to be brats and were treated as grown up; Cousin Winston was kindness itself to Tom and me and he was loved and admired by us. We also admired Clementine, who with her sister-in-law Lady Goonie Churchill epitomized beauty and grace in our eyes. Lady Goonie's children, Johnny, Peregrine and Clarissa were often at Chartwell, and Johnny became a great friend.

Christmas holidays at the Cours Fénelon were very short; I had to go back to Paris early in January. The idea that I might travel alone was never considered, and to save the expense of a chaperon it was kindly suggested that I might go with Randolph and his father. They were on their way to Rome to visit Mussolini, who was greatly admired by Winston.

Randolph and I chatted the whole way over except on the boat. The sea was rough and Randolph was sick. 'Poor little boy!' said Cousin Winston when I told him this as he emerged from his cabin at Calais. How kind he is, I thought; nobody pitied us if we were sick on the Channel. Randolph recovered in a trice, and we all had a wonderful luncheon at Calais before we got back into the train for Paris. I was sad to say good-bye to them, and wished I could go on to Rome.

At the Gare du Nord an old woman was on the look-out for me, and I was handed over to her while the Churchills shunted off to the Gare de Lyon.

She was one of two old sisters who took English girls in their flat; they had been chosen because they lived on the corner of the avenue Victor Hugo and the rue de la Pompe, and once more I was to be allowed to go to the Cours by myself. And not only to the Cours. In spite of my minus quantity of talent I was still having violin lessons; piano I had given up, for the contrast between me and Tom was too painful. My violin master lived near the Lycée Janson, a hundred yards away; I was also to be allowed to go down the hill to the Helleus in the rue Emil Menier. In other words, for the first time in my life I had a certain freedom.

In London we could not so much as go to Harrods from Rutland Gate by ourselves. This meant—since we had no footmen like the girls at the Cours Fénelon—that either one had to find a sister willing to go, or coax Nanny out, or else stay at home. It was extremely tiresome and frustrating, but we took it as a matter of course; most of the girls we knew followed the same rule. I never travelled alone on a train until I was twenty-two; even after I was married there was always somebody with me.

At Asthall it was different; we were supposed to ride two together, but we could walk wherever we liked. I used to walk along the tarmac main road, day-dreaming that a beautiful young man would stop his car, get out, and propose that we drive together to the far ends of the earth. If some crazy individual had really suggested carrying me off in this way I am sure I should have gone with him, so possibly Farve was not so far wrong in trying to circumvent disaster.

I now found myself in Paris knowing, through Nancy and Pam, quite a number of young people, if not with freedom then at least with endless possibilities for manœuvre within permitted limits. I took instant advantage of this. If I was invited to go to a cinema with a young man I told the sisters that my violin master wanted me for an extra lesson, or that I must go to Helleu for a sitting. When I came out of the Cours my friend and I would fly off in a taxi and he would drop me back at the avenue Victor Hugo in time for dinner. Except for an occasional thé dansant, given by people I was allowed to visit, this was the extent of my dissipation.

In his white drawing-room Helleu made several drawings of me. While he worked he talked. He made me feel what

Americans call 'good', and as if he would rather be drawing me than doing anything else in this world or the next. He took me to Rouen to see the rose window in the cathedral of which he had done a painting.* We lunched in a nearby restaurant where the owner was delighted to welcome him, we had sole dieppoise and Sancerre and lingered until it was time for the Paris train. He took me to the Louvre, to Versailles. He talked all the time about pictures or about people. I had hardly ever heard of the people. 'Je vais exposer à Londres l'année prochaine,' he told me. 'Lady Cunard m'a proposé son salon.' But I had never heard of Lady Cunard. He did a pointe sèche of me, drawing straight on to the sheet of copper as was his wont.

Helleu's daughter, Paulette, was a year or so older than I; we were friends. Unlike her father, she was very critical and frank; she thought my clothes awful, which they were, particularly compared with hers, and she contradicted whatever I chose to say. Nevertheless I was very fond of her; her attitude towards me was no more unflattering than my sisters' and I was perfectly accustomed to snubs—they were the normal thing; it was admiration that astonished.

Helleu had another beautiful daughter called Madame Orosdi who lived in the avenue du Bois. He and I used to walk in the avenue after the Cours at midday, and sometimes we met his grand-daughters and their governess. He said the avenue du Bois was not what it had been; motor cars spoilt it. He loved women, horses and sailing boats, he said; and he really was a relic of the belle époque who disliked everything modern, including short hair and the fashions of the twenties.

Occasionally he took me to see friends of his: Sem, the caricaturist, was one; Troubetskoy the sculptor another. When we were ushered into Troubetskoy's studio he was at work on a head of Venizelos, the Greek politician. 'Bonjour, Monsieur, la voici la Grèce!' cried Helleu in his enthusiastic way, pointing to me. Venizelos turned a lack-lustre eye upon me, and I felt a fool; my exuberant old friend had gone too far.

'Sûrtout, soyons classique!' he used to say, and he told me he was le petit-fils d'Ingres, because Ingres had taught the man

* '. . . for interiors of cathedrals, I know of none to equal in beauty those of the great painter Helleu.'

Marcel Proust, *La Bible d'Amiens*

who taught him. He asked me which was my favourite picture, and did not altogether disapprove when I said it was *Le déjeuner sur l'herbe*. I have often wondered since why I so loved that picture when I was sixteen. It may have been because of the subject. Just as in what already seemed the old days at Asthall with Jim Lees-Milne, my ideal was bohemian life in a warm climate. In Manet's picture the people must have been warm enough although it was so green, because otherwise the woman could never have sat so naked and relaxed.

The flat where I lived was on the ground floor, flush with the street; my bedroom window could only be opened at night, when the shutters were locked, otherwise any passer-by could have stepped in for there was no area such as London houses have. Early in the morning I heard footsteps hurrying past on the pavement close to my bed, and the sound of men clearing their throats and spitting. At night I sat up in bed and wrote my diary.

The flat had a lavatory at the end of the passage, its only window gave into the kitchen which I thought improper. There was no bath. Twice a week the maid brought a shallow round tin, the same as Degas so often painted, into my room. She poured half an inch of boiling water into it, and left it with a jug of cold water standing by. One had to add some of the cold water in order not to be scalded in the basin, but however little one put in it mysteriously turned from boiling hot to stone cold. It needed courage to wash in this object, and then to dry oneself on a towel the size of a handkerchief. I wrote and complained to Muv, and she sent me enough money for an occasional bath at the Villas St. Honoré d'Eylau, which the old sisters considered perfectly ridiculous, very extravagant and rather insulting to their elegant dwelling.

They were great despisers, and their worst strictures were reserved for anywhere that was not Paris. Some parts even of Paris itself were not approved of: 'La rive gauche! Ce que ça fait province!' they said.

I loved Versailles, and sometimes went down with Helleu to walk in the wintry park. If I was unwise enough to mention this at dinner they were on to me like a ton of bricks. 'Vous aimez ça? Ah, ça je ne comprends pas alors. Versailles! C'est d'une tristesse! Et ce que ça fait province!' they said in chorus.

One of them did the cooking herself; the food was excellent but there was not enough of it for me. At that time I was always hungry though I ate like an ogre of everything I was given; fussiness had been replaced by greed. The old ladies laughed rather crossly about my insatiable appetite; I suppose I ate more than they had reckoned each child should when they fixed the price to be paid. It was well known that I was hungry; sometimes Helleu or one of my other friends would meet me at the Cours at the end of the morning and take me to Pruniers down the avenue for a sandwich before luncheon. Helleu loved to see me eat: 'Mais prenez, prenez donc!' he said when I lunched with them, heaping my plate with heavenly food, roast veal, bœuf en gelee, îles flottantes.

'On ne vous donne pas assez là bas,' kind Madame Helleu said gently. She and Paulette invited me to their sitting-room for the goûter; we had weak tea and slices of rich black chocolate cake. She was raffinée and elegant, 'la multiforme Alice', as Robert de Montesquiou called her, 'dont la rose chevelure illumine de son reflet tant de miroirs de cuivre.'

At the Cours Fénelon I no longer found it difficult doing my lessons in French. I even allowed myself to copy the other girls who, the moment Mlle Foucauld's back was turned, threw open the lids of their desks and got busy with looking glasses and powder puffs. Some of them also used lipstick; but this, in spite of my new freedom, I would not have dared to do. One beautiful creature, as smart as I was dowdy, told me that her mother dressed her at 'les grandes maisons'; I was still so ignorant of such things that I supposed she was referring to the Galéries Lafayette or the Printemps, shops which were beyond my wildest dreams. All my clothes were still home-made.

The end of my stay in Paris was made desperately sad by the illness and death of Helleu. When I heard how ill he was I went to the flat; Paulette opened the door. 'May I see him?' I asked. 'Of course *not*,' was the reply.

I felt his death deeply. I was his devoted admirer, and loved his gaiety and liveliness and enthusiasm. I went back to London, carrying the pointe sèche he had done of me. It had been reproduced, a full page in the magazine l'*Illustration*, and this had put me on the map at the Cours Fénelon. Indulgent Mlle Foucauld said it was 'très ressemblant', but I knew in my heart it was flattering. The old sisters hastened to plant a dart. 'Helleu?' they said. 'Non, Helleu ne me dit rien du tout. Franchement je trouve que ça fait très avant guerre.'

As I have said, nothing could exceed the slender distinction of Mme Helleu. Everyone knows what she looked like because Helleu loved to draw and paint her. In his life of Proust, George Painter says that Helleu was Elstir in the novel, and from this he deduces that Mme Helleu was 'a lady of ample charms who was not quite presentable in society'. Mr. Painter here confuses Mme Helleu with Mme Monet; Monet being another artist who was part of Elstir.

The change of scene, and being back in my usual place in the family soon comforted me for the loss of my old friend; the Easter holidays in London were agreeable, and I was delighted to see the others again. Nanny, in her new nursery, clicked and sniffed rather over my Paris adventures when she bothered to listen at all, but life was pleasant and I looked forward to the summer term at the Cours Fénelon. Then the bomb fell.

One day Pam and I were out for a walk in the Park. On our way back I stood still and my heart gave a thump. My diary! I had been writing it after breakfast on, of all places, Muv's writing table in the drawing-room, and I suddenly remembered that I had left it there, lying open, when somebody called me out of the room. I had clean forgotten it, and Muv must have seen it, and most likely read it too.

Mabel opened the door; 'Her ladyship wants you,' she said. A hollow voice rang down the stairs: 'Diana, Diana, come here at once.' I was never called Diana in the family, except for scolding purposes. Muv called me Dana, Farve Dina, Nancy Bodley, Pam and Unity Nardy, Decca Corduroy and Debo Honks. The very word, Diana, was in itself sinister. Useless to protest the harmlessness of what I had done; to have been to a cinema alone with a young man, in Paris, even in the afternoon, was a frightful disobedience and an almost unforgivable crime. For two or three whole days nobody spoke at meals; my parents looked too black and threatening. Telegrams flew to Paris cancelling all arrangements for the summer term; there was no question of my going back.

At first the others were sympathetic to me about the trouble I was in, but as the gloomy days dragged by they turned on me.

'How *could* you be such a fool! Leaving your *diary* about! In the drawing-room too. How could *anyone* be so stupid!'

I imagine Muv and Farve must have conferred for some time about what they could possibly do with me. I was not yet seventeen, too young to come out, and in any case the summer was already full enough of arrangements for Nancy and Pam. I should be very much in the way at Rutland Gate. The Buildings were not yet fit for habitation; workmen were busy putting the finishing touches to Farve's house. With all her worries over us to occupy her, Muv still failed to go down and see what he was up to there.

Finally it was decided that I should be sent to Bucks Mills with Unity, Decca, Debo, Miss Bedell and Nanny, to a cottage belonging to our great-aunt Maude Whyte. It was a pretty cottage in a village near the sea, but I suffered an agony of boredom there, the terrible, deathly essence of boredom. I had not enough books and no money to send for more. Every afternoon I walked up the hill to the village shop and collected the *Daily Mail*. It had a serial of *The Story of Ivy* by Mrs. Belloc Lowndes. The moments spent reading about Ivy were the best of the day, but it was a cruelly short extract. On Sundays even Ivy failed me; I ached from morning till night.

How long were we at Bucks Mills? Two months—three—I have no idea. It seemed an age without a name. Aunt Maude had told some of the neighbours about us, and one of them wrote to me. 'Dear Miss Mitford' the letter began—it was from a lady called Mrs. Pine Coffin, and she wrote 'miss' with a long s—'pray use my valley'. We sometimes did use it, to walk in. But I never felt in Mrs. Pine Coffin's valley as though somebody might come along in a fast car and carry me off. I had lost heart.

6

Swinbrook

WHEN AT LENGTH we left glorious Devon it was to go
straight to the new house at Swinbrook. The rest of the Asthall
furniture was in it, but we all thought the house monstrous.
Muv blamed herself for not having paid more attention while
it was being built; the fireplace in the drawing-room, for example, a sort of rustic affair in un-cut Cotswold stone, was
unnecessarily ugly.

From our point of view the worst part was that the library
books had been squeezed into the business room, where one was
not always welcome. There was no distant, solitary library
which we could use as our own. The piano was in the drawing-
room; Tom hardly ever played; he did not care to when people
were dashing in and out, banging doors, as they naturally did
in the drawing-room used by us all. In place of the Barn with
its peace and delicious smell of books and polished wood where
Tom and I had spent so much of our time at Asthall there was
a squash court, hardly ever played in and yet impossible to use
as a retreat, with its hateful echoes and bare, windowless walls.
There were now more of us 'downstairs' than ever; only Debo
remained to keep Nanny company in the nursery.

True, we each had a room to ourselves. This boon, however,
did not count for very much, because—possibly the newly-
finished plastering and painting may have been to blame—
Swinbrook was always cold, and we were not allowed fires in
our bedrooms.

I only lived there for just over a year, and even during that
time we were often in London. I spent hours in the linen cupboard, a tiny room with a window; hot water pipes ran to and
fro so that it was warm summer and winter. When Annie and
Muv found me there: 'Go out, darling,' said Muv. 'Of course
you're cold if you sit indoors reading all day.' The favourite
authors now were Lytton Strachey, Bertrand Russell, Aldous

Huxley and J. B. S. Haldane. I loved them for their wit and irreverence and their rejection of accepted standards.

Farve was much less happy now that he had his wish and lived on the hill near the pheasants. No doubt he felt our heavy disapproval. Children imagine that their parents—at least parents of his sort—are so strong, so impregnable, that they cannot be hurt, however many the pin-pricks. He no longer laughed when Nancy teased him about the Buildings, but roared, perhaps with pain. I think he realized we truly hated our new home; we did not trouble to conceal it. Sometimes a visitor would inadvertently turn a knife in the wound. 'But it's charming, Sydney, what a lovely drawing-room. Of course it's not Asthall, how you must miss it! Asthall was so lovely, but all the same it's very nice here.'

Farve would growl that he was thankful to be 'out of that damned hole'; but he must have minded. Even the pheasants seemed to have lost their savour, and he never fished now. He went away as often as he could; Rutland Gate was let, but he stayed in the Mews at the back of the house and took refuge from us in the Marlborough Club; in the summer holidays he went to Scotland to shoot.

When I stayed at Chartwell that summer of 1927 Sickert was a fellow-guest. Cousin Clementine told us that as a girl, at Dieppe, she had asked him once: 'Mr. Sickert, who is the greatest living painter?' 'My dear child, I am,' was the reply.

He helped Cousin Winston with advice and theories about painting. He said that as the light that came through the studio window from out of doors was always changing, it was best to paint a portrait by artificial light. On lovely summer afternoons they would shut themselves up with blinds and curtains drawn and the electric light on. Randolph told me that when his father was painting Sarah it was so airless that she fainted, I could easily believe it. This pre-occupation with light was new to me; Helleu never seemed to notice whether the sun went behind a cloud or not when he was working in his white drawing-room.

Cousin Winston asked Sickert at luncheon one day: 'Suppose you had to send a single work of art to Mars, to show them the very best we could do on earth, what would you choose?' Sickert thought for a while and then he said he would send

Tintoretto's *The Origin of the Milky Way*. When I got home I asked Tom the same question about music, and he chose Mozart's Jupiter Symphony.

Eddie Marsh was very often at Chartwell. He was kind, gentle and witty, everything he said in his high-pitched squeaky voice sounded specially amusing. He fired us all with enthusiasm for various second-rate painters and some first-rate ones too, but his chief interest was the theatre. The Churchill children said that if he was asked what he thought of the play he would reply: '*All* plays are divine, but some are diviner than others.' Eddie was the first grown-up person I ever met who treated me as an equal, in the sense of being ready to discuss a subject without the slightest trace of didacticism. This was a result of his exquisite politeness, and of course he taught us far more than do most of the usual run of dogmatic older people.

Another regular at Chartwell was Professor Lindemann. He was not always busy with Cousin Winston, he found plenty of time to spend with us. We loved his company and his brilliant cleverness. Eddie Marsh had taught us a patience called, like the tea, Earl Grey. Prof would look over one's shoulder while one was puzzling what to do, and say: 'That won't come out. There's no point in going on,' or else: 'You can get that out in three moves.' He was a real magician, a human ready-reckoner of lightning speed.

He played a lot of tennis with Cousin Clementine and the other guests; he played to win. There was no thought of an exhilarating volley with Prof about; his method was to drop the ball just over the net with a spin on it to stop it bouncing, if his opponent was on the back line; or if the enemy was up at the net, he would scoop up the ball so that it fell dead on the back line before it could be reached. He must have been most tiresome to play against but it amused me to watch.

Randolph told of Prof's brave exploit at Farnborough during the war. Until 1916 if an aeroplane went into a spin it crashed and the pilot was killed. The Prof worked out mathematically how the pilot could get his machine out of a spin. He then learnt to fly, took up an aeroplane, put it into a spin and successfully demonstrated the truth of his theory.

Another story Prof would neither confirm nor deny; it was

3

that when the Dean of Christ Church reproached him for never going to communion he had replied: 'I can't. I'm a vegetarian.' Randolph insisted: 'You *did* say it, didn't you, Prof?' The Prof gave his little titter and changed the subject.

We used to discuss undergraduates I knew; he disapproved of all of them. 'A dreadful person' was his usual summing-up, and of one cherished friend, Brian Howard, 'Oh, you can't like him. He's a Jew.' Unlike Muv, he definitely preferred people to be rich, and looked upon poverty as a fault. Rich himself, he bestowed rich gifts; he gave me a beautiful watch made of three different coloured golds.

That summer at Chartwell I admitted to the Prof, under questioning, how bored I often was. 'Why don't you learn German?' he said. 'Learn German and read Schopenhauer's *Die Welt als Wille und Vorstellung.*'

When I left and we said goodbye: 'Come and see me next term at Christ Church,' said the Prof, 'and tell me how you are getting on with your German.'

'Oh, she won't be allowed to,' said Randolph. 'Didn't you know? Cousin Sydney has read her diary.'

'Oh, shut up, Randolph,' I said—not for the first time, nor for the last.

When I got back to Swinbrook Farve was there. He looked rather pleased to see me, so I summoned up courage to ask him, 'May I learn German?'

'Certainly not.'

'Oh, Farve, *why* not? After all, Tom's learning it.'

'That's different. Tom's a boy.'

Strangely enough, at that very moment Tom was in Vienna, learning German. Yet Farve could not have been more put out if I had asked to learn the can-can. Tom had gone to Vienna for another reason as well; he thought he could take a final decision in that musical city as to whether he should devote his life to music, or whether he should go to the Bar.

The Bar was thought to be an excellent profession for Tom because he loved arguing. He loved it so much that he offered a shilling an hour to anyone who would argue with him. By the time we got to Swinbrook we no longer argued; instead, we walked in the walled garden. His favourite flowers were the mallows; they reminded him of a Greek poem he knew. 'Ay me, the mallows,' he said, 'when their pride is gone.' The summer ended; he went back to Austria, not to Vienna but to Bernstein, a castle in the Burgenland belonging to a Hungarian, Janos von Almasy, a curiously fascinating man who became one of Tom's dearest friends. He was a perfect companion for a clever boy, intellectually stimulating and with a Don Juan-like temperament. He took Tom to all the neighbouring castles; in one of these, Kohfidisch, lived two sisters, the Countesses Erdödy. Tom at the age of nineteen was rather in love with the younger of the two, Baby; he was also very much in love with German music and German literature.

That autumn Diana Churchill and her mother stayed with us for my first ball; it was at Oxford, the Radcliffe Infirmary Ball was its unpromising name. Prof telephoned next day to ask how many proposals we had had? None, was the disappointing answer.

As our London house was let I sometimes stayed at 11 Downing Street with the Churchills when there was a ball in London and Diana and I went together. At Christmas Tom came back and we visited various friends for hunt balls. One became almost as cold on the way to these entertainments as we used to be in the Morris Cowley when we went to the dancing class. There was no chance of leaving again, however cheerless the town hall, until one's hostess thought everybody had had enough fun. Hunt balls were not my idea of what glamorous grown-up life should be.

The following summer I went to dozens of balls in London. Sometimes Muv came too, and sometimes Farve. I waited until they were at supper or engaged in close conversation on the chaperon's bench to escape to a night-club. The charm of night-clubs was the fact that they were forbidden. After a short time we would return to the ball; there was poor Muv, very sleepy, dying to go home, and only hoping we had enjoyed ourselves. Parents are no longer expected to perform this intolerable corvée; looking back, I see how good they were to put up with it, year after year, for daughter after daughter.

In July I had a proposal from Bryan Guinness, which I accepted. 'Oh no,' said Muv when I told her. 'You are much too young. How old is he?'

'Twenty-two.'

'Oh no, darling, that's ridiculous. Of course you can ask him to stay if you like, but you must wait two years.'

'*Two* years?'

'Well, one year. You are too young to make up your mind.'

7

Bailiffscourt

I WENT, ACCOMPANIED by Nanny, to stay at Bailiffscourt. This was a piece of country by the sea in Sussex which the Guinnesses had bought a couple of years before; they had saved it from speculators who had planned to ruin the entire coast.

Bailiffscourt itself was a small farm-house at Climping, notorious as the home of Colonel Barker, a woman who pretended she was a man and married a Brighton girl. We loved this story which had filled the newspapers and I was considered very lucky to be going to see the place formerly hallowed by the presence of Colonel Barker. I soon discovered, however, that one must not mention Colonel Barker at Bailiffscourt; her name was taboo and Lady Evelyn preferred to forget that she had ever existed.

Lady Evelyn, her children, their Willoughby cousins, and two nurses lived in the Huts. These really were huts, made of pitch pine and set on brick foundations. They smelt deliciously of raw wood and salty air. They were planted down in the middle of a cornfield, and at the bottom of the field was the sea. There was a quite exceptional glare in summer outside the Huts; the flat treeless landscape, the enormous sky, the ripe corn and the sea reflecting back the light of the sun almost blinded one.

Lady Evelyn, like Farve, was a builder. She was going to build a very strange house; already her mind was full of her plans for it, but meantime the family put up in the Huts. Bryan and I wandered about the fields or sat on the beach. Sometimes we all went for a picnic on the Downs. Lady Evelyn, Nurse Helche, Grania, Rosalie, Peregrine, Pink McDonnell, Bryan and I. When we reached the chosen spot the drivers of the cars unpacked a huge tea, a frying pan, a pat of butter, and eggs. 'Diana's so clever, Mummy, she can *cook*,' said Bryan, bursting with pride.

'I've never *heard* of such a thing, it's *too* clever,' said Lady Evelyn in her whispery little voice.

'I can't really. Only fried eggs. Anybody can do fried eggs,' I said modestly, but Lady Evelyn and the nurses took up the refrain. To cook! It was *too* wonderful.

Grania was exactly Debo's age, eight. She had gold curls, an exquisite, agile figure, and she was a ballet dancer. 'She doesn't do many lessons because of her dancing,' said Bryan. One of her masters had been the great Massine himself. As Diaghilev and all his dancers were my heroes and heroines I looked at Grania with awe.

Bryan's brother, Murtogh, never came for the picnics, nor was he seen on the beach or in the cornfield. He stayed in his room with the blinds drawn against the glare, making toy cinemas. He reminded me of Colin in *The Secret Garden*; I wondered he was not ordered out of doors, but Lady Evelyn never dreamed of crossing her children in their slightest whim.

At that time she was in her early forties; a very pretty, slight, fair-haired and blue-eyed person with a very tiny voice. Her voice was not exactly soft; it was more like a miniature hard voice, scarcely audible. She never raised it. She had a ferocious collie called Lady which bit men visitors. 'Lady! Lady! What do I see you doing?' Rather naturally, Lady never noticed this reproof, what with her own growls and the exclamations of her victim.

Lady Evelyn loved wild flowers growing among the corn and did her best to encourage them. Not only in the fields near the Huts were poppy and cornflower seeds strewn in profusion; all the way down in the train from Victoria to Arundel she would lean out of her carriage window in spring-time, scattering weeds and seeds as she went. 'I'm afraid Walter doesn't quite approve,' she told me. Walter, Bryan's father, was Minister of Agriculture.

I had been invited to go to Scotland; I was not anxious to accept and would have preferred to stay at the Huts with Bryan, but Muv said I must go. She thought it would help me to make up my mind; it was a good plan to see as many people as possible. Nanny and I set off. First we went to the Malcolms at Poltalloch, and then to Meikleour. Margaret Mercer-Nairne thought of nothing but horses. When I told her about my engagement she said: 'Yes, marry Bryan, and then you can live in Leicestershire and hunt.'

This was in fact the last thing I wanted to do; I had had enough of the country for a lifetime. People, an eternity of talk, books, pictures, music and travel—these were my eighteen-year-old desires.

Margaret, her mother Lady Violet Astor, and I rode through fertile, un-Scotch country every morning while the men were on the moors. They had their horses at Meikleour to get them fit for the season's hunting. We joined the guns for luncheon, trudged with them all afternoon, and ate a huge dinner sitting in stuffed armchairs. I loved Margaret and her comfortable house full of beautiful French furniture; next to Diana she was my greatest friend at that time.

When I got back to Swinbrook I told them my mind was still made up. Lady Evelyn was on our side, but said she could not write to Muv and Farve. 'I shouldn't *dare*,' she whispered. While Parliament was in recess Bryan's father was away on his yacht—far away. He did not go to the Mediterranean, but to distant, savage lands.

In September he was expected back. Lady Evelyn and the children left the Huts and went to Heath House, Hampstead. 'I wish we could stay on at Bailiffscourt,' she said. 'Such beautiful weather. But I must go at once because of Christmas.'

'*Christmas*, Lady Evelyn?' I cried. 'But that's three months off!'

'Oh yes,' said Bryan, 'but it takes Mummy a *good* three months to do her Christmas. In fact she's really at it the whole year.'

This astonished me so much that I asked Rosalie and Pink McDonnell about it one day. 'Aunt Evelyn's Christmas is terrific,' said Rosalie. 'In fact Uncle Walter can't stand it. He always leaves England the moment Parliament rises because of the Grosvenor Place Christmas.'

Bryan came to stay with us at Swinbrook. Every time he said or did something uncountrified I glowed with pride and pleasure. Uncle George used to say the country was 'all mud and blood'. I was beginning to agree, and I saw in Bryan the antithesis of a squire.

The only time his vagueness unnerved me was at breakfast, when we helped ourselves. He would stand by the sideboard, holding a plate in one hand and a spoonful of sticky porridge in the other, which he shook violently in an attempt to dislodge it into the plate, looking away and talking to us the while. Farve slightly ground his teeth, but bore it in silence for my sake; and I was grateful, for I knew how much it cost him. Bryan, in fact, never spilt; not even the porridge; but one always felt he might just be going to. He seemed to love being part of our huge family and could not understand my complaints about the lack of solitude; the more sisters the better for him, and he particularly loved the little ones. I loved them too, but Swinbrook had no charm for me, I wanted to go away and never come back. The schoolroom atmosphere exasperated me and it was that which Bryan most enjoyed.

Colonel Guinness, who turned up eventually, had a long talk with Bryan. I was invited to stay at Heath House; Bryan met me at Paddington and drove me to Hampstead. When we arrived his mother was gardening. She was walking along a path with a watering can, watering it here and there, if that is the word, with milk. 'Mummy's encouraging the moss', explained Bryan.

The garden was quite big by Hampstead standards; it looked rather sad. Ugly tufts of murky, un-tended grass and weeds sprouted everywhere, there were over-grown hedges with holes and gaps in them, and not a flower was to be seen except the odd dandelion and thistle. 'Mummy can't bear garden flowers,' Bryan told me. 'She only likes wild ones, and of course they don't do very well in London.'

Lady Evelyn pointed vaguely here and there. 'You can't imagine what a perfectly *ghastly* pergola there used to be,' she said, adding in a horrified whisper, 'And there were *hideous* roses—in *beds.*'

Inside, Heath House had also been transformed to Lady Evelyn's taste, and one saw what Bailiffscourt would eventually become.

Colonel Guinness seemed not to notice either the garden or the house. He talked about politics, people and health.

'What! No vitamins?' he said when I refused some raw carrot. The food was excellent; we ate it off a worm-eaten refectory table. I felt very shy of Bryan's father. He was kind but distant to me; but he had promised Bryan to write to Farve.

Every evening we dined early and went to a play. In the mornings Lady Evelyn did her Christmas shopping, and in the afternoon she scattered milk over the grim garden.

Farve gave in and we were officially engaged. I spent my time between Swinbrook and Grosvenor Place, where the Guinnesses returned in October. Lady Evelyn shopped all day now, as there were only about seventy shopping days till Christmas.

Grosvenor Place was like Heath House only much, much more so. When you approached the great, ugly Victorian imitation of a French château and walked up the steps the door opened at once. This was the work of George, the door man, who sat all day watching the entrance from a little window in the porch. He was by way of being clumsy. 'Did George knock you down?' was Lady Evelyn's first question when one arrived. George led the way across a dark hall with stripped pine panelling to the lift, which looked like a tiny mediaeval closet. The lift whizzed up several floors and was opened by a nursery-maid. Tea, and in fact most of life, was spent in Grania's nursery. Lady Evelyn herself slept in one of the night nurseries. The day nursery was a large cheerful white room with a bright fire, plenty of toys and books, and sofas covered in chintz. While the rest of the house was almost pitch dark, lights blazed in the nursery. Lady growled and made little dashes, but she only bit men guests; Raymond and Edward Greene, great friends of Lady Evelyn, always came to Grosvenor Place wearing riding boots because of the collie.

If one arrived for luncheon or dinner George handed one over to the head parlourmaid and the full oddity of Grosvenor Place was unfolded. The downstairs rooms were lined— panelled is not the word—with rough, blackened wood. The fires were encouraged to smoke and smoulder, because the effect Lady Evelyn wished to create was that of a house so 'early' that chimneys had not been invented. The furniture, besides refectory tables black with age—or with simulated age—one did not always quite believe in the Grosvenor Place furniture—consisted of dozens of Spanish chairs, of various sizes but similar design, a strip of dark, hard leather for the back, another for the seat, with many a rusty nail to catch a stocking here and there in the crumbling wooden frame. The lamps were made of bent pieces of iron holding sham yellow candles with yellow bulbs of about five watts shaded in thick old parchment—tallow, not wax, was the note. This ground floor was just as dark by day as when the glimmering lights were lit, for ancient leaded windows of greenish hue had been fitted in place of the Victorian plate glass. The dining-room gave on to a small courtyard, on the other side of which a carved stone gothic door had been built into what was really the wall of the Mews. There was also a gnarled tree, which, I was told, had been lifted roots and all by a giant crane over the Mews at the back of the house. These amenities were guessed at rather than seen as one peered through the tiny panes of primitive, almost opaque, glass.

On the tables were pewter pots containing bunches of grasses and wild flowers, and there were polished pewter plates and dishes to eat off. The forks had two prongs. The pewter things were made by Day, the head chauffeur, in a garage. He had given up driving and spent his whole time making more and more pewter plates, because Colonel Guinness liked to have dinner parties of over a hundred people. Lady Evelyn thought entertaining a tiresome bore, but she did it for his sake, only insisting that there must be enough pewter for everybody. To have had to fall back on silver or china would have been too humiliating.

On the day of a dinner party the cars went out of London at dawn, crowded with maids; when they got to the country they filled baskets with cow parsley, grasses and buttercups and then hurried back to London and changed into their medieval gowns made of stuff with a pattern of wild flowers on it, to be ready by the time the guests began to arrive.

The guests behaved rather badly; they all pretended to get hay-fever from the floral decorations. I sat next to Philip Sassoon at one of these dinners; he was quite furious because Lady Evelyn could just as well have had orchids everywhere instead of cow parsley and moon daisies, and gold rather than pewter. He loudly disapproved of her eccentricity.

Grosvenor Place had two of everything because it was numbers 10 and 11 knocked into one house. One of the big staircases was entirely taken up by Murtogh's slide. After a visit to a fair he had said to his mother: 'Why can't we have a slide from the top of the house to the bottom?' and immediately a beautiful, polished wooden slide was built and fitted on the staircase. Everybody, not only Murtogh, played on the slide. It was a marvellous idea perfectly executed.

Lady Evelyn's father was still alive. His children and even his grandchildren called him the P.A. This stood for Pocket Adonis; Lord Buchan was a tiny man and had been a handsome dandy in his youth. He and Granny Rose no longer lived together; the P.A. hardly ever came to England, but preferred Paris and Fontainebleau. His only son, Uncle Ronny, was a bachelor of about fifty. He was charming and rather eccentric; he believed in the Hidden Hand and the Jewish World Plot. Colonel Guinness had no patience with Uncle Ronny's pet theories, but as he was a member of the government Uncle Ronny deluged him with literature about them which went straight into the waste-paper basket.

In the dark and gloomy rooms at Grosvenor Place Lady Evelyn and Grania looked more fairy-like than ever, they were so graceful and slender and had such bright, pale hair. There was no question of home-spun to go with the decor, Lady Evelyn dressed at Paquin and Grania at Wendy, a shop for children's clothes kept by her aunt, Lady Muriel Willoughby.

As soon as our engagement appeared in *The Times* wedding presents began to pour in. In those days even nodding acquaintances sent wedding presents. Some of them were useful, or pretty; many of them I treasure to this day; but the majority were frightful, and they came in cohorts—fifteen lamps of the same design, forty trays, a hundred and more huge glass vases. They were assembled at Grosvenor Place, where the Guinnesses had kindly offered to have the wedding party; Rutland Gate was let. When the presents were all arranged Lady Evelyn looked at them reflectively.

'The glass will be the easiest,' she said. 'It only needs a good kick.' She said silver was much more of a problem. 'Walter and

I had such luck, *all* ours was stolen while we were on our honeymoon.'

Farve looked grave when I repeated this boutade. 'It is so kind of people to give you presents,' he said.

Just before my wedding day Decca and Debo got whooping-cough; they could not be bridesmaids. It spoilt the wedding for me; I could have spared anyone else more easily than them. The Dulvertons lent us their house in Wilton Crescent, and there I was dressed in a white satin gown made by Hartnell.

Lady Evelyn had given me lace for my veil; I found it impossibly difficult to arrange. Nanny and Gladys were standing by; Farve was ready to start. He had been begged not to get me to the church half an hour early; he was an excessively punctual person. 'We won't get there ahead of the game,' he promised; but now it really was time for us to be off, and my veil was awry. In my nervousness and despair I snatched away from the helping hands. 'Never mind, darling,' said Nanny soothingly, 'nobody's going to look at you.' As I hugged her, all my bad temper vanished, I guessed, rightly, that I was hearing these words for the last time.

Bryan's friend Michael Rosse was his best man. Although if anything rather younger than Bryan, Michael had constituted himself the mentor of his contemporaries, who received letters containing fatherly advice. These letters afforded much amusement; they were irresistibly comic in their artless pomposity. But Bryan was very fond of Michael.

As I walked up the aisle on Farve's arm followed by a flock of bridesmaids in tulle sylphide dresses I saw Bryan and Michael waiting, and thought how neat and handsome they looked.

All I remember of the marriage service is that Tom had got hold of a wonderful trumpeter who filled the church with triumphant sound when the choir sang Handel's 'Let the bright seraphim in burning row', and that the clergyman pressed his hand on my head so hard that the rickety wreath and veil arrangement almost fell over my eyes.

At Grosvenor Place there were crowds of people; Bryan's Oxford friends were all there. Robert Byron suggested we might meet in Cappodocia later in the year. 'Oh yes,' I cried, 'we will. Let's all meet in Cappodocia *soon*.'

'I don't particularly want to go to Cappodocia,' said Bryan drily.

Lady Evelyn was a vision in cream velvet trimmed with sables. Just as we were going away Bryan rushed over to where she was standing and threw his arms round her. 'Good gracious, Bryan!' she said, in the little voice usually reserved for Lady.

8

Buckingham Street

NEXT DAY WE took the train to Paris. Exactly two years before I had been on that train with Randolph and his father; then I was a child, sent hither and thither at the will of the grown-ups. In this short space of time I had become a grown-up myself, with a husband and a maid and a trunk full of new clothes made by Gladys. Miss Osmond was at Victoria to see us off, she gave us sheaves of newspapers and our tickets. The papers had descriptions of our wedding and pages of photographs. There was nothing unusual about this; every big wedding filled the newspapers and there were lists of guests and of wedding presents in *The Times* which probably partly accounted for the deluge of lamps and vases.

We went to the Guinness's flat in the rue de Poitiers. Lady Evelyn's bedroom had a grey satin canopy over the bed with pink satin roses, three-dimensional ones, sewn on it. The curtains matched, and there was a day-bed with little lace-covered pillows near the fire. It was a wood fire, it had a fine-meshed brass blind which one could let down when one left the room to stop the sparks flying. The whole thing was charming. In the drawing-room, for the most part faux Louis XVI, there were touches of orange, purple and black here and there where art nouveau had left its mark, but it was pre-gothic.

Bryan's parents almost never used the flat, and the people there seemed pleased to have us. The cook made a wonderful pudding called tête de nègre which I asked for every day. Soon we went on, to Sicily; I saw the Mediterranean for the first time, and Greek temples among almonds in blossom and olive groves. I would willingly have stayed there for ever. It seemed to me a mystery why anyone who is not obliged to do so by work should choose to live elsewhere; the shores of the Mediterranean had everything the human heart could desire in those days. Too many people have since had the same idea; they have ruined the coast with concrete and polluted the once sparkling sea.

A Bar examination loomed for Bryan and we went back to London, stopping in Paris on the way. I bought a dress; white faille with a wide pale blue sash, from Louiseboulanger.

We went to live at 10 Buckingham Street, a pretty house designed by Lutyens. The furniture had been bought in a hurry; Bryan had insisted on a certain amount of refectory tables and worm holes. Two empty rooms were stacked with wedding presents. My bedroom was pink, with a blue brocade bed on a dark blue velvet dais; fixed to the back were lamps set in silvered iron-work. I knew it was hideous, but it was not altogether my fault; the bed lady had taken the bit between her teeth while I was abroad. Colonel Guinness did not interfere with the choice of house: he only stipulated that we must have a bathroom each. 'There is nothing so barbarous as for a husband and wife to share a bathroom,' he said. 'Barbarous' was a favourite word with Bryan's parents. Later that summer when Lady Evelyn was presenting me at Court on my marriage she said just as it was about to be our turn to go into the throne room: 'We ought to have been practising our curtsies all day but I forgot.'

'So did I,' I said, 'I've been doing household accounts.'

'Household accounts!' in horrified tones. 'How *barbarous* of Bryan.'

The accounts were nothing whatever to do with Bryan, but had been urged upon me by Muv whose hobby they were. She gave me a leather-bound book for them with my initials in gold, but it remained virgin for I never thereafter returned to this barbarous occupation.

We found some new faces at Buckingham Street, and a few old ones. May, Bryan's favourite parlour maid from Grosvenor Place, had come, and Turner from Swinbrook as driver. The cook was very good and I was only too thankful to leave the food to her. Faced with a bit of blank paper on which to write a menu only one idea came—dressed crab. I was making up for lost time by eating all the dishes proscribed by Moses, but one could not live exclusively on dressed crab.

Farve had a black labrador retriever he called Rubbish; at the time of my marriage he no longer wanted this dog, which was gun-shy; he knew I loved him and he offered him to me.

As soon as we got back Rubbish was sent from Swinbrook. He was the most exceptionally sweet dog, and the joy of my life, though his nervousness made me anxious.

After a few weeks we decided to go to Berlin. 'You will love Berlin, my dear,' said Brian Howard when I told him. 'It is the gayest town in Europe; in fact, my dear, you'll never have seen anything like it.'

We went to all the famous night-clubs where men pretended to be women and vice-versa. At one of them there was a telephone on each table, but we could not see a soul worth ringing up. The night-clubs were not in the least amusing; grim would have been a more appropriate word.

At the embassy we made the acquaintance of Harold Nicolson. 'You are very young,' he said to me. 'What you must do is plant trees, *now*. Then you will enjoy them when you are middle-aged.'

'Yes, but where?' I said. 'We haven't got a country house.'

'Well, get one *at once*,' said Mr. Nicolson.

We wrote to Turner to meet us at Harwich, with Rubbish. The car was there, but no dog. 'He's ill,' said Turner. 'He ran away one night when they took him out. The police brought him back. He's very ill.'

'Oh!' I cried, 'but I said he was never to be let off the lead.'

'I know,' said Turner, 'but he just got away.'

What had happened was that he heard a car back-fire and thought it was a gun. With one leap and tug he had torn away from the maid who was holding him, and hunt and call as they would he was not to be found. Two days later the police had brought him back with terrible gashes in his side; he must have speared himself on some railings he was trying, in his panic, to jump. When I saw him lying in his basket unable to move I knelt on the floor with my head on his, imploring him not to die.

The vet said he must on no account lick his wounds, and arranged a huge cardboard funnel round his neck to prevent it. He could soon walk again and I took him out in the quiet little street; he found it difficult to sniff a lamp post, the funnel was in his way. 'I can't help laughing at your dog,' said Chips Channon, who lived across the road. 'I've never seen a dog wearing a lampshade before.'

We went to Berlin again another year to see Tom who was studying law at the university. He was full of German politics. 'There are fights all the time among the students,' he told us. 'Sozis against Nazis. The other day one lot threw the other lot out of a window.'

'Out of a *window!*'

'Well, not a very high window. But sometimes they do kill each other.'

This was the first time I ever heard the word Nazi.

'Do you take sides?' I asked.

'Oh no,' said Tom. 'It's their own affair. But if I were a German I suppose I should be a Nazi.'

'Would you?' said Bryan.

'Yes; no question. It will be either the Nazis or the Communists.'

In May 1929 there was a General Election. We joined Lady Evelyn and Colonel Guinness in his constituency, Bury St. Edmunds. Their prettiest house was in Bury, a panelled, Georgian house giving on the street with a garden at the back. Lady Evelyn went there so rarely that, like the rue de Poitiers, she never bothered to gothicize it. It was full of chintz and muslin furbelows in the taste of the early years of her marriage.

Walter Guinness hated electioneering. He was a clever, knowledgeable but very fastidious man; he was not much good on the platform. He had a little book of jokes and tried to weave them into his speeches and give a popular touch, but the whole business bored him. He told me once that he always drank half a bottle of champagne before any constituency function to help him to get through it. He was being driven in a car to stay the night with constituents where he knew he was going to be very bored, opened his writing-case, found his champagne and drank it straight out of the bottle. To get rid of the body he threw the empty bottle out of the window and in so doing managed to break the glass. The chauffeur stopped, but Colonel Guinness told him, 'Drive on, it's quite all right.' It was so impossible to explain to his hosts what had really happened to the window of their motor that he did not even try. 'I didn't mention it,' he said, 'and nor did they.'

At this election the 'flappers' voted for the first time, in other words women of twenty-one and over. I was not yet nineteen and therefore had no vote but in any case I could not have voted for Colonel Guinness for I was strongly anti-Tory; I should have abstained.

My father-in-law was returned with a reduced majority, the Tories were beaten and a Labour Government was formed. Out of office, Colonel Guinness boarded his yacht even earlier than usual.

One evening at the opera we saw Lady Cunard; Lytton Strachey was in her box with her. She invited us to go back to supper afterwards, and when we arrived at 7 Grosvenor Square we found a large party, and supper tables laid in the upstairs drawing-room where the Marie Laurencin pictures were. Lytton Strachey sat down beside me and we became instant friends. He was everything I loved best; brilliantly clever and willing to talk for hour upon hour. He never seemed to be in a hurry, or to want to go away. To begin with I was rather shy of him, and afraid of boring him, but as time went on this feeling disappeared and gave place to admiring affection.

Emerald Cunard also became a great friend, though almost my first remark rubbed her up the wrong way. 'You knew Helleu, didn't you?' I asked, hoping to be able to talk of my dear old friend of two years before.

'Helleu? Of course I knew Helleu. Everybody knew Helleu,' she replied, almost angrily. I soon found out that she could not abide to be reminded of dead friends: it was only the living she cared to think about.

We were lent a small house at Bailiffscourt almost on the beach. Pool Place was frankly hideous; it had been built just before Lady Evelyn's arrival and she meant to pull it down. Meanwhile we painted its inglenooks white and went there from time to time.

At the end of the summer we stayed there with Rubbish; Nanny and Decca and Debo came too. Lady Evelyn was at the Huts nearby.

Great changes had come about at Bailiffscourt since my visit the summer before. The landscape was no longer treeless. Forest trees had been bought where they stood and dug up, with their roots. The roots were wrapped carefully and individually; the trees were hoisted as gently as invalids on to trailers and driven across country to Bailiffscourt. There huge holes awaited them, into which they were lowered by cranes, the roots being unwrapped one by one and friable soil packed round them. When they were in position each tree got a coat of plaited straw and a rubber belt put round it, or rather a wire hawser concealed in rubber, to which a dozen guy-ropes were attached, their ends firmly pegged to the ground. This was because of the wild gales to which they must inevitably be subjected in that exposed position so near the sea.

Even in crowded England, I thought, surely a seaside place might have been bought where at least there were trees—ordinary trees—and even, possibly, an old house? I put this to Rosalie one day. 'Not for Aunt Evelyn,' she said. 'It would never be quite right. She must do it all herself.'

While we were there that summer Rubbish got hysteria. He tore round in circles, giving little cries. I caught him at last and we lifted him into the car and flew to the vet, who gave him a calming injection. 'It's no good,' said the vet. 'He'll bite somebody in the end. They never recover.' So he died, and with him the last scrap of my childhood. He had been a link between me and Farve, between me and home.

We went away to Paris, and with us a great new friend—at least he was new to me, though Bryan had known him at Oxford—Evelyn Waugh. That autumn and winter we were seldom apart. It was at the time when Evelyn's short-lived marriage with Evelyn Gardner had come to an abrupt end; she had left him. He was by way of being shattered by this, but I must admit he showed few signs of it. Possibly his pride suffered, but never was anyone more amusing and high-spirited. There was no hint of painful depression, a misery I subsequently often encountered in other friends, and to which he himself was no stranger in after years.

He stayed with us at the rue de Poitiers and so did Nancy. Bryan was writing a book; Evelyn and Nancy were writing too. While I sat in bed in the mornings reading, everyone wrote. When the ink would not run Bryan shook his pen violently and spots appeared all over the grey satin curtains. I was expecting a baby. All day long wherever we might be, in Paris, or in

London, or at Pool Place, kind Evelyn was there to chat and keep me amused. We went for little walks or drives or sat at home; when Evelyn was there it was impossible to be dull for an instant.

Back in London Bryan bought me a huge puppy. The last thing I wanted was another dog but of course I soon got fond of him. He was a tall and gawky Irish wolfhound called Pilgrim, who had overgrown his strength. Evelyn told me that Wenborn, the man at Pool Place, had said to him: 'That Pilgrim! He'll *never* make a dog.' In order to prove him wrong, I fed the wolfhound myself; he was fussy and only liked to eat his disgusting raw meat if it was offered to him between finger and thumb. I could hardly bear to touch it, but my reward was to see him grow strong. I even took him to a dog show at the Crystal Palace where he won various silver goblets and prizes.

The Grosvenor Place Christmas was terrific, as Rosalie had said. First came the traditional food, and on each plate there were three or four little parcels as well as elaborate crackers. Then we all went up to the drawing-room and one was given a pair of scissors. Huge piles of presents were grouped in the corners and along the walls. Having found one's name the opening began. Every parcel was a work of art, like the parcels some Paris shops produce with multiple bows of satin ribbon and tinsel and flowers decorating them. They represented the concentrated work of weeks. I think Grania's nurse gave a hand, but the bulk of it was done by Lady Evelyn herself. After an hour or so, all the presents opened, we were given log baskets in which to carry away our loot. The curious thing was how little loot there seemed to be. It was almost impossible to believe it had shrunk to this little measure. Of tissue paper and cardboard boxes and ribbon there were mountains, of course.

Later in the day Evelyn came to Buckingham Street. He told us he had been to midnight Mass with Tom Driberg on Christmas Eve. It was high Anglican, he had not yet become a Roman Catholic. Our friend Henry Yorke, who wrote under the name Henry Green, had just published *Living*, his novel about a factory. We gave away twenty copies of it that Christmas; now they would be rarities, I imagine.

Evelyn's delightful companionship made the remaining

months of my pregnancy go by more quickly but each baby
seems to take an age. Grandmother said that January: 'When
do you expect the baby?'

'In the beginning of March,' I replied. 'In fact it might be
born on the 13th.' The thirteenth of March was Farve's
birthday.

'Oh, I hope not!' cried Grandmother. 'Poor darling Dowdy!
Always so unlucky!'

At the time, her remark surprised me. My parents still
seemed to me impregnable beings, the masters of their fate, and
certainly not associated with luck.

Bryan had a real passion for the theatre. In theory I loved it
too. As children we had been taken to Stratford-on-Avon every
summer, and in Paris to the matinée classique on Thursdays. I
soon realized, however, by working through almost every play
in the list, that Eddie Marsh was only too right about some
plays being diviner than others. It is extraordinary how boring
a boring play can be, how draughty the theatre in which it is
performed can seem, how unending the intervals. On the whole
it was worth while because there were plays by Ibsen, Strind-
berg, Shaw, Tchekov, and Shakespeare as well as new plays, a
few good, many mediocre. Bryan belonged to various clubs for
Sunday performances.

Occasionally, if there was nothing left to see, we went to
musical comedies. A year or two later at the first night of Noël
Coward's *Bitter Sweet* I ran into Eddie Marsh. 'What do you
think of it? Isn't it divine?' he said, his monocle glittering with
delight.

'Well, not *very*,' I said, 'but I'm glad we came because it
won't run, will it?' I thought it was bound to flop.

'My dear Artemis, it will run for ever,' said Eddie. He knew
what was what. I loved being invited to luncheon with him in
his flat at Gray's Inn. The walls and even the doors were stuck
all over with pictures and drawings. He showed me the first
picture he ever bought, a landscape by Richard Wilson: for the
most part his collection was by living English painters.

That winter if we had an evening at home I dined in bed and
the guests at a table in my room. 'Mind the step!' I said after
dinner when they tripped over the stupid daïs as they came to
sit on my bed for chatting purposes.

In March my son Jonathan was born. When I saw him sleeping in his elaborately trimmed cot beside my bed I felt completely happy, and it was the same when each of my sons was born. Unlike Muv, who thought her babies too ugly for words, I thought mine perfect and love for them blotted out any memory of pain or of the boredom of pregnancy. Many women feel depressed after childbirth; I felt elated, and as they grew I loved and admired the babies more and more. Before Jonathan's birth I had bought clothes for him from Wendy. I chose the prettiest dresses no matter whether they were for boys or girls, they were like doll's dresses covered in frills and furbelows. Nobody now would dress a newborn baby in such elaborate clothes. Even the nightgowns, made of fine linen lawn with hundreds of little tucks had pearl buttons so tiny that they and the fiddling little buttonholes were almost invisible. Doing them up took ages, and while the unfortunate baby was dressed in this absurd way he screamed and made himself into a furious arch with scarlet face in his despair at having to wait for his food. It was not the mothers who insisted upon all this, but the nurses and nannies, who would have been so ashamed to belong to a baby dressed in a single comfortable garment that they would have given notice on the spot.

Jonathan's godfathers were Evelyn and Randolph, who met for the first time at the font. A stormy friendship then began which ended only when death parted them.

Grandmother came to the christening and there was a photograph in the newspapers of her and Cousin Clementine leaving the church together—the last ever taken of Grandmother. Nanny Higgs came to look after the baby; she had been Nanny to Diana and Randolph when they were very small; she idolized Diana. She was a 'character' and became a dear friend, but she scarcely allowed me to touch the baby, he must be admired from a distance. I enjoyed her day out when I took him in the Park; on other days I had to make do with Pilgrim.

We went to many balls and parties that summer, which Evelyn did not approve of. He disliked such entertainments and preferred to sit and talk, but I was pleasure-loving. There were fancy dress parties given by what the papers called the Bright Young People, a description that always made us laugh. Evelyn used it of our particularly serious friends, Bright Young

Roy Harrod, or Bright Young Henry Yorke. Brian Howard had a Greek party, the guests brought their own wine. There were also conventional dances. Margaret Mercer-Nairne asked me to bring a dinner party to a ball her mother was giving at their house in Carlton House Terrace. One of my guests was Robert Byron.

Late at night Robert was apt to do an imitation of Queen Victoria. He put a napkin on his head and pulled his eyes down and he looked like a very jaundiced edition of the Queen in her old age. No sooner had we arrived at the ball than Robert became Queen Victoria, and remained so until persuaded into a taxi some hours later. I felt responsible for him and was embarrassed every time I looked into the sitting-room where he had installed himself with a bottle of champagne. Napkin on head, he was surrounded by surprised debutantes and their young men. Older persons turned away in disgust. This was not the only time I tried to mix two worlds, but it was one of the least successful.

I missed Evelyn badly and could not think what to do to get him back. It was through him that we had made friends with the Lambs, who were to come and stay with us in Ireland; Lamb was to paint our portraits. I begged Evelyn to come too but he said no, certainly not. From then on he bestowed his incomparable companionship on others. I had to be content with the dedication of two books: *Vile Bodies* and *Labels*.

Henry and Dig Yorke came to Ireland, and the Lambs, and Lytton Strachey. Lytton was not quite easy as a guest and I think he rather wished he had stayed at home. One evening we were going, as usual, to the theatre. Knockmaroon is near Dublin and we went regularly twice a week to the Abbey Theatre, every time the programme changed; after a couple of visits one had a strong feeling of having seen the play before, partly because all the Abbey plays had a distinct family likeness and partly because one got to know the actors so well. Since he had already endured a few evenings with Irish actors pretending to be Irish people Lytton refused to come to any more Abbey Theatre plays. 'Oh *do*,' I said. Generally he gave in at once if I wanted something, but he was adamant. Admittedly one play we had seen was so abysmally dull that we left in the middle; many years later I read Lytton's letter describing this scene, to Carrington, in Michael Holroyd's biography of him.

He had a way of retreating behind spectacles and beard which was rather alarming; in this mood he could not be reached.

I knew from Pansy that where he lived in the country there was a couple, the Ralph Partridges, who shared the house with him. Mrs. Partridge had been called Carrington, her maiden name, since her Slade School days. 'Should I like her?' I asked.

'I can't even imagine you with Carrington,' said Henry Lamb.

'Why not? Would she hate me?'

'Yes, she might. You never know with Carrington,' said Pansy. 'She's always enthusiastic about something or other.'

I thought a good deal about Carrington, and when Lytton invited us to stay at Ham Spray I almost dreaded her. Ham Spray was an old house in pretty country near Inkpen. Its centre was upstairs where Lytton had his library; here he worked and thought in peace. Carrington did most of the cooking; one had typical Bloomsbury fare—that is, a distant cousin of French bistro food, with a drop of wine and a few herbs added to every dish.

I loved her at first sight. She did wonderful pictures in silver paper, and arrangements of shells; on the door of Lytton's library she had painted rows of books and thought of clever names for them, like ISLAM. I suppose she was enthusiastic in her way, but my idea of an enthusiastic person is a loud, undiscriminating sort of bore, while Carrington was quiet as a mouse. She lived for Lytton; nobody else really counted. He accepted her worship in a slightly distant way, I thought. The Bloomsburies—at any rate the ones I knew—although they were a mutual admiration society about their painting, writing and criticism, and despite myriad love affairs within the group, seemed in friendship to be more reserved and chilly than most people. There was something disconcerting, for example, in the way that staying in a country house they would all slip off without wishing one another goodnight. It was supposed to hurt a Bloomsbury if you said goodbye or goodnight.

Possibly to begin with they were copying Lytton's behaviour, just as they imitated his way of talking with its exaggerated emphasis on one or two words in a sentence and the other

words hurrying along as best they could. In Lytton's case there
was exceptional fastidiousness and reserve; for some of the
ebullient younger members of the sect to carry on in this way
when they were neither fastidious nor reserved was rather
absurd. It was the same with the voice; just because Lytton,
who talked wittily and sparingly, made an impression of such
brilliance upon his audience, the use of the Strachey family
voice for non-stop gossip and literary chatter only served to
emphasize the contrast between him and his disciples.

On the Sunday evening Carrington made a rabbit pie. I was
terribly poisoned by it and quite thought I was going to die. I
asked for a doctor at 4 a.m. He came, and gave me a glass of
brandy and a pill while Bryan and Carrington hovered. High
fever kept me in bed a couple of days more, and that was how I
made such great friends with Carrington. She sat all day chatting
in my room.

At Pool Place I considered the advice we had been given
about planting trees, but it seemed unpromising. The house
was almost on the beach, nothing would grow in the disgraceful
garden except nettles. 'What *can* we do about the stinging
nettles?' I asked Lady Evelyn one day.

'I don't know I'm sure,' she said, 'unless you get some dogs.'

'*Dogs*, Lady Evelyn?'

'Yes. I believe every time a dog lifts its leg on a plant the
plant *dies*. We must get *dozens* of dogs.'

That year we went to Venice, to heavenly Greece and to
Constantinople, which seemed in those days a dying city. Since
Ataturk had moved the capital and Piraeus had captured most
of the sea-borne trade there was an overpowering atmosphere
of decay. There were crowds of beggars, intent on exhibiting
their dreadful deformities, at the entrance to mosques and
churches. I was quite pleased when we boarded the Orient
Express for the endless journey home.

Inside St. Sophia the Turks were allowing the Byzantine
mosaics to be uncovered. There was scaffolding, and the white
paint and verses from the Koran were being scraped away to
reveal the glorious six-winged seraphim. One day we lunched
with our ambassador Sir George Clerk. I was to see him ten
years later in very different circumstances. He told me that as a

young man he went out riding in the Row every morning with Grandfather Bowles. 'He was so clever,' said Sir George Clerk. 'He taught me all I know about politics.'

Bryan was now a barrister. Everyone finds it a struggle to get the first briefs, and to begin with Bryan thought his idleness at the Temple quite normal. One day he invited a young man who was in the same chambers to dinner. After dinner this person became communicative. 'Of course,' he said, 'I'm afraid you'll never get any briefs.'

'Why not?' asked Bryan.

'Well, because when there's a brief going for one of us the clerk always gives it to me. He says Mr. Guinness doesn't need three guineas.'

This was very depressing news for Bryan; how could he ever get off the ground at the Bar if he was never to be allowed to plead? After a while he stopped going to the Temple and resumed his writing.

Henry Lamb painted a large square picture of Bryan, the baby and me, with Pilgrim standing over us; in the background was the valley of Knockmaroon. We sat separately, often in his London studio. Like Sickert, Lamb was preoccupied with light; he had a yellowish net curtain which he pulled across the window on clear days to simulate the more usual atmosphere. I have sometimes wondered whether the curtain might not have been to blame for the rather gloomy colours which often mar his work and make it seem jaundiced. The picture was a success, but Eddie Marsh, though he admired Lamb, criticized it as a likeness. 'You see, you don't look like a peasant, so what is the point of pretending you do?'

We were now to have a house of our own in the country, and settled on Biddesden. Three times in my life I have had the great good fortune to live in a beautiful house; the first was Biddesden. It was built of brick with stone ornaments in the early eighteenth century by General Webb, one of Marlborough's generals. In the hall, two stories high, hangs a vast picture of General Webb on his battle charger. The picture goes with the house; if it is removed General Webb's ghost rides up and down the stairs making the house uninhabitable until it is put back where it belongs.

At Biddesden we were not far from Ham Spray; there was a great deal of coming and going. Carrington would telephone: 'Lytton says, may we come over?' They were my dearest and most welcome guests. We discovered a short cut to them across the downs and through the narrow leafy lanes. About half way there was a deserted cottage. It was old, with an overgrown garden and orchard and a well; I always stopped and looked in the windows, it had a magic atmosphere. These were the days of terrible agricultural slump, tenant farmers could not pay their rent or the wages of their labourers. Perhaps it had been a shepherd's cottage; keeping flocks was no longer profitable. I often thought of buying it and retiring there from the world, never to return.

In the summer of 1931 I was expecting my second child and Muv and my sisters came to stay at Biddesden. Carrington described them to Lytton: 'I went with Julia to lunch with Diana today. There we found 3 sisters and Mama Redesdale. The little sisters were ravishingly beautiful, and another of 16 very marvellous and grecian.' This was Unity, and Carrington wrote of Debo: 'The little sister was a great botanist, and completely won me by her high spirits and charm.'*

Lytton and Carrington sometimes visited Rosamond Lehmann and her husband Wogan Philipps. Once they came to see me next day. 'How was Wogan?' I asked.

'He was *ten*. Now he's *eight*,' was Lytton's reply.

That summer while Bryan was abroad I often lay sleepless in my lovely bedroom with its five long windows, and fancied I heard footsteps on the paving stones outside. I was afraid, as in the old days at Asthall. As the months passed this feeling entirely left me. It was Lytton Strachey who cured me of night terrors; I confessed them to him. I told him I was afraid at Biddesden, and that I had been afraid at Renishaw, where we stayed with Osbert Sitwell. Lytton raised both hands in a characteristic gesture of despairing amazement. 'I *had* hoped,' he said, 'that the age of reason had dawned.'

John Betjeman was staying with us once at Biddesden when he had a terrifying dream, that he was handed a card with wide black edges, and on it his name was engraved, and a date. He knew this was the date of his death.

* Carrington, *Letters*, ed. David Garnett.

Like me, John was very partial to hymns. He even knew
Nanny's hymns, 'Shall we gather at the river?' and 'There were
ninety and nine'. We used to sing them after dinner; we had to
wait till port time because May refused to be in the dining-room
during the hymns and the under parlourmaid had to manage by
herself. May was usually indulgent to us, but she thought there
was a time and a place for everything.

Another person who sang after dinner at Biddesden was
George Kennedy. He was an architect and a great friend of the
Lambs. He was often with us because he designed a domed
gazebo we were building at the edge of the garden; it was to
be reflected in water, and the water was to be deep enough to
swim in.

We left Biddesden and went to Buckingham Street where my
second son, Desmond, was born in September 1931. To pass
the long waiting time we went to the theatre nearly every night.
One evening, at a very exciting play called *The Front Page*, I
knew during the last act that I ought to go home because of the
baby but could not bear to miss the end. Early next morning
he was born.

In those days the doctors ordered one to stay in bed for three
weeks without putting foot to the ground; visitors were a
consolation. Lytton came to see me. 'Take the baby to your
room,' I told the monthly nurse half an hour before he was due
to arrive. 'Mr. Strachey can't bear new-born babies.' I remembered his shudder of horror when he saw a photograph of me in
the *Tatler* with Jonathan in my arms.

While Lytton and I were talking the door opened and in
came the nurse carrying the infant. She could not believe in
anyone being eccentric enough not to want to see him. 'Isn't he
lovely,' she said to poor Lytton, uncovering the scarlet head
almost under his nose.

'What long hair!' said Lytton, faithfully doing his best.

'Oh,' said the nurse briskly, 'that will all come off.'

Lytton gave his faint shriek: 'Is it a *wig*?'

When we got back to Biddesden we found Carrington had
done a surprise. On a blank window she had painted a girl
peeling an apple; it looked from a little way off like a real person
sitting on the window-sill just inside.

That winter Lytton became ill and stayed in bed. Poor

Carrington nursed him with loving care, but he got steadily worse, it was discovered afterwards that he had cancer. In January he died.

Carrington was in deep despair. Next to Lytton, the person she loved most was Dorelia John. 'Oh, Mrs. John,' I cried, 'what can we do about Carrington? Couldn't she spend half her time with you and half with me?' Mrs. John said of course Carrington would be more than welcome to go to Fryern for as long as ever she wished, but I sensed that she was doubtful and I am sure she knew that Carrington had no intention of living anywhere now that Lytton was gone.

Friends surrounded her and did their best to comfort and distract. One day when I was away she came over to Biddesden and borrowed a gun from Bryan. She seemed much more cheerful and normal, almost her old self. 'What do you want that gun for?' asked somebody when they got back to Ham Spray.

'To shoot rabbits.'

'But there aren't any rabbits.'

At that moment a rabbit ran across the lawn.

'There!' said Carrington.

She shot herself with the hateful gun when her guests had gone back to London. The deaths of Lytton and Carrington were a heavy blow to me. My life seemed absolutely useless and empty.

At this time I saw a good deal of Tommy Tomlin, the sculptor, who was married to a talented Strachey, Julia. I loved them both. He was, I think, the best talker among all the clever Bloomsburies I knew. His conversation had sustained brilliance and did not rely on any trick of voice or use of paradox. Tommy often suffered from depressions and after Lytton and Carrington died he was plunged into a deep and lasting one. We used to go for long walks in London. One day he stopped still—I can see him now, with deathly pale face and eyes almost white too—and said: 'Everything in the whole world is terrible, but there is one *good* thing, and that is that Hitler has lost ground in the German elections.'

9

Cheyne Walk

I WAS EIGHTEEN when I went to live at Buckingham Street, and twenty-one when we left. They were happy years. My two eldest sons were born there. We had innumerable parties and I loved the company of brilliantly amusing friends: Harold and William Acton, Robert Byron, Evelyn Waugh, John Betjeman, John Sutro, Roy Harrod, the Yorkes, the Lambs, also my childhood friends Cela and Derek Keppel, Diana and Randolph Churchill. In the older generation Lytton Strachey, Emerald Cunard, Mrs. Hammersley, Osbert Sitwell and many more, and of course there were my sisters and Tom.

It was at Buckingham Street that we arranged the Bruno Hat exhibition. This was Brian Howard's idea. He wanted to paint twenty pictures and invite all the art critics to a private view. Evelyn wrote the preface to the catalogue: *Approach to Hat.*

Brian painted his pictures in John Banting's studio; he used cork bath mats instead of canvas, and framed them in white rope, but I believe this was a measure of economy rather than an attempt to be original. They were a sort of cross between Picasso and Miro; rather decorative. Brian and Banting rushed up the stairs with several pictures under each arm, and their excitement when the whole lot were hung in the drawing-room was contagious. Rather against Brian's wishes we disguised Tom as Bruno Hat with a black wig and moustache and he sat in a bath chair; a mad idea, because if he was a cripple, as for some reason I have forgotten he pretended to be, how was it that he had managed to paint all the large pictures which covered the walls? In any case he was installed in his invalid chair in a corner of the room, and to our joy not only all our friends but also the critics came in droves.

Photographers elbowed their way in with immense cameras and were firmly directed by Brian away from the bewigged Tom and persuaded to photograph the art. Bruno Hat was supposed to be a German who knew no English; this was to discourage journalists from probing. But he was also supposed to have been discovered by us in Sussex, painting these glorious pictures out of his imagination without ever having visited Paris. Nobody believed any of these tales, everyone knew the whole thing was a joke. Lytton Strachey bought a picture to please me, and I stuck a red spot on it.

Next day the papers were full of the 'art hoax'. One of them said that Maurice Bowra had addressed Hat in fluent German and that Hat had been unable to reply, but this was an invention, for Tom's German was much more fluent than Maurice's. I believe in his heart of hearts Brian was very disappointed. He had hoped for a Hollywood-style miracle, and that he would be 'discovered' by an astonished art world as a master.

Throughout his life there were to be a succession of disappointments for Brian Howard. Talented, attractive, very good company, it is hard to say why he achieved nothing at all. He had been a precocious leader of his generation at Eton and even at Oxford, and he was to see his contemporaries outstripping him one by one. I suppose he wanted the palm without the dust, but more disastrously he despised what was within his range. He might have made a success in journalism, or even fashion, but he aspired to greatness and thought such things beneath him. He wanted to be Rilke, or Nietzsche, or Picasso. The sad thing is that Brian's life was unhappy; he sought release in drugs, he swerved between depression, elation and profound discontent, and he died by his own hand.

A frequent guest was our old friend Mrs. Hammersley, loved by us all for her cleverness and pessimism. She went with the Sitwells on a journey in North Africa where she inconveniently fell ill. Osbert published an unkind story about this incident entitled ' . . . that flesh is heir to'; its theme was that Mrs. Ham was a germ-carrier who suffered every ill that flesh is heir to and handed on the germs to anyone unwise enough to consort with her. Mrs. Ham was hurt; there was a coolness. One day I boldly invited them both for luncheon; after a moment of embarrassment they embraced and made up.

We stayed with Osbert at Renishaw, a memorable visit because his parents were there. Lady Ida was vague and distant but Sir George was a delightful old gentleman who had made elaborate gardens at Renishaw of which he was very proud. He was not yet world-famous as one of the comic characters of all time, for Osbert's autobiography was yet to be written, but stories about him—Ginger, as Osbert called him—flew about. They were relished by Gerald Berners, particularly the one where Sir George, at Montegufoni, threw a lighted twist of straw down a well in order to demonstrate its great depth to his guests. As they peered into the well Osbert was heard saying to Sachie, 'I wish Father would light his beard and throw *himself* down.' Renishaw, if one looked out of the windows at night, was seen to be ringed by distant flames which glowed and sometimes flared up to the black sky. It was an oasis among dark satanic mills and blast furnaces.

In London we sometimes went to tea with Edith Sitwell; one climbed stone stairs to her cheerless flat and was given stale currant buns. We loved going and revered the poetess, who was as a rule nourishing some violent quarrel or feud upon which she discoursed.

The Acton brothers had an immense house in Lancaster Gate full of rococo furniture. At about the time our Buckingham Street years came to an end they left London; Harold went away to live in China. Tom and I missed him very much and so did his many devoted friends; cultivated, charming and witty, we loved his company. His conversation like Lytton's owed something to his irresistible voice. He and William, despite English schools, had retained certain Italian inflections from their Florentine childhood. Tom loved to hear Harold talk in his exotic way about everyday, commonplace things familiar to them both: 'Tell about your rowing at Eton, Harold.' Harold's eyes glistened: 'My dear!' rolling his head, 'I once fell out of my *whiff*! It was swept over the *weir* and shattered to *atoms*!' Next time they met: 'Do tell us again what happened to your whiff, Harold,' Tom would say. Once we were dining together somewhere and a fellow guest was a painfully matter-of-fact woman who obviously felt she should disapprove of Harold. '*You're* not the sort of young man I can imagine doing things underneath a car,' she said in a rude way.

Harold smiled and screwed up his eyes. 'Ah!' he answered slowly, 'It all depends *who with*!'

We moved from Buckingham Street to a house on the river, 96 Cheyne Walk. It had once been Whistler's and was the east end of Lindsey House, two doors from where Farve was born. The panelled drawing-room had windows at each end, on the river and on the garden. We painted the panelling grey and white with a little gilding on the cornice; it had been 'pickled' in the fashion of the moment and my paint was criticized. Bryan's father gave a huge Aubusson carpet. 'Do you like them? Yes, have it by all means,' he said. Opening on to the garden there was a big dining-room like a country room with lily chintz, and here I loved giving large leisurely luncheon parties which seldom ended before late afternoon.

A few days after my twenty-second birthday we had a ball to which we invited everyone we knew, young and old, poor and rich, clever and silly. It was a warm night and the garden looked twice its real size with the trees lit from beneath. A few things about this party dwell in my memory: myself managing to propel Augustus John, rather the worse for wear, out of the house and into a taxi; Winston Churchill inveighing against a large picture by Stanley Spencer of Cookham war memorial which hung on the staircase, and Eddie Marsh defending it against his onslaught. I wore a pale grey dress of chiffon and tulle, and all the diamonds I could lay my hands on. We danced until day broke, a pink and orange sunrise which gilded the river.

While we were at Cheyne Walk Augustus John painted my portrait. I sat in his studio at Mallord Street. I admired some of his portraits and was flattered to be asked to sit, but it was not enjoyable. Although he was then in his fifties he had already become quite an old man, with sparse hair and blood-shot eyes. I never found him good company, but Bryan was fond of the whole family and we stayed once or twice with them at Fryern. Pubs and shove hapenny are not among the entertainments I enjoy and a little of Augustus went a long way, though I liked Dorelia and her daughters. The sittings were drear. There was always an atmosphere of morning after the night before at Mallord Street, an ugly modern house built

4

of dark bricks. The conversation was desultory and John was grumpy. This was probably my fault, but so it was.

Another who painted me that year was John Banting. He did a head and shoulders of vast dimensions, the canvas being about six feet by four. Bryan bought the picture because Banting was very poor, and it travelled with me to various houses for many a year, never hung but always surfacing during a move and then going back into the box room. Now, huge though it was, it is lost. How one could lose an object of that size is a mystery; but it has disappeared. The John portrait I never cared for. It had been his idea that he should paint me, not mine, so there was no question of having to buy it. It ended up forty years later at Christie's and now belongs to Desmond.

In the hall at Cheyne Walk there was a wall painting in sepia of the river with little boats sailing on it, which I thought rather absurd. Not wishing to destroy it and yet not wishing to live with it either, we had canvas on stretchers fixed to the walls and whitewashed. When the house was ready I invited Mrs. Harington Mann, a great friend whose shop I constantly used for stuffs and upholstery, to come and see it. As we walked into the hall I began to tell her about the now invisible fresco. She seized my hands. 'Promise not to mind what I'm going to say,' said Mrs. Mann. '*I* painted the river and the boats.' Before there was time for the full horror of my gaffe to sink in she went on: 'I don't like it either, I did it ages ago, and if this house were mine I should simply have painted it over.'

Good, kind Mrs. Mann; I think she really meant what she said, but it was a horrid moment for me. Probably stories about this incident went the rounds. Many years later I was told that people were saying I had destroyed a fresco by Whistler at 96 Cheyne Walk, which only shows once again that people will say anything.

In the summer of 1932 Cochran had an idea that he might produce *The Winter's Tale* in a London theatre; he wanted to surprise the public with a new face, never before seen, for Perdita. He offered the part to me. I was rather pleased, and inclined to accept. Dr. Kommer, a friend full of kind flattery who, rather like Helleu, made one feel 'good', knew a great deal about the theatre. When I told him of Cochran's suggestion he poured gallons of cold water on the project; he even went to Cochran and talked him out of it. Kommer had never seen me act so much as dumb crambo, but he must have known instinctively that I should have been hopelessly bad. It was as if he had been in the ballroom at Batsford when I was eight and watched the play Muv forbade us to perform. I was rather cross about Perdita at the time, but no doubt Kommer prevented me making a fool of myself.

When he was in London Kommer had a *Stammtisch* at the Ritz where his friends were always welcome for luncheon. He showed me his visiting card; engraved upon it was: Dr. Rudolf Kommer, and in one corner *aus Cernowitz*.

'But you don't live in Cernowitz do you?' I asked. He was always on the move between New York, London and Salzburg.

'No,' he replied, 'but in America they always say Kommer? that lousy Jew from Cernowitz? So I put it on my card.'

He worked for Reinhardt, whose hideous and vulgar productions had wide acclaim in the Anglo-Saxon world. When in Salzburg they lived at Schloss Leopoldskron, a baroque castle on the hill. I liked Kommer; fat, bald, clever and kind.

On our way to Italy that summer Bryan and I motored through the south of France with Barbara Hutchinson and Victor Rothschild who were engaged to be married. We visited the Saintes Maries de la Mer and Aigue Morte and churches and the Aldous Huxleys and we stayed a few days at the Jules César at Arles. One morning I awoke with a sore throat which quickly became so swollen that I could no longer speak. My companions decided to take me to Avignon where they put me to bed and got hold of a bearded doctor from the Institut Pasteur. He diagnosed diphtheria. He kindly allowed me to stay in my hotel room rather than removing me to an isolation hospital, and every few hours he gave enormous injections. His treatment was so effective that in little more than a week I was able to travel to the sea. When I told my London doctor he said crossly: 'Oh well, kill or cure I suppose.'

However, our troubles were not over. The doctor had given anti-diphtheria injections to the others and the unfortunate Victor suffered a violent reaction. He became bright red, swelled up and had a high temperature. He was tormented by a painful, itching skin. I can see him now, under his mosquito net, his bed so full of talcum powder that it looked as if he was in a snow storm. I felt it was all my fault that this brilliant young man had been laid low. When he recovered we all spent a few days swimming and then Bryan and I left for Venice.

Venice that summer was full of friends staying in various palaces and hotels and spending their days at the Lido. Our countrymen were not on their best behaviour; at one dinner party, a picnic on Torcello, there was a fight.

Randolph was being very much himself; one day at luncheon at the Lido Taverna he teased Brendan Bracken by calling him 'my brother'. Up jumped Brendan and Randolph rushed away down the beach to escape from him. When Brendan caught up with him Randolph reached out, snatched off his spectacles and threw them in the water. Brendan, half blind, stood in the shallow sea roaring like a bull and peering short-sightedly at the sand until somebody retrieved the spectacles, broken, for him. An American was heard to say: 'Fon is fon, but that Randolph Churchill goes too far.'

Tom was there, staying at Malcontenta with Baroness d'Erlanger; and Doris Castlerosse, Bob Boothby, Kommer, Mona Harrison Williams of the aquamarine eyes, the Mosleys and their children, Tilly Losch, Edward James, Baba de Lucinge, Lifar, and many Venetian friends. On the beach we congregated round the hut of Princess Jane di San Faustino, an old American lady with a sharp eye and a sharp tongue. Emerald was also in Venice, and Sir Thomas Beecham, but she was cross and not at her best.

We sat on the Piazza San Marco during 'l'heure exquise' when the setting sun lit up the gold mosaics on the church, then went to change and dined somewhere in the delicious airless heat, and we slept under mosquito nets, for in those days mosquitoes came in swarms off the canals to eat one alive.

Although the city is as beautiful as ever, the tragedy of Venice since the far-off days of which I write has been the foul rash of industrial development on the mainland, so close as to pollute the whole atmosphere and hasten the decay of the glorious place. That some who have made fortunes out of this evil desecration have also busied themselves on committees to 'save Venice' cannot exonerate them in the eyes of real

Venetians. The resultant feuding has not been helpful. Paradoxically, the great flood of 1966 alerted the whole civilized world to the danger that Venice could sink beneath the waves. Much has since been done, and Venice is 'rising', the flood proved a blessing.

Forty-five years ago Palladio's Malcontenta was a house of noble beauty in a bleak and lonely setting which emphasized its grandeur. Now it is surrounded and encroached upon; trees have been planted in an attempt to screen it, and succeed only in emphasizing the miserable truth: it has been wantonly spoilt, like so many other places in Europe which, spared by war, have since fallen victim to money grubbers. An obvious example is St. Paul's cathedral, dwarfed and hidden by office blocks.

10

Mosley

THE 'NATIONAL GOVERNMENT', elected at a time of national panic and world-wide slump in the autumn of 1931, was a depressing phenomenon. Now aged twenty-one, I had a vote but did not use it. Had there been a Lloyd George Liberal in our constituency I should have voted for him, but there was not. The over-blown Tory majority and the—as it seemed to young people then—absurd figure of Ramsay MacDonald pretending to lead it as prime minister were a despairingly inadequate combination.

Bryan's father came back from his summer cruise; he had not stood for parliament and that winter he accepted a peerage. He called himself Lord Moyne and chose for his motto *Noli Judicare*. He was an admirably unprejudiced man who lived up to the motto. Sarcastic about the 'National Government', that autumn he often looked in at Buckingham Street for a chat and I grew very fond of him.

It was not necessary to have a particularly awakened social conscience in order to see that 'something must be done', in the renowned words of King Edward VIII some years later. The distressed areas, as they were called, contained millions of unemployed kept barely alive by a miserable dole; under-nourished, over-crowded, their circumstances were a disgrace which it was impossible to ignore or forget. The Labour Party had failed to deal with the problem, the Conservatives could be replied upon to do a strict minimum, yet radical reform was imperative. Could it be beyond the wit of man to manage the economy of a powerful and rich country which 'owned' a quarter of the globe in such a way that its citizens could eat their fill and live in decent circumstances?

The waste of the talents of gifted, inventive and hard-working people under leaders like MacDonald and Baldwin made one almost as angry as did their surely unnecessary privations. For the rich, however, life went on much as before the crisis. Nothing will stop young people enjoying themselves; there were parties and balls, concerts, operas and plays, travels abroad, country house visits, hunting, shooting, racing. Early in 1932, not long after the deaths of Lytton and Carrington had left a painful gap in my life, I first met Oswald Mosley. I shall henceforward refer to him as M. He has never been called Oswald, and his nickname, Tom, was my brother's name, which leads to confusion. In the collection of Carrington's letters so brilliantly edited by David Garnett there is a letter from Carrington to Lytton Strachey in which she says: 'I had a nice chat with Diana over the fire after dinner alone. She told me a great deal about Tom's character.' After 'Tom' the editor has put in brackets, 'Mosley'. This letter was written in July 1931, before I ever met Mosley. It was Tom Mitford's character we were discussing.

M. and I were put next to one another at a dinner party given by the St. John Hutchinsons for Barbara's twenty-first birthday. He told me he had seen me before, once at Venice, and at a ball at Philip Sassoon's. 'You were sitting with Billy Ormsby-Gore,' he said. From that moment we met everywhere, and I listened to him as he talked.

He was completely sure of himself and of his ideas. He knew what to do to solve the economic disaster we were living through, he was certain he could cure unemployment. Lucid, logical, forceful and persuasive, he soon convinced me, as he did thousands of others. He seemed to be the one person who had the answer, and as R. H. S. Crossman was to write many years later: 'Mosley was spurned by Whitehall, Fleet Street and every party leader at Westminster, simply and solely because he was right.'

In terms of experience M. was light years ahead of me. When the first war began I was four, but he was seventeen and as he was at Sandhurst was immediately engaged. He had fought in the air and in the trenches. Invalided out before he was twenty, the tremendous and shattering experiences of those years propelled him into politics. In the khaki election of 1918 he became Conservative M.P. for Harrow. His meteoric rise has been described many times. Very clever, quick, fearless, sharp as a needle, he excelled in debate in the House of Commons, while

on the platform he became the best speaker of his generation.
He soon left the Conservative party, and sat as an independent.
The Liberal *Westminster Gazette*, edited by A. J. Spender,
wrote that M. was 'the most polished literary speaker in the
Commons, words flow from him in graceful epigrammatic
phrases that have a sting in them for the government and the
conservatives. To listen to him is an education in the English
language, also in the art of delicate but deadly repartee. He has
human sympathies, courage and brains.'

On the platform he was as effective as he was in Parliament.
'When Sir Oswald Mosley sat down after his Free Trade Hall
speech in Manchester and the audience, stirred as an audience
rarely is, rose and swept a storm of applause towards the platform—who could doubt that here was one of those root-and-
branch men who have been thrown up from time to time in the
religious, political and business story of England. First that
gripping audience is arrested, then stirred and finally, as we
have said, swept off its feet by a tornado of a peroration yelled
at the defiant high pitch of a tremendous voice' wrote the
Manchester Guardian soon after the 1931 election.

Public speaking is now a lost art, but in the twenties and
thirties and indeed right up to the time when television finished
it off it was an essential part of the equipment of a politician,
the amulet of power. Vast crowds gathered to hear him speak
all over the country.

M. had crossed the floor of the House, in company with the
Cecil brothers, Lord Henry Bentinck and Aubrey Herbert in
1920. He subsequently joined the Labour Party, and in 1929
became Chancellor of the Duchy of Lancaster in Ramsay
MacDonald's government. He, J. H. Thomas, Lansbury and
Johnstone were to deal with unemployment. With another
clever young Labour M.P., John Strachey, who was his P.P.S.,
M. studied this intractable problem and devised an economic
solution. He wrote a memorandum, described thirty years
later (1961) by R. H. S. Crossman: '. . . this brilliant memorandum was a whole generation ahead of Labour thinking.' When
his plan was rejected he resigned, in May 1930. The *Nation*
wrote: 'The resignation of Sir Oswald Mosley is an event of
capital importance in domestic politics . . . We feel that Sir
Oswald has acted rightly—as he has certainly acted courage-

ously—in declining to share any longer in the responsibility for inertia.' He had become increasingly disillusioned with the leaders of the Labour Party, who were content to remain in office and do nothing about a worsening situation. He wrote a Manifesto which was signed by sixteen M.P.s including Aneurin Bevan, and by Arthur Cook the miners' leader. Nothing was done on any front, and caught in the world depression the government fell.

M. decided that in order to be able to translate his ideas into action none of the old parties would be adequate, yet of what use were ideas unless they were acted upon? He formed his New Party, and all the candidates were defeated in the 1931 Tory landslide. Public meetings were his only means of propagating his ideas; he had no daily newspaper. His meetings were frequently attacked, therefore his supporters stewarded them and threw out the smashers. Hecklers he welcomed, for a clever speaker can always amuse his audience at their expense. M.'s movement evolved from New Party to British Union of Fascists as a direct result of smashed meetings; he could no longer be silenced by the meaningless noises of a few rowdies, as in the days before his followers wore black shirts. He called his movement Fascist because it would have been dishonest not to recognize that fascism was a universal movement in the Europe of the period, although it took very different forms in different countries. He was convinced that the English form would transcend the others. M. had a regard for Mussolini as a man who had brought order out of chaos in Italy, but he thought the corporate state, now so widely imitated, was too bureaucratic.

I went to dozens of his meetings, in halls and out of doors, during the next few years, one or two of which I shall describe.

For three years before the war M.'s meetings were perfectly orderly; they culminated in the demonstration at Earl's Court in July 1939 which filled the biggest indoor hall in Europe. All this was in the future; when I first met him in 1932 M. was about to launch his Fascist movement. Fascism seemed at the time the only dynamic movement led by the only politician in England who combined the experience, the force, the intellect and all the other essential qualities of leadership to make possible the difficult task of shifting the dead weight of Baldwinites on the right and MacDonaldites in the centre with the rump of Labour led by Attlee on the left, which was smothering the country with inertia and complacency. The only notable politicians of the older generation, Lloyd George and Churchill, were both excluded and isolated. This suited the Tory rank and file, who mistrusted brilliance. Like the sphinxes in Goethe's *Faust*, their motto seemed to be: 'Im heiligen Sitz, lassen wir uns nicht stören'. (Do not disturb our sacred repose.)

Very briefly stated, M. had a national plan to end unemployment and poverty in the midst of plenty; a plan to develop the Empire, a quarter of the globe neglected even by the Conservatives; and he advocated a foreign policy designed to unite Europe rather than seeking always to divide it in the out-dated manœuvres of balance-of-power politics. He also, two years before Churchill began his campaign, demanded re-armament and parity with any other country in the air. England must not be disarmed in an armed world, he said.

With his lucidity and intelligence and his gift of oratory, M. appeared to me then, as he does still, the cleverest, most balanced and most honest of English politicians. Above all, it was his generosity and his hatred of cant that made him attractively unlike the general run of men in English public life. He was not what Churchill called 'one of the goody-goodies' any more than was Churchill himself.

In private life M. was the best of companions; he had every gift, being handsome, generous, intelligent and full of wonderful gaiety and *joie de vivre*. Of course I fell in love with him, and decided to throw in my lot with him. Forty-four years have since gone by; we have had our ups and downs and sorrows and joys and never have I regretted the step I took then. If I have a regret, it is that I could not have done more to help him and further his aims, for there is no doubt in my mind that the disasters which have befallen our country and our continent need never have been.

M. himself did not underestimate the difficulty of his attempt to change the course of history. He knew the inertia of the mass and the cowardice and petty ambition of politicians as well as anyone. But taking it all into account and with uncanny foresight of what the future would hold for England if the old politicians remained in charge, he wrote prophetic words:

'Better the great adventure, better the great attempt for England's sake, better defeat, disaster, better far the end of that trivial thing called a political career than stifling in a uniform of blue and gold, strutting and posturing on the stage of little England amid the scenery of decadence until history, in turning over an heroic page of the human story, writes of us the contemptuous postscript: "These were the men to whom was entrusted the Empire of Great Britain, and whose idleness, ignorance and cowardice left it a Spain." We shall win; or at least we shall return upon our shields.'

Bryan and I were divorced. We were the recipients of a great deal of advice from friends and relations, but our minds were made up. Roy Harrod, a great friend of us both, wrote me long letters; he thought, as most people did, that we were making a great mistake. Years later I was staying in the same house as his son Henry and on the hall table I saw the well-known tiny handwriting and square envelope used by Roy. I picked up the letter and saw in the nick of time that it was not addressed to me. 'You've got a lovely thick letter from your father,' I told Henry. He said, 'Oh,' and put it in his pocket. I had a feeling that it might have been, like the ones I used to get, a mine of good advice.

Advice is given by the unworldly. Perhaps worldly people know from experience that it is never taken. Emerald, for example, and Gerald Berners, forbore to cavil.

Bryan soon married again; a Scotch girl who, like me, was one of a big country family. They had many children and lived happily ever after.

For me there was no question of marriage, for M. was married already. I looked forward to a long life alone, seeing my beloved M. when he could spare time from his all-absorbing political work and the family to which he was devoted.

I took a small house at the eastern end of Eaton Square. Nanny was rather pleased because it was within easy reach of the park and the other nannies; she had never cared for Cheyne Walk. Nancy was also quite pleased; she had her room at Eaton Square and we saw more of one another than formerly. Everyone else was cross, predicting disasters. None of my friends approved. However, having delivered a few lectures they soon settled down, and Eaton Square was full of the old familiar faces.

Then a devastating blow fell upon M. His wife, Cimmie, was operated upon for acute appendicitis, got peritonitis and died. This could hardly happen now, but before the discovery of antibiotics it was fairly common. She left three children, Vivien, Nicholas and Michael.

M. immersed himself in his political work; his life was entirely given to it. Except that occasionally we went to Paris for a few days, and sometimes I stayed with him at a country house he had at Denham, we saw one another from time to time at Eaton Square or at his flat in Ebury Street, and my friends became accustomed to my unsociable habit of changing plans at the last minute. For me, M. always came first. He had little leisure, he worked long hours and travelled all over the country, speaking.

That summer saw the end of Nancy's love for Hamish St. Clair Erskine, an unfortunate attachment which had lasted for several years. It was obvious that unless a break was made Nancy would remain faithful to the idea of him which she had imagined to herself. Now the break came, and she immediately got engaged to Peter Rodd, a handsome and clever man who despite his undoubted intelligence and even charm managed to be an excruciating bore, buttonholing one and inexorably imparting information upon subjects one was only too happy to know nothing about. Jonathan and Desmond, aged three and two, were pages at Nancy's wedding in December 1933. Very young and very wild, they were constantly being asked to be pages and every time I dreaded some act of indiscipline which might disrupt the proceedings; however they always behaved perfectly. The solemnity of church and the ladies in feathered hats who gathered for fashionable weddings subdued them.

Nancy's letters to Mark Ogilvie-Grant show that for some time she was happy with Prod, as she called him, and thought him a paragon. There can seldom have been anyone whose geese became such glistening swans as Nancy's. They were very poor and she wrote novels to supplement their income, and also wrote for various magazines. Not for publication was her story *The Old Ladies of Eaton Square* about herself and me. In it we were frequently visited by an old gentleman who wore a butter-coloured wig, and lived at the other end of the square: Mark. Sometimes our visitor failed to arrive and we knew he had been caught and detained by a pretty young lady in Eaton Terrace, Anne Armstrong-Jones. As well as being much more attractive, she was much cleverer than the old ladies; she could sew her own dresses and was once found by the Old Gentleman sitting on the floor ironing her shoes. We were jealous of her and her talents. This story was the beginning of Mark's name of Old Gent, or O.G., and of the legend of the butter-coloured wig, which recurs in so much of Nancy's voluminous correspondence with him and which puzzled her biographer Harold Acton.

2 Eaton Square was a comfortable, sunny little house looking down the length of the square gardens. The dining-room was minute, and I could no longer give the big luncheon parties I used so much to enjoy at Cheyne Walk. There was just room for six, three a side on red velvet banquettes. Emerald said: 'Diana's dining-room is very nice, once you get in,' an incomprehensible remark to anyone who had not been invited to squeeze on to the banquette.

At about this time her own parties changed character. One saw fewer writers and painters at 7 Grosvenor Square. More and more she loved to entertain the princes and their friends; that is, the Prince of Wales and Prince George. Partly in order to get more money for Sir Thomas Beecham, the Opera and music in general she tried very hard to enlist the help of the King and Queen, but here she had no luck at all. One realized this rankled; she often said: 'Who do the King and Queen *see*? Who is in the King's *set*?' I remember her putting this question to an old courtier, Sir Harry Stonor. He was very deaf, but when at last he understood what she was asking him he blinked his disapproval. The mere thought of the King and Queen having a 'set' made us all laugh. The princes were another matter; they often went to Emerald's, and soon the Prince of Wales began to be accompanied by Mr. and Mrs. Simpson; the three of them used to troop in together. This in itself was hardly calculated to commend Emerald to the King and Queen, but in any case she had given them up as a bad job.

Emerald was always in love. She kept the capacity—as rare in old age as it is common in youth—for concentrating her affection, esteem and illusions upon an individual. The love of her life was Sir Thomas Beecham; George Moore's adoration she accepted with an uneasy mixture of pleasure and embarrassment. She never knew what he would do next in the way of poetical reminiscences and flowery dedications: Dear Lady of my Heart, dear Lady Cunard. There was more *Dichtung* than *Wahrheit* in his writings. 'To Lady Cunard', he wrote, 'a woman of genius. Her genius is manifest in her conversation, and like Jesus and Socrates, she has refrained from the other arts.'

The audience for this marvellous, intelligent, inconsequent conversation was formed by her luncheon and dinner guests, and although she often invited clever men some of the company was not as amusing as it was fashionable. 'There are people about that are of no interest to me, as little intelligent they seem as squeaking dolls,' complained George Moore, and once, with a nip of sarcasm: 'I was glad to see you brightening as usual the lives of dull people.'

Sir Thomas she found it impossible to corral, he was always breaking out in various directions. He was often very unkind to Emerald, but probably her love irked him. To console herself she tried to become infatuated with a series of younger men; they all conformed to a recognizable physical type. The antithesis of the ebullient and irrepressible Beecham who was short, stout, rapid, witty and sarcastic, they were tall, languid, gentleman-like and vague. 'He's an *idealist*, dear,' she used to say of one of them. There was nothing physical in these love affairs; for Emerald they were less than satisfactory, the love all on her side.

It was this need of hers, together with her vivid intelligence and wide reading, that lifted her into an altogether higher category from the general run of snobbish worldly 'hostesses' of whom one has known so many. This is not to suggest that worldliness and snobbishness had no part in her; they had, but there was more to her besides.

Emerald had lived in England for forty years or so; perhaps she sometimes forgot she had ever lived anywhere else. She once rented a friend's house while 7 Grosvenor Square was being re-painted; she was loud in her complaints of the rigours of her temporary home.

'There are no faucets near the basin,' she announced in her high-pitched voice.

'Faucets, Emerald? What *are* faucets?' asked several of us. She became quite furious.

'*Faucets!* Everybody knows what a faucet is.'

'It's American for tap,' said somebody.

She was very much put out, and one had the feeling she disliked being reminded in this way of her origins.

Harold Acton was the only person who succeeded in being friends with both Emerald and her daughter Nancy, until he went away to Peking. Nancy usually lived in France, but she brought her negro friend to London and they stayed at Stulik's Eiffel Tower. In a moment of spite Lady Oxford informed Emerald of this fact which everyone else knew already. There was a bitter quarrel between mother and daughter; Nancy wrote a polemic 'Black man and white ladyship' attacking Emerald, and after that their friends had to choose between them.

Nancy Cunard was rather beautiful; if Emerald was bird-like she was snake-like. She may have been a good poet, I cannot judge; she was certainly a good writer, and her book about George Moore, 'G.M.' deserved a success it never had. Her favourite sport, shocking the bourgeoisie, became such an over-riding passion that she wrecked herself and was more or less crazed with drugs and other excesses. Her black friend, a simple soul, had been taught by Nancy that he must admire everything African. He equated African with large size: 'Is this *African?*' I once heard him ask, pointing to one of William Acton's enormous rococo Italian tables.

Sometimes Emerald took me to rehearsals at Covent Garden. Sir Thomas allowed her to go but she was not supposed to bring her friends, so I kept in the shadows at the back of her box. One day Beecham was annoying Lotte Lehmann, as he often annoyed singers, by rushing the orchestra along at top speed so that I suppose she felt she could not develop the full beauty of her magnificent voice. After he had taken the same few bars three times and left her behind each time, Lotte Lehmann stamped her foot and burst into tears. I felt as embarrassed as

someone who inadvertently witnesses a row between husband
and wife. Beecham was a great conductor, but his tempi and his
sarcasms were exasperating for the singers.

It is absurd to pretend that Lady Cunard and Lady Colefax
were twin hostesses in pre-war London. There was no comparison between them. Lady Colefax liked to see famous people
at her parties, but when she had got them there she had no idea
what to do with them. If at her table some clever man began to
talk she quickly interrupted; the conversation was stillborn.
Emerald made her guests perform to the best of their ability,
so that the atmosphere was exhilarating and charged. She
fanned the spark of intelligence, fun, interest and amusement
into the flame of conversation in a way that was rare in London,
where as a rule each person talked only with his neighbour.

Sibyl Colefax, in order to induce people to come to her house,
held out the bait of lions as fellow guests. She invited by postcard, scrawled with initials, and one was supposed to be able to
guess that 'N.C. and W.S.M. are coming' meant Noel Coward
and Somerset Maugham. Gerald Berners sent her a postcard
inviting her to luncheon 'to meet the P. of W.' Lady Colefax
accepted with alacrity, and when she arrived Gerald introduced
the Provost of Worcester.

He sometimes teased Emerald. She had a positive passion for
the charming Bertie Abdy, whom she extolled in extravagant
terms. 'Bertie knows *all* about art,' she announced one day. 'In
that case,' said Gerald, 'how do you account for the fact that he
has bought two Fragonards which have turned out not to be by
Fragonard after all?' Emerald was undefeated. 'They *weren't*
art!' she said firmly, and the logic of her reply gave Gerald
intense pleasure.

John Betjeman brought Lord Alfred Douglas to see me at
Eaton Square. We tried hard to like him, but we failed. We
tried, because he had been ostracized for so many years; we
failed, because he was a self-centred bore. All traces of the
beauty which had so entranced Oscar Wilde were vanished.
Lord Alfred, prompted by us, spoke freely about Wilde, whom
he called 'O. W', but he had nothing of interest to tell; it was
a well-worn twice-told tale. John looked upon him as an ancient,
though minor, Victorian monument. Acquaintanceship with

'Bosey' probably inspired his marvellous poem about the arrest of Oscar Wilde in the Cadogan Hotel, which he read to us at that time.

Another ancient monument who often came to Eaton Square was Gladys, Duchess of Marlborough. She quarrelled bitterly with the Duke, whom she called Little Ogpu. She was living in his house at Carlton House Terrace, where Ogpu, in an attempt to dislodge her, had the electricity turned off. Her lawyer insisted that she must nevertheless stay there. One hot summer evening after dinner we were sitting on the balcony overlooking the Mall; it was quite late, and the empty house was getting dark. Gladys, who must have heard the tinkle of a distant bell, got up and ran through the drawing room to the top of the stairs. I was slightly alarmed when I heard her call down; 'Come along up, Duchess, come along up!' There was an eccentricity about Gladys that made me wonder whether she might not be a little mad, and I thought she was talking to herself. However, a few moments later the Duchess of Hamilton appeared. We sat on the balcony until it got quite dark, the duchesses talking about dogs, a passion they shared. Then we felt our way down the stairs and out into the lighted street.

Gladys Marlborough had been a beautiful and clever girl during the belle époque in Paris and Rome at the turn of the century. I often questioned her about this remote and fabulous pre-first-war world. Speaking of Ida Rubinstein, the dancer, she said: 'Oh, she insisted on the grand luxe.'

'What *is* the grand luxe?' I asked.

'A carpet of fresh blossoms on her bathroom floor, renewed twice a day,' was one example Gladys gave.

She was the victim of an early and disastrous attempt at face-lifting. The idea had been to give her a perfect Grecian nose; some sort of wax inserted under the skin where the nose joins the forehead had slipped to the lower part of her face, which consequently looked like a collapsed balloon. She was unself-conscious about it, and her large blue eyes remained as evidence of her former beauty.

Gladys Marlborough, accompaned by dozens of Blenheim spaniels, went to live in the country; she became a hermit, and would see nobody. A few years later her mind gave way; she gradually sank into the sad and lonely world of madness.

11

Munich and Rome

UNITY WAS ONE of us who, despite my father's dislike of the idea, did go to school, or rather to schools in the plural. She loved her schools but she was always expelled from them; she could never keep the rules.

'*Not* expelled,' Muv used to say. 'Asked to leave.' The result was identical.

Her sins were so trivial that Farve took her part; he once went so far as to suggest throwing a headmistress who had got rid of Unity into a pond, but even if he had done so it would scarcely have induced her to change her mind. I have never been able to understand how anyone could abide school, but I sympathized with Unity as one after another of these dreadful establishments rejected her. Once she was expelled because she refused to be confirmed.

All this was in the past, and she was now nearly nineteen. In the summer of 1933 it was with Unity that I made a journey which changed her life.

In the spring of that year Mrs. Richard Guinness had invited me to come and meet 'a very interesting German'. When I arrived the interesting German was playing the piano in her drawing-room.

'He is a personal friend of Hitler,' said Mrs. Guinness. 'He plays the piano for him when he is exhausted after a great speech. He is David to Hitler's Saul.' I hardly realized at the time what a wonderfully inappropriate analogy this was.

Putzi Hanfstaengl was a huge man with an exaggerated manner. He got up from the piano and began to talk in fluent English about his idol—for he left us in no doubt that Hitler was everything in the world to him, as leader and as friend. He had known him for twelve years; it was to Hanfstaengl's wife and his sister that Hitler had fled after the failure of the 1923 putsch, when sixteen National Socialists had been shot dead as they marched past the Feldherrnhalle. Hitler, marching with them arms linked, had been thrown to the ground when his comrade was killed, and his shoulder was wrenched out of joint. In the Hanfstaengls' house at Uffing he had been arrested.

The Hanfstaengls had got plenty of American dollars because the family firm which made art reproductions had a branch in New York. Putzi had helped Hitler to buy a newspaper, the *Völkische Beobachter*, during the inflation. Now that Hitler was in power he had given Hanfstaengl the post of chief of a bureau dealing with the foreign press.

All I knew of Hitler was what I read in the English papers. 'How about the Jews?' I asked.

'Oh, the Jews, the Jews, that's all one ever hears in London, what about the Jews,' shouted Hanfstaengl. 'People here have no idea of what the Jewish problem has been in Germany since the war. Why not think for once of the ninety-nine per cent of the population, of the six million unemployed. Hitler will build a great and prosperous Germany for the Germans. If the Jews don't like it they can get out. They have relations and money all over the world. Let them leave Germany to us Germans.'

He boomed on all evening; I had often met drawing-room communists who breathed fire and slaughter; he was my first drawing-room Nazi. He said if ever I came to Germany I must look him up and he would introduce me to Hitler. 'You must all come to Germany,' he told the assembled company. 'You will see with your own eyes what lies are being told about us in your newspapers.'

A few months later Unity and I decided to go abroad somewhere together and I suggested Bavaria, partly because I had never been there and partly because I wanted to 'see for myself'.

She told me afterwards that at the time she would have preferred France or Italy, but she agreed and we went to Munich. We found some English friends of Tom's and went sightseeing with them, baroque churches and castles, and we went to the opera.

Unity and I called at the old Brown House, afterwards to be rebuilt, and asked the man at the door how we could find Dr. Hanfstaengl. He had not given me his address because, according to him, everybody in the new Germany would know where to find him; he gave me to understand that his name was a household word. The hotel people seemed never to have heard of him, but at the Brown House they said they would try to forward my note.

At that time I knew about twenty words of German and Unity none at all. I could put a simple question but I never understood the answer. Unity began to be disappointed because I had promised we should meet Hitler and so far it had been nothing but churches and picture galleries.

Next day Hanfstaengl telephoned. 'You have come at exactly the right moment,' he said. 'We are having our Parteitag tomorrow, I will get you tickets and a room in Nuremberg.'

He met us at the station. The Parteitag turned out to last four days, not one as we had imagined. The old town was a fantastic sight. Hundreds of thousands of men in party uniforms thronged the streets and there were flags in all the windows. There were three different uniforms but Putzi wore yet another one he had designed for himself, of a darker shade of brown. Unlike the other Politische Leiter, who were in trousers, he had breeches and riding boots. Unity thought him wonderful and very funny; he was most kind to us and took us to all the speeches and parades. He had an adjutant, and in our party there was also an American lady who knew Germany well and explained things to us. I often went to the Nuremberg Parteitag in after years, but never again was the atmosphere comparable with this first one after Hitler came to power. It was a feat of improvised organization to bring such numbers of men from all over Germany and feed and house them and get them to the right places at the right moment. Most of them lived in tents near the town. The gigantic parades went without a hitch. A feeling of excited triumph was in the air, and when Hitler appeared an almost electric shock passed through the multitude. In other years the whole thing had become an established political circus marvellously synchronized and with permanent installations to contain the million or so performers; in 1933 it was a thanksgiving by revolutionaries for the success of their revolution. They felt the black years since their defeat in the war were now over and they looked forward to a better life. There were almost no foreigners; later on the diplomats and assorted guests came, but not in 1933. By a strange chance, Unity and the American lady and I witnessed this demonstration of hope in a nation that had known collective despair. We heard the speeches Hitler made, most of them very short, and we understood not a single word.

There was not much in the English papers about the Parteitag; when they mentioned it at all it was to describe it as 'militaristic', though it was not even as militaristic as a torchlight tattoo in England. Hanfstaengl at this time still professed the deepest adoration for the Führer, though a querulous note came into his voice when some of the other members of the government were mentioned. He called Dr. Goebbels a 'kleiner Rigoletto'. As Propaganda Minister he had a finger in Putzi's pie.

'When are we going to meet Hitler?' Unity asked two or three times a day. She was put off with a variety of excuses, which ranged from his being far too busy to more personal matters. 'You mustn't wear lipstick, the Führer doesn't like it.' We were quite accustomed to make-up being disapproved of; it was a phobia of Farve's, but in those days it was the fashion and Unity was firm. 'I couldn't *possibly* do without it,' she said.

We left Germany without having met Hitler, but Unity was determined to go back as soon as she possibly could. She set about persuading my parents to allow her to learn the language, in Munich, with obsessive determination.

Soon after getting back to London from Germany I set off again, this time to Rome for a visit to Gerald Berners. He had become a great friend of mine the year before. We often met at Emerald's and we had been fellow guests of Mrs. Ronnie Greville's at Polesden Lacy, a luxurious house where Gerald approved of the cuisine. His house in Rome looked on to the Forum, the Forum was our garden, where we sat in the sun and wandered about. Gerald's cook, Tito, bred canaries which sang all day and kept him company when Gerald was in England and he was alone in the house. An enemy opened the doors of all the cages and the canaries flew away into the Forum where they perched singing and twittering on bushes and trees. There was no food that day; Tito was in the Forum from morning till night coaxing and whistling to his birds. They all came back, and even seemed pleased to find their familiar cages once again. He made delicious things, in particular there was a cake, hard chocolate outside and inside sour cream, sponge, rum, angelica and candied cherries which I have often thought of since but never achieved.

Our days followed a pattern. Gerald got up early and worked, composing at the piano, playing a little phrase and then writing it down. His music had a dying fall, there was a superficial gaiety in it accompanied by an underlying sadness. He had written the music for a Diaghilev ballet, *The Triumph of Neptune*, and was to compose *The Wedding Bouquet*, a ballet with chorus, the words by Gertrude Stein.

In the afternoon we went sight-seeing; Gerald knew Rome well; he was en poste there as a young diplomat and since then had his own house. Luncheon and dinner were devoted to people; Gerald loved company and the Romans loved him. When one first arrived it took a day or two to get the trend of the scandals of the moment which were discussed in every house and all the time. I thought the Romans exceptionally beautiful to look at and also exceptionally spiteful about one another. They themselves would not have agreed, for Gerald told me that when Dorothy Radziwill visited Rome after a long absence they said of her disapprovingly: 'Oh! Elle a la méchanceté d'avant guerre!'

Half way through the morning Gerald would telephone from the landing outside my room, making plans for parties and expeditions. 'Pronto, pronto, e Lord Berners,' he began. His Italian was fluent but he made no concessions, he pronounced it as though it were English. He never embarrassed with a good accent like some of one's compatriots.

He loved it when the Romans translated literally from Italian to English. 'No, it wasn't amusing,' said one, referring to a party, 'there were only four cats there.' And another when she heard Gerald and I were going for a walk along the Via Appia: '*Not* the Via Appia! I *hate* the Via Appia. Mama and I used to have such annoying talks on the Via Appia!'

Gerald was clever and witty, we laughed all the time. He did not do imitations and he was not a raconteur; his stories and jokes were short and abrupt and took only a few seconds

to tell. When he laughed himself it was a sort of delighted
sneeze. Like most of the wittiest and funniest people I have
known he was fundamentally sad and pessimistic. Happy
extroverts are doubtless to be envied, but they do not make
the best companions.

A year later, when I was once again staying at Foro Romano,
Gerald was writing *The Girls of Radcliffe Hall*. It was a roman
à clef about a school of which he was the headmistress; many
of our friends, lightly disguised, were the pupils. Every morning
he came and sat on my bed to read the latest instalment. The
book made us scream with laughter; he had it privately
printed.

During the golden month of October we saw beautiful
things day after day; it was perfect happiness. Sometimes we
motored out to Frascati, to Prince Aldobrandini's villa, or to
the Villa Medici, or to Caprarola. Once we lunched with the
Caetanis at Ninfa, the most romantic of houses surrounded by
streams. There is nowhere as green as Ninfa, or so it seems
compared with the sunburnt campagna. We often lunched
with Princess Jane di San Faustino; she had a parrot which had
belonged to Marshal Ney, I was deeply impressed by this aged
bird.

Gerald went out with his painting things and he and Princesse
Marie Murat painted side by side. She lived with the French
ambassador, the Comte de Chambrun whom she subsequently
married. Sometimes we wandered in Rome, not yet the wild
noisy hub of crazy traffic, tearing motor bicycles, scooters and
cars, every driver pressing a klaxon, that it was to become after
the war. We climbed the dome of St. Peter's, a rather terrifying
climb up a steep stair set at an angle, hidden between the inner
and outer shells of the dome. We walked on the roof of the
great church where the San Pietrini live, selling Vatican stamps
and postcards. We ate ices in the Piazza Navona.

On one of these long visits to Gerald Phyllis de Janzé
joined us for part of the time. I was fond of her; she was
beautiful and intelligent and had been a great friend of Carrington at the Slade. But she tiresomely criticized all things Italian
for not being French.

'If you've lived in France,' she said, 'everything here seems
coarse.' We argued about it. 'Diana and Phyllis quarrelling

in the back of the car,' Gerald called it. It seemed to me then and it seems to me still although I have lived for a quarter of a century in France, that next to Greece we owe nearly everything in architecture to the Italian Renaissance, above all to Michelangelo and Palladio. The Gothic north may be sublime, but 'sûrtout soyons classique' as Helleu used to say. Furniture is of course another thing altogether, and here France reigns supreme.

Gerald, Desmond Parsons and I motored to Paris from Rome in easy stages in a lumbering Rolls Royce driven sedately by an English chauffeur. We visited Max Beerbolm in Rapallo and he showed us his latest books of photographs transformed with touches of Indian ink into fearful caricatures and monsters; an art Gerald himself excelled in.

On our way through France we lunched at the Pyramide in Vienne, a temple of gastronomy to this day among the greatest in all France (which is equivalent to saying in the whole world). It is named after a Roman obelisk which local people formerly called the tomb of Pontius Pilate, probably because he was the only Roman whose name was familiar to them.

When we got to Paris we dined with Violet Trefusis. She said to Gerald how amusing it would be for them to pretend to be engaged and get a deluge of presents. A day or two later we were all back in London and their forthcoming engagement was announced in the gossip column of a newspaper. Violet telephoned Gerald: 'I've had dozens of telegrams of congratulations.'

'Have you really?' said Gerald, 'I haven't had a single one.'

Her mother, Mrs. Keppel, who happened to be in London, thought the joke had gone too far and issued a denial. Gerald said he was going to put in *The Times* 'Lord Berners has left Lesbos for the Isle of Man'.

Later that winter, probably as a result of overwork, M. had a recurrence of his old trouble, phlebitis. We went to Provence for him to recover in a charming house he rented from Sir Louis Mallet, near Grasse. Despite his illness M. and I were very happy there; we sat out in the sun by day and dined in front of a wood fire. I went for long walks in the hills, coming upon washer-women beating their linen on oaken boards in the bright streams and chatting together as they worked, like Joyce's washer-women in *Anna Livia Plurabel*.

At Eaton Square I saw old friends and made some new friends. Adrian Daintrey painted me at that time, and during the sittings he talked about Proust. I had read an essay on Proust by Clive Bell in which he made out that *A la recherche du temps perdu* was as difficult to read and as hard to understand as a manual of physics. Adrian told me this was complete nonsense; he urged me to try the Scott Moncrieff translation. This I did, and fell under the spell. I have been under the spell ever since. Bryan gave me the N.R.F. edition; he had the sixteen volumes bound in pink cloth for me; a gift which has produced more amusement and pleasure over the years than anything else in my library. It must be admitted that the English translation, though brilliant in its way, is quite different from the original; however for those who cannot read French it is a hundred times better than nothing.

The same year, 1934, I was painted with my two boys by Tchelichew. At that time he was well known in Paris but not in London; Edward James brought him over to design the sets and costumes for a ballet in which Tilly Losch was to dance. Tchelichew's dream-like decor for *Errante* was romantically beautiful.

He had painted a rather gloomy portrait of Harold Acton and many superb portraits of Edith Sitwell. His style, constantly evolving, was at its most poetic at this time. His portrait of me and the boys is the picture I love far the best of all the many painted of me. Pavlic imagined long flowing golden hair for us, all three, hair like rain, and our faces gold with blue shadows and blue eyes. He had a bad time with the boys, then aged four and two and a half. He was unable to entertain them as he spoke no English. They sat separately, accompanied by Nanny Higgs, and she came back from the sittings full of complaints. 'Mr. Tchelichew was so kind, oh he was kind, but Desmond turned his head and wouldn't look, even when Mr. Tchelichew gave him a sweet.' However the result was not only a magic work of art but exactly like both children. Pavlic's design had been for three heads and six hands, but he had to paint out Desmond's right hand which was lovingly posed on my shoulder. The sight of it enraged Jonathan. 'I won't have Desmond hugging her. *I won't sit,*' was his threat, and Pavlic gave in.

Edward brought Kurt Weill to dine with me once or twice. I had heard the *Dreigroschenoper* in Berlin and Lotte Lenya's marvellous gravelly singing voice. Kurt Weill had not yet been canonized for his association with Brecht and his tunes were not yet known to the English public. There is an early portrait by Lucien Freud of a short man standing among potted plants, the short man is the very image of Kurt Weill as he was in those days, soon after he fled from Germany.

That summer M. took a furnished house by the sea in the south of France for his annual holiday where I stayed for a couple of weeks with him and his children. From there I flew to Rome, on my way to stay with Edward James who had got the Villa Cimbrone at Ravello. When I arrived I telephoned Cimbrone; Edward had not turned up, though he was expected any day, I was told. None of the acquaintances I had made during my visit to Gerald was in Rome in August. The only exception was Mrs. Strong, an old English lady archaeologist. Gerald said that when she was young, at the turn of the century, Mrs. Strong lectured on archaeology from behind a screen because her beauty was sublime and it distracted the students. By the time I knew her she had become a noble Roman matron. I went to see her a few times and when several days passed and still no Edward appeared, and Rome was hot as an oven, I asked her advice as to what I should do.

'Is your maid with you?' she asked.

'Yes.'

'In that case, go to Cimbrone and wait there for Mr. James,' said Mrs. Strong. This I did, and spent a few lovely days in the scented garden with its pool and distant view of brilliant sea sparkling far below.

Then Edward arrived, accompanied by Henri Sauguet, composer of the Diaghilev ballet *Les Forains.* Edward, kindest of hosts, whizzed us about in a huge open motor. The coast road made one feel sick; at every hairpin bend there was a warning; SVOLTA! Sauguet and I dreaded these twists and turns; 'La supplice des svoltas' he called them.

We went to Paestum. In those days the temples stood quite solitary in the flat swampy landscape. Unlike Agrigento, unlike Athens, there was no spectacular rocky setting. Yet in many ways Paestum seemed to be the very essence of classic Greece, uncompromising, bare, even grim; superb.

In the evenings up at the villa we laughed all the time as we sat under the stars in the warm scented air. Sauguet, like most Frenchmen in those days, was not a traveller; I believe he was seeing Italy for the first time. He is brilliantly clever and witty, with an incomparable gift of mimicry. His imitations were supreme

People who possess this gift of mimicry have amused and delighted me all my life. The most talented I have known were Sauguet, John Sutro, Oliver Messel; and, many years later, Elizabeth Winn, and my son Max.

There was no shadow upon this visit to Edward at Ravello; I look back more than forty years and see perfect beauty and amusement and enjoyment; sun, sea, Greek temples, scented gardens, and the wild laughter and fun of the fantasies of our brilliant French companion.

12

Hitler

MEANWHILE UNITY HAD got her way; she had spent
several months in Munich, learning German. She stayed with
a dear old lady who took English girls; Pempy and Angie
Dudley Ward had both been there and were the adored
favourites of Baroness Laroche. The Baroness was not a
National Socialist, far from it, but she was well accustomed to
the girls in her care having this or that Schwärmerei. Often it
was for opera singers, but often too for Hitler, long before he
came to power. Never before, however, had she known a girl
like Unity, who set herself with passionate single-mindedness
to learn German so that when she met the Führer, as she felt
convinced she would one day, she would be able to understand
what he said.

After leaving Ravello I joined her in Munich. We had
planned, through Hanfstaengl, to go to the Parteitag again.
This time he refused to help. He had no tickets to give away,
he said, and he told Unity he had been criticized the year
before for being surrounded by foreigners who all wore lipstick.

This was very bad news. He was our one hope, and not only
had he failed us but he indicated that in any case we should be
unwelcome. Unity was rather cast down. He had strongly
advised her not to go to Nuremberg; there would be bigger
crowds than ever, he said, and certainly not a room to be got
anywhere near the town. Every hotel room had been requisitioned for the week.

Unity told me all this and we pondered what to do. I was for
giving up; there was so much to see around Munich. I envisaged us sitting up all night in the Nuremberg station waiting-
room. Unity, of course, would not hear of such weakness; we
must go, she said, even if it was only inside a day. We took an
early train next morning.

There was a vast mass of people crammed into the town.

Every café and restaurant was packed, the streets were jammed solid with humanity. It was like a dozen Cup Final crowds concentrated in a town the size of Oxford.

Unity was undaunted, in fact her spirits rose and she kept saying, 'Aren't you glad we came? Isn't it lovely? *Do* be glad we came.'

I could not help wondering where we were going to sleep that night; going back to Munich was quite out of the question, Unity would never consent to it while this jamboree of her dreams was in progress.

'It doesn't matter about not having a room, does it? It's really all the better, because we can get such marvellous places for seeing the Führer go by tomorrow if we stay in them all night,' she said.

At that moment we spied two men getting up from a table in a beer garden; we nipped into their chairs, thankful to sit down. Unity spoke politely to the other occupants of the table; I had been struggling with Hugo's *German Self Taught* and could understand most of the talk. The easiest thing, in a foreign language one is learning, is small talk which runs along familiar lines. These lines were boringly familiar: 'Are you English? (Or sometimes are you Swedish?) How do you like it here in Germany? Are you a student?' and so on.

One old man with white hair sitting at our table was wearing the gold party badge, which meant he was one of the first hundred thousand members of the NSDAP. Unity spotted this at once. 'Yes,' he said. 'I am a very old member. I am number one hundred in the party.'

'Number a hundred!' Unity was very impressed. 'Then you must know the Führer?'

'Oh yes, I knew him in those days,' said the man.

When he discovered that we were in Nuremberg with no tickets and no room to stay in, number 100 looked very sorry for us. He wrote something on a bit of paper and told us to go to the office which arranged accommodation. On our way there Unity was hopeful. 'Nard,' she said. 'Can you imagine the luck! Parteigenosse Nummer Hundert! I'm sure he will introduce us the Führer.' She had quite lost faith in Hanfstaengl.

We were given a room in a little inn and tickets for everything, as a result of the kind intervention of Number 100. We found him and thanked him, and next day he sent us a book he had written called *Zehn Tausend Kilometer Heimweh*. I think it described the campaign of White Russians in Siberia after the first war.

That year the Arbeitsdienst paraded with their shining spades; this was said to be militaristic by the English press. Again we listened to speeches. They gave an account of the astonishing progress made in a year, unemployment dwindling, houses built, new roads begun, industry and agriculture flourishing. When the hectic exhausting days were over I went back to England and Unity to Munich. I resolved to learn German and went a few times to the Berlitz School.

I asked M.'s advice and he agreed it would be a good idea to go to Munich for a few weeks and learn German. Unity found me a charming flat with Biedermayer furniture and a good cook; she stayed with me there and we followed, in a rather desultory way, a special course for foreigners at the University. At twenty-four I was by no means, to my surprise, the oldest person in the lecture room. There were several white heads among the students. I loved Munich. It is bitterly cold in winter but the houses have double glazing and efficient central heating. The icy air out of doors had a special smell, so that had one been set down there blindfold one would have known at once it was Munich. Possibly the smell was of brewing, combined with the little cigars the men smoked. On Sunday mornings before it was light there was quiet movement in the streets; hundreds of people making their way to the station carrying skis on their backs. In less than an hour they were up in the mountain sunshine and they came home when it was dark once more. It was not only the rich who could afford these outings, which cost very little and meant that young people in Munich never lost their brown holiday looks even in mid-winter. Another thing they enjoyed for nearly nothing was music. Standing room at the opera cost 50 pfennigs, about eightpence, and quite a good seat two marks, less than three shillings. The Alte Pinakotek had a superb collection of old masters; the gallery was bombed in the war and they are now in the Haus der Kunst, one of the few things Hitler built not to be blown up by the Allies after the war was over.

We often had guests at the flat, girls from Baroness Laroche's and acquaintances of Unity's. Among them was a handsome Norwegian boy, son of the Nobel prize winner Knut Hamsun; he had been allowed to join the S.S. as a favour to his father who was a great admirer of the new Germany.

Unity had discovered from her German teacher that Hitler often lunched at the Osteria Bavaria when he was in Munich. He stopped there on his way to the Obersalzberg. 'He goes there as a private citizen,' said Fräulein Baum. It was a tiny restaurant with a little garden at the back where one could eat out of doors in summer. Unity knew as if by instinct when he was likely to be there. She followed his doings in the newspapers, chatted to the doorman at the Brown House, looked to see if there was a policeman in the Prinzregentenplatz where he had his flat. If she considered it possible that he would turn up at the Osteria we lunched there. He kept Spanish hours, it was after two o'clock that a couple of black Mercedes cars drew up, he walked in and sat at his table in the corner, accompanied by an adjutant and a few friends. Nothing would induce Unity to leave until he did. She willingly waited an hour and a half if necessary for the pleasure of seeing him go by her table on his way out. Naturally he noticed her; she was what the Germans call *auffallend*, tall and beautiful.

Two of the waitresses at the Osteria were her friends; Ella and Rosa. They were like kind old parlourmaids. One day Ella said to Unity: 'The Führer asked me who you were.'

'Did he?' said Unity. 'I hope you said an English Fascist and not just an English student.'

She urged me on with my German. 'You will feel such a fool if we meet him and then you can't understand everything he says.'

We stood in the crowd outside the Theatinerkirche on the 9th of November to see the ceremony commemorating the sixteen men who had died in the narrow street near the Feldherrnhalle during the 1923 putsch. My English maid went too, and was given a place where she was very near Hitler. 'What did you think of him?' we asked.

'Well, he was quite different from what I thought he would be.'

'In what way?'

'He's got such beautiful hair,' was the unexpected answer.

I left Munich after five or six weeks and Unity installed herself in a Studentinnenheim. I was as usual pleased to get back to Eaton Square, with my little boys upstairs and M. rushing in and out and Tom not far away, and to see my friends again.

I went to the theatre less often than formerly, but Tom and I went to concerts and I was a cinema fan. In the seventies one dreads disgusting films in which people bash and torture, or get eaten alive by sharks, or where every sexual cruelty imagined by Sade in his prison is dwelt upon in revolting detail. In the thirties there were also films to be dreaded; the sugary and embarrassing sentimentality and drivel coming from Hollywood was hard to bear. Sometimes in those days I went to the cinema with Nigel Birch. We chose our films with care, but there was no guarantee that a child, or a dog, would not loom up on the screen. Nigel simply refused to look. He kept a large handkerchief which he put on his head and which hung over his eyes until the scene changed. It was called 'covering up'. 'I'm afraid I shall have to cover up,' he would say, and one told him when the time came for him to uncover again. Henry Yorke, another hypersensitive cinema companion of mine, also detested sentimental scenes; once we had to go out in the middle of a film. It is strange that popular taste should have changed thus radically, from idiotic slush to unendurable violence and violent sex. Presumably the film moguls cater for popular taste, for they must know what fills the coffers.

I often stayed with Gerald Berners at Faringdon. It was a mecca of beauty and fun, delicious food and comfort. Once I took Jonathan and Desmond with me, a foolhardy enterprise. Forty years later Desmond published a description of this visit: he remembered Gerald's pigeons dyed saffron yellow, shocking pink and turquoise blue which fluttered about the garden looking exotic, also the printed notice Gerald had found and hung on the stairs: MANGLING DONE HERE. The little boys, aged six and seven, were made to share a bed; it was a huge bed but my heart sank when I saw it. I put a bolster between them, but they were still much too near together and I felt sure there would be a fight or a series of fights. They might very well burst out of their room and fight on the landing, and wake everybody up in the middle of the night. I implored them not to. Desmond recalls, 'My brother was horrid to me, so clever, and forever reading books with the light on,' but he adds, 'there was a magical atmosphere at Faringdon, the house of a musical eccentric.'

Mrs. Hammersley, with her deep hollow voice and black shawls and veils, always looked and sounded tragic, but in reality she was not only witty and original but often in high spirits. One day she telephoned and asked me to go round; it was when she was living in a house in Tite Street that had been Sargent's studio. Like all her houses she had made it lovely, and her portrait by Wilson Steer, dressed in a voluminous white satin gown holding a straw hat and sitting beneath a Gainsborough-like tree was shown there to best advantage.

When I arrived I realized something was very amiss. She was lying on a chaise longue, her face yellow with incipient jaundice, and with tears squeezing out of her tightly-shut eyes. She told me that deep depression had got her in its grip. She said I must talk to her and invent a thrilling journey we could make together; we could motor to Cornwall, for example. I did as I was bid, though the mere idea of motoring to Cornwall with Mrs. Ham, and of the unending complaints, was daunting. However, she did not wish, as the Christian Scientists say, 'to make a reality of it.' She simply wanted to be told stories that would help to lift the clouds of misery engulfing her. I did my best. She recovered fairly quickly, and Cornwall was forgotten.

In the future I was to go through similar agonies with Gerald. It is no good exhorting people suffering from depression to count their blessings, no good telling Mrs. Hammersley how lucky she was to be lying in her lovely drawing-room with friends at beck and call. She knew it already and was none the less in despair. Depression is irrational. Once I said to Gerald: 'Remember, you've been like this before, and you've always come out of the tunnel into the light,' but he replied: 'One doesn't always. My mother had depressions and she died in the middle of one.' I could think of no optimistic rejoinder.

Boris Anrep, a Russian mosaicist who was a Bloomsbury figure, asked me to be one of the nine muses in a group he was doing for the floor of the National Gallery. Osbert Sitwell sat for Apollo, Clive Bell for Dionysos, and the muses were mostly friends of the artist with the exception of Greta Garbo, a star

5

from a distant firmament. I was to be Polymnia, muse of sacred music and of oratory, the latter presumably in honour of M.

Boris's floor is still there, one walks upon it every time one visits the gallery. Strangely enough the portraits are very like the models, but the colours are typical dreary Bloomsbury colours. If Anrep, who had real talent, had lived in Paris rather than London after he fled from his own country his mosaics might have been influenced by the brilliant gaiety of a Matisse rather than by the puritanical muddiness of a Roger Fry.

One day at about this time I went down to Oxford to visit Roy Harrod and we had a strange adventure. There is a drain, or water tunnel, linking the two branches of the river. Roy hired a boat and we rowed into the tunnel; the arched roof was festooned with ferns and mosses. After a while as we left the entrance behind it became too dark to see much, but it was obvious that the water was high and that we were very near the roof; we crouched in order not to be beheaded, and the space on either side of the boat was too narrow for rowing so Roy shipped his oars. We were carried along by the current. I was profoundly thankful when light appeared and we came out into the sunshine, and I pretended a sang-froid I did not feel when it seemed a distinct possibility that we should drown in the dark.

Early in 1935 Unity's wish came true. Hitler, seeing her sitting so often by herself in the Osteria Bavaria, sent over to invite her to join him at the table in the corner. She wrote an ecstatic letter and begged me to come to Munich so that I too could meet Hitler.

During one of our periodic visits to Paris M. had given me a pretty and elegant Voisin car. I went back when it was ready, and accompanied by a driver from the Voisin works I set out for Munich. Although it was March there was a heavy fall of snow in the Black Forest and we got stuck fast in a drift of soft new snow. The thought of spending the night in the car with the poor old chauffeur who was grumbling away under his breath was almost more than I could bear. After a bad quarter of an hour, when the sun had already set and light was fast fading I saw, quite a long way off across the snow, a peasant with a team of horses. I got out and shouted to him as loudly as I could. By great good luck he heard; he turned towards us and his horses pulled us out of the drift and set us on the road once more.

Country men and sailors will always help the traveller in distress; townsmen more often pass by on the other side. They dread becoming involved. There is a terrible description in one of Montherlant's diaries: feeling deathly ill he was obliged to lie down on the pavement of a busy Paris street. Nobody offered to help. Probably they imagined he was just another drunk.

The rest of our journey was without adventure, and when we got to Munich I sent the old Frenchman back to Paris. Soon after my arrival Hitler came to the Osteria and we lunched with him.

During the next four years I saw him fairly often, though not nearly as often as Unity did. Since she is no longer here to tell what he was like in private life I will do my best to describe the man I knew. It is only what the French call 'la petite histoire'; but even in small matters the truth is sometimes interesting.

Hitler, at this time aged forty-five, was about 5 feet 9 inches in height and neither fat nor thin. His eyes were dark blue, his skin fair and his brown hair exceptionally fine; it was neatly brushed; I never saw him with a lock of hair over his forehead. If he was out of doors in the sun and wind all day, as he was for example the last day of the Parteitag every year, he quickly got sunburnt, but it did not last for his skin was pale. His hands were white and well-shaped. He was extremely neat and clean looking, so much so that beside him nearly everyone looked coarse. His teeth had been mended with gold, as one saw when he laughed. At the Osteria he was generally in civilian clothes, he wore a grey suit and a white shirt and a rather furry soft hat which he called 'mein Schako'. His most unusual feature was the forehead. He had a high forehead which almost jutted forward above the eyes. I have seen this on one or two other people; generally they have been musicians. At this little bistro he was in relaxed mood; if he had not been so he would have lunched at his flat. Besides the adjutant, usually Brückner or Schaub, there were often a few old friends, mostly men but also some women; Frau Troost, wife of the architect, was there occasionally. Frequently Hoffman the photographer and Herr Werlin of Mercedes Benz were with him. We rather dreaded the conversation turning to motor-cars, for the Führer took a deep interest in engines and was apparently expertly knowledgeable on the subject, very boring to us. However like most politicians he enjoyed talking politics, and often Reichspressechef Dietrich would give him a sheet of paper with a résumé of the news, which set him off on more interesting themes. One of his abiding interests was architecture. Without ever having visited Paris, for instance, he knew its beauties and where they stood in relation to one another. Albert Speer was quite often at Hitler's table; at that time a young architect he has grown into an old writer. On the occasions when I saw him he gave a wonderful imitation of being fascinated by his host; or perhaps he really was fascinated.

I never heard Hitler 'rant' and almost never heard the famous monologue, though I should have been interested to listen to it. In my experience he liked conversation. In certain moods he could be very funny; he did imitations of marvellous drollery which showed how acutely observant he was.

Although I often saw him at luncheon and dinner and in the afternoon when Germans drink coffee, I never once saw him eat a cake of any sort, let alone a cream cake. His food was dismal. He was a vegetarian, he ate eggs and mayonnaise and vegetables and pasta, and compote of fruit, or raw grated apple, and he drank Fachingerwasser. At the Osteria they knew exactly what he liked, he had been there for years past.

His guests ordered whatever they pleased. In his flat, if one was invited, delicious food was sent along from Walterspiel, one of the world's greatest restaurants, but this was for the guests: his own menu did not vary.

He was extremely polite to women; he bowed and kissed hands as is the custom in Germany and France, and he never sat down until they did. Such trivialities would not be worth recording were it not for the acres of print about Hitler in which his rudeness and bad manners to everyone are emphasized. I have read books by dons as well as by sensation-seeking journalists in which it is asserted that he had no idea how to behave in company, or that he always hogged the conversation so that

nobody but he could say a single word, or that he had no sense
of humour, or that he guzzled cream cakes. Novelists have now
taken up the theme, and possibly—just possibly—it may be
worth while to set down the truth about these little things in
so far as I know it from my own observation.

Unity decided to come back to Paris with me and we took it
in turns to drive the Voisin. Bryan was at the rue de Poitiers
flat with Nanny and the boys, and I wanted to be there for
Jonathan's fifth birthday.

While we were in Paris Unity and I visited Brancusi in his
studio, of which there is now a model in the Musée de l'Art
Moderne. We were taken there by Marie-Laure de Noailles
with whom we had been lunching at the place des États Unis.
Brancusi was a beautiful god-like old man with a flowing beard.
He showed us his sculptures; Unity was entranced and knew
at once what they represented. She went from one to another,
naming them. 'Mai oui, c'est ça, c'est exactement ça,' said
Brancusi. Many of the marvels we saw that day I admired
again not long ago in New York. Brancusi's *Muse endormie* is
an object of veneration to me.

I was still in Paris with the children and Unity had gone
back to Germany when M. went to Munich to see Hitler for the
first time in April 1935. It was a private visit and he was received at the flat in Prinzregentenplatz. After their talk they
went into the drawing-room where a number of people were
gathered before luncheon. Hitler had invited three ladies to
meet M., all of them with English connections: the Duchess of
Brunswick, only daughter of the Kaiser and a great-grand-
daughter of Queen Victoria, Frau Winifred Wagner, the
English-born daughter-in-law of Richard Wagner, and Unity.
He hoped thus to give Unity a great surprise, the thrill of meeting M., but of course they knew one another already. This was
the first time she had been formally invited, and not just asked
to join Hitler at the Osteria. She asked him afterwards what he
thought of M. and he replied: 'Ein ganzer Kerl!'

It is sometimes suggested that there was something deeply
wrong, in 1935, in having wished to lunch and dine and talk
with Hitler. The war and its attendant horrors were in the
far future, but there are those who say: 'Ah, but Roehm had
been shot in 1934. Surely that in itself was a reason for avoiding

him?' Hitler came to power when his party polled more votes than any other; nevertheless he was a revolutionary who emerged from a violent society. From the time when the NSDAP was started again after his release from Fortress Landsberg, early in 1925, until he became chancellor almost eight years later, one of his followers was killed on average every nine days, in fights with the red front. There were six million unemployed. In 1932 a conservative M.P.* wrote in his diary: 'Europe is on the brink of starvation and bankruptcy.'

In 1934, seventeen months after Hitler took office, unemployment was dwindling and order had been restored. This did not suit everyone. The head of the Sturmabteilung, Ernst Roehm, was a professional revolutionary who looked with distaste upon the potentially stable country which was taking shape. He had no wish to see his hundreds of thousands of S.A. men reduced to performing boring tasks of reconstruction. He hoped to stir up the nether world. Hitler, faced with threatened civil war, had Roehm and his co-plotters shot. His prompt and violent way of dealing with a situation as dangerous for Germany as for himself was rightly condemned in the law-abiding democracies, where politicians in modern times had not been faced with any such dilemmas. Despite the circumstances prevailing in Germany, Roehm should have had a fair trial.

Winston Churchill wrote soon afterwards:† 'It is not possible to form a just judgment of a public figure who has attained the enormous dimensions of Adolf Hitler until his life-work as a whole is before us . . . History is replete with examples of men who have risen to power by employing stern, grim and even frightful methods.' He went on: '. . . he has succeeded in restoring Germany to the most powerful position in Europe' and 'It is certainly not strange that everyone should want to know "the truth about Hitler".'

Churchill wrote these words at the time I first made the acquaintance of the extraordinary individual whom he thus described.

Lloyd George went to Germany to meet Hitler in 1936. Two years previously he had said to Frances Stevenson‡ that he con-

* Victor Cazalet.

† *Great Contemporaries* published 1935, re-issued 1942.

‡ *Lloyd George, A Diary*, by Frances Stevenson.

sidered him 'a very great man'. The visit has been described by A. J. Sylvester* and Thomas Jones,† who wrote: 'Hitler was forty-six, Ll G was seventy-three, alike only in their perfect grooming and the brilliance of their blue eyes, these two actors exchanged courtesies.' Hitler gave his guest a signed photograph, and Lloyd George said 'how honoured he was to receive the gift from the greatest living German.' Back in England, Lloyd George wrote:‡ 'He is a born leader of men. A magnetic, dynamic personality . . . The old trust him. The young idolize him.'

All this by no means implies that Lloyd George approved of everything in Germany. He applauded Hitler's economic measures, the way he had dealt with unemployment, his land reclamation, but he surely condemned the concentration camps which still held men in prison without trial. Lloyd George himself, in the early years of the century, had denounced in many a fiery speech the concentration camps set up by the British in South Africa. Four thousand Boer soldiers were killed in battle, and more than twice that number of Boer women and children died in the camps. Nor did he approve of Hitler's attack on the Jews. 'We put up with them in our country,' he said to Sylvester, and some years previously he had this to say of anti-Semitism: 'Of all the bigotries that savage the human temper there is none so stupid as the anti-Semitic. It has no basis in reason.'

Many years after the time I am describing, millions died as a result of orders given by Hitler. In his book *My Life*, M. writes 'How did this man come to be responsible for one of most execrable crimes in all history? For to kill prisoners in cold blood, whether Jew, Gentile or any other human being, is a vile crime . . . Hitler must, in the end, bear responsibility for it.'

No one who has been a prisoner can fail to imagine in the very bones the horror of it. To be killed in circumstances where you have no hope of defending yourself is frightful. Our century has been the most violent and bloody in history.

More millions died in Stalin's camps, in peace time; and most

* *Life with Lloyd George.*
† *Lloyd George.*
‡ *Daily Express* 17/9/36.

of all were killed by Mao Tse-Tung in China. 'Foreign special-
ists . . . estimate that since October 1949 at least twenty million
Chinese have been "deprived of existence". This does not
include 23 million who are believed to be held in forced labour
camps. In no previous war, revolution or holocaust from Tamer-
lane to Hitler, have so many people been destroyed in so short
a period.'*

When I knew Hitler the Russian crimes were actuality, the
Chinese holocaust was in the future and so was the German.
Yet recently, long after the facts about Mao Tse-Tung were
well known, respected politicians from the west visited him and
found a delightful old poet. The fact that they went to see him
shows that 'morality' has nothing to do with the case. When the
Chairman died, the obituaries and messages from heads of state
were fulsome.

Possibly the truth is that only men of compelling and unusual
charms and gifts acquire the power to commit crimes of such
magnitude. With regard to atrocities, Hitler was not unique.

* *Reader's Digest,* July 1956.

13

Accident

ONE HOT EVENING in July 1935 I was dressing for dinner when M. telephoned. We had planned to motor down late to his house at Denham, but he found he could not leave till next day. I told him I would drive myself down and sleep in the country air.

I was dining with the Dunns where I sat next to Lord Beaverbrook. There was amusing talk, and it was after midnight when I got home. Everything was ready, I changed in a trice, put my spaniel in the motor and was off. At the junction where five roads meet between Belgrave Square and Cadogan Place an enormous Rolls Royce loomed up and crashed into me. I was only half unconscious, a strange sensation. A little crowd gathered and two policemen dragged me out of the battered car and laid me on the pavement; one of them held my head in his lap. Voices faded, and then came back, and faded again. I half opened my eyes. Two women went by, they were taking their dog to a lamp-post. 'Don't look, it's too horrible,' I heard one of them say. This struck me as comic; I was an 'accident', too horrible to look at, drenched in blood.

'My dog,' I said to the policeman. 'Please take him home. He's very nervous.'

'All right, all right,' said the policeman soothingly. After a while an ambulance drove up and they lifted me in. I was unconscious during the drive, which was very short, but just before the waves engulfed me I managed to say:

'Take me home, please. It's near. Two Eaton Square. And my dog. Please take us both home.'

'All right,' said the policeman, but they were carrying me up the steps of St. George's Hospital.

'Where's my dog?'

'He's all right, he's gone home,' said the policeman. This was untrue. He spent a frightening night among strangers at the police station. What with the crash and seeing me covered in blood, this dreadful experience affected his nerves for the rest of his life.

At the hospital I heard them say cheerfully: 'We've brought you another street accident.' I was lifted on to a table and they found no broken bones but a very battered face.

'Where's the thin thread?'

'Night Sister's locked it up.'

'Well, haven't you got a key?'

'No, and she's gone off.'

One of those bright institutional conversations was taking place over my body. My head was dizzy but thoughts came and went. My anxiety about the spaniel had been calmed by a lie and I began to worry about M. Suppose he saw it in the morning paper, and suppose nobody at Denham or at home knew where I was, or knew whether I was alive or dead?

'We must use the thick thread then,' the voice was saying. 'This is going to hurt,' he went on putting his face close to mine. 'I can't give you an anaesthetic. It's going to sting.'

'I see,' I said. 'Can I telephone?'

'Oh no,' said the doctor, 'you certainly can't. You wouldn't be able to stand for one thing.'

'But I *must* telephone,' I said. 'You can carry me on the stretcher to the telephone.'

'We'll see,' said the doctor. He dug his needle into the side of my nose. After two stitches he said: 'I'm afraid this stings.' Sting was a mild way of putting it.

'Yes,' I said, awake now, 'and if I don't scream will you let me telephone?'

'Yes, all right,' he said making another jab. He sewed up my nose and then my jaw, and then, unwillingly, they carried me to a telephone which was fixed to a wall in the passage. I dialled M.'s number; he must have been asleep, it was after two.

'I'm in St. George's Hospital and I'm quite all right.'

'What? Where did you say?'

'*Quite all right,*' I repeated and rang off. It was as much as I could manage.

They put me in a huge ward full of poor old ladies who had had major operations. After about three hours of snores and groans and strange night noises the nurses came pattering along waking everybody up. I was only too pleased, since I was awake already. My face hurt. My neighbours in the beds either side were pleased to see me; they told me the accident ward was shut for the summer and they enjoyed having the accidents in their ward, it made a change. They were there for weeks and months and bored to death.

When an important nurse came by I asked if I could go home. 'We'll see,' she said. I was carried away to be X-rayed, and after a bit: 'You can go home if you hire an ambulance,' I was told.

Tom came and fetched me in an ambulance. He looked worried. 'Your face,' he said. All one could see among the bandages was my eyes peering out.

'Oh, I don't think it's much. They've sewed me up,' I told him. I was carried into Eaton Square and put in my own bed. M. came, and Bryan came. It was Bryan's father who thought of what to do; he telephoned: 'You must see Sir Harold Gillies at once. Don't wait. I'm going to get hold of him *now*.'

When Sir Harold Gillies undid the bandages he was angered by what he saw. He pulled the thick thread out, which hurt. 'What on earth is this?' he said.

'Well, they couldn't find the thin thread,' I answered. Sir Harold said that if he had left the stitches in my nose and jaw I should have been marked for ever by them, as well as having a pugilist's nose. He would operate after a week when the swelling and bruising had gone down, meanwhile he put two huge stitches from one part of my face to the other to hold the cuts together and he told me not to talk or laugh more than I was obliged. Lord Moyne sent a kind nurse and she came with me a week later to the London Clinic. I still did not know what I was in for.

As it was the silly season the papers had headlines about my crash and the house filled up with flowers and letters and telegrams. I sent masses of the flowers on to St. George's to my friends in the operation ward. The *Daily Express* had a short leading article on the mutability of human fortune; doubtless Lord Beaverbrook, like Tom and everybody else but me, imagined my poor face was wrecked for ever.

But for Sir Harold Gillies it would have been, though it never occurred to me. I felt sorry I had smashed my car, annoyed at being stuck in London and having my plans upset, grateful for the flowers and the kind visits of M., Bryan, Tom, Lord Moyne and my sisters; but I thought the newspapers very exaggerated.

After Gillies had operated on my nose and jaw I woke up in real pain. It felt as though somebody had banged my head with a hammer for a very long time. After three days I asked the nurse for a looking-glass. Lifting an eyelid with my finger, because the eyes were still closed by bruising, I saw a sort of pudding with no features sticking out of it. However, a few days more and the swelling went down and there was my face again.

After an X-ray I was told I must have another operation, on the antrum. This was gloomy news. Back into the London Clinic, hope deferred. The second operation was less painful but almost more hateful. I began to feel very sorry for myself. Farve came to the Clinic.

'I shall never get well here because I hate it so much,' I told him.

'What do you want to do?' he said.

'I want to fly to Naples, but they say I must stay another week.'

I knew the habits of the Clinic. Farve came with his car before dawn when the night nurses were at breakfast and the day nurses still asleep. I dressed quietly and he helped me down the stairs. We dared not take the lift in case we were caught. He drove me to Croydon and saw me into the aeroplane. At Marseille I changed to a seaplane, flew to Rome and got to Naples that evening.

M. had taken the Rennells' villa at Posillipo. It was perched above the sea with the celebrated view across the bay to Vesuvius; an absurd house. According to Gerald, he and Gerry Wellesley and some others at the embassy in Rome twenty years before had held a competition for designing the most hideous house imaginable, and the winning drawing had been stuck on the wall of the Chancellery. Lady Rodd happened to see it. 'My dream house!' she exclaimed, and asked if she might borrow the drawing. She used it for the Posillipo villa, a crazy jumble of styles.

The warmth and the sun soon cured me, though to begin

with I could not manage the hundreds of steps down to the sea, nor bear the noonday light. After a few days I recovered from my injuries, swimming in the deep sea with M.

Unity had lost no time in telling Hitler of our Parteitag adventures, of how Putzi, having invited us in 1933 and promised to introduce us to him, then did his best to prevent us going to Nuremberg at all in 1934. 'Why?' he wanted to know.

'Because of our lipstick,' said Unity.

Hitler laughed. He said it was typical of Hanfstaengl, who had bored him over and over again with old American women, not to introduce just for once somebody he would have liked to see. He was amused about our gate crashing and Parteigenosse Nummer Hundert. This year he promised we should be his guests. One night we were invited to a huge picnic-like out-of-doors dinner party on the Burg. I was put next to a little man with poached-egg blue eyes who was wearing dozens of medals on his brown shirt. I started to speak German but he said, 'Let's talk English,' which I was only too pleased to do. When I asked how it was that he spoke so fluently, 'Well, you see I'm an Eton boy,' was the surprising answer. He was the Duke of Saxe-Coburg. He told me Hitler had visited him; asked to write something in the duke's copy of *Mein Kampf* he put: '*Mein Himmel auf Erde heisst: Vaterland.*' (My heaven on earth is called Fatherland.)

There was a performance of *Meistersinger* at the opera, the rows of boxes had been garlanded from stalls to gallery with swags of fresh flowers.

Before Hitler's last speech at the closing session in the Congresshalle an orchestra played a Bruckner symphony. Like so many Germans, Hitler had a passion for music. For some obscure reason this love of music is hardly allowed to exist by his English biographers. (After the war I read a book by Alan Bullock in which he rather absurdly says that Hitler 'did not get much further than Beethoven'. Musically speaking, what is further than Beethoven? Hoping to discover the answer to this conundrum I went to a lecture by Alan Bullock on Hitler at, of all unlikely places, the Army and Navy Stores. To my disappointment at the end of his lecture the lecturer disappeared; there were no questions. On the way out I found myself next to

Sheila Birkenhead. 'Too sad there were no questions,' I said, to which, giving me a searching look, she replied, 'I expect it was just as well.')

In February 1935 a plebiscite had been held in the Saar. For fifteen years the province was ruled by France; now, in accordance with the peace treaty, the Saarlanders were to choose their own future. They could vote for the status quo, or for League of Nations rule, or to join Germany once again. English soldiers ensured the secrecy of the ballot.

There was much speculation in the press, because although the Saarlanders were German the theory was that since Hitler was now in power nobody of his own free will would vote to be incorporated in the Reich. Probably the journalists genuinely believed this, for they cannot have hoped to influence the vote in a German-speaking province. The referendum on one subject or another had been a fairly frequent feature of German politics during the previous two years and the result was always a large majority for the National Socialist government, but according to English newspapers either these votes were simply faked or else people had been dragooned by 'jack-booted storm troopers' into going to the polls and putting an X in the required place. The result of the Saar plebiscite, run by the League of Nations, was almost exactly the same as for plebiscites within Germany itself, ninety-seven per cent voted for incorporation in the Reich. This was a great disappointment to the English press as well as the English Left, but after a while, assuming that the circumstances of the Saar vote had been forgotten by their readers, the old theory about faking and dragooning cropped up once more in the newspapers.

The truth is that Germany supported Hitler. As to the Jews, thousands of whom had come in from eastern Europe after the war, most Germans probably hoped they would remove themselves to some other part of the globe. World Jewry with its immense wealth could find the money, and England and France with the resources of their vast empires could find the living space, it was imagined. English, French and American newspapers were at one in describing the Jews as Germany's cleverest and most desirable citizens, hence it was assumed by Germans that they would get a warmer welcome in any of these countries than proved in fact to be the case. The Jews who left did not make things easier for those who remained behind. Their virulent attacks upon all things German and their insistent calls for trade boycotts, military encirclement and even war, hardened the hearts of the many Germans who were well-disposed towards them. The anti-Jewish laws were passed in Germany in the thirties with the object of inducing the Jews to leave the country. As Arthur Koestler has written: 'The Old Testament laws, racial and economic, against the stranger in Israel could have served as a model for the Nuremberg Code.'*

Since those days there have been many rough and cruel expulsions of unwanted citizens by intransigent nationalist governments, the Indians driven out of East Africa, for example, or the Israeli bulldozing of Arab villages, not to mention millions of Germans forced out of Prussia, Silesia, Pomerania and Bohemia. These uprootings have been among the most painful episodes in our violent and barbarous century. It was a tragedy that world Jewry did not make a greater effort in the thirties to accommodate its co-racialists from central Europe elsewhere in the world.

When Hitler came to power, large numbers of his political opponents were arrested and put in concentration camps. This blot on the régime was always condemned by M., who said that imprisonment without trial was wrong in itself and a sign of incompetence in a government. Imprisonment without trial was used by the English government in Northern Ireland, and political opponents were constantly being imprisoned in India and in our African colonies. Pandit Nehru spent sixteen years in British prisons in India. Ignoring these well-known facts, English journalists and politicians pretended to think that such practices were unique to Germany.

As the years went by almost all the prisoners in Germany's camps were released; what happened during the war is another matter. By then, we ourselves were imprisoned and silenced.

* In *Scum of the Earth*.

14

Wootton

MEANWHILE IN LONDON, since launching the British Union
of Fascists, M. had held a number of successful meetings at
the Albert Hall. It was always full to capacity and people had
to be turned away, therefore in the summer of 1934 he hired
Olympia which, almost twice the size, holds an audience of
fifteen thousand.

The communists decided to wreck this meeting. For weeks
beforehand the *Daily Worker* drummed up its supporters to
gather at Olympia and smash fascism. It even printed a map
showing them how to get there. A few friends dined with me
before the meeting but they went off without me; I had a
temperature and felt far from well. I have always regretted
this, for the Olympia meeting and its fierce fights have
been argued about ever since and I wish I had seen it for
myself.

The communists and their allies came well armed with
razors and such like and there is a first-hand account of the
behaviour of two of them in Philip Toynbee's book *Friends
Apart*. He describes how he and Esmond Romilly bought
knuckledusters at an ironmonger to help them smash fascism,
but they were thrown out of the meeting, in tears, before they
could do much harm. No doubt our people were very ready
with their fists, but they did not fight with razors and knuckledusters, and it was their own meeting they were defending.
There was a great controversy in the days that followed, letters
to *The Times* and so forth, but it was Lloyd George who hit
the nail on the head: 'It is difficult to explain why the fury of
the champions of free speech should be concentrated so exclusively, not on those who deliberately and resolutely attempted
to prevent the public expression of opinions of which they disapproved, but against those who fought, however roughly,
for freedom of speech. Personally, I have suffered as much as

anyone in public life today from hostile interruptions by opponents determined to make it impossible for me to put my case before audiences . . . and I feel that men who enter meetings with the deliberate intention of suppressing free speech have no right to complain if an exasperated audience handles them rudely.'*

M. was invited by the BBC to discuss the violence at the meeting on the wireless. After he had said his say, Gerald Barry, editor of the *Weekend Review*, spoke. M. was not allowed to answer a number of untrue allegations he made, and Barry had the last word. Nowadays, with television, there would presumably be a face-to-face confrontation, a much fairer procedure. This broadcast in 1934 was the last permitted to M. by the BBC for thirty-four years. It was not until 1968, and after he had brought an action in the High Court, that he, like every other politician, was able to speak for himself on the wireless and television controlled by the BBC, although he had throughout been the subject of frequent comment by other people, and wildly hostile comment at that.

Our opponents exaggerated the violence at Olympia. If half their stories had been true the hall would have been strewn with dead and dying and the hospitals full of casualties. As it was they gave themselves a bad fright, and on the whole subsequent meetings were quieter.

Forty years afterwards Harold Macmillan wrote a book about prominent politicians entitled *The Past Masters* in which there is a photograph of M. holding what looks like a fleur de lys. In fact, it was the top of a London park iron railing, and was part of the arsenal of weapons used against him to be confiscated from the reds by his supporters at Olympia.

Two years after Olympia there was a meeting in Oxford at the Carfax Rooms which has also been the subject of legend and controversy. I happened to be there as I was on my way from Swinbrook to London and decided to wait in Oxford and hear M. speak. The hall was full; in the front sat some youngish dons. I recognized Frank Pakenham and Richard Crossman, and some undergraduates. At the back were rougher looking men. When M. began to speak the undergraduates opened large newspapers and pretended to read them. At first M. paid no

* *Sunday Pictorial.*

attention to this absurdity, nor to various interruptions and
shouts, but when they began ostentatiously rustling their
papers he said: 'I am glad to see the young gentlemen are
studying, I believe they are very backward in their lessons
this year,' a mild sarcasm which was the signal for all the
undergraduates and their rougher allies in the rows behind to
jump up and start shouting. After the customary three warnings
from M. 'to give order or leave the hall' our stewards began
putting the noisy men out. Crossman leapt at the platform
and was immediately seized and chucked out. The iron chairs
were freely used as weapons against the stewards and there was
a great noise and pandemonium. I flattened myself against the
wall in order to keep as far as possible from the assailants.
Within twenty minutes calm was restored, all the trouble-
makers had been put out in the street, and M. resumed his
speech. A large and peaceful audience listened to his economic
policy for an hour, and then put questions to him for almost
another hour. This was a typical 'violent' meeting. It was
always a surprise to see how few in numbers the noisy interrupters had been—a couple of dozen in an audience of several
hundred on this occasion. Needless to say the fight, which had
been short and sharp, was all that was reported in the newspapers. The peaceful meeting which followed was not
mentioned, nor, obviously, the points made by M. in his
speech.

There was a sequel many years afterwards. When Robert
Skidelsky was writing his life of M. he went to see Maurice
Bowra, the Dean of Wadham, who had described the meeting
in his memoirs. Maurice said: 'I think you should see this,'
and he gave Robert a letter written to him by the man who had
been Chief Constable of Oxford in 1936. The Chief Constable
said he had read Maurice's book and his (second-hand) account
of the Carfax Rooms meeting, and felt it was unfair to M.
That Sir Oswald was very patient with interrupters until they
all jumped up and began shouting and fighting, was the gist of
the letter.

It was honest of Maurice to show Skidelsky the Chief
Constable's letter; since, however, his book of memoirs was
already published when he received it his contribution to the
controversy is the usual condemnation of 'fascist violence'. As

the memoirs, unlike Maurice himself, are dull, no second edition ever gave the Chief Constable's reaction.

The Oxford meeting reputedly made Frank Pakenham, at the time a conservative, into a socialist. He got a bang on the head in the melée. How true this is I do not know, but M. subsequently claimed full credit for 'putting him on the Labour front bench'.

In 1936 M. and I decided to get married. I also made up my mind to leave Eaton Square and live in the country. I asked the agent to look for a house within reach of Manchester, because M. spent so much time in the Midlands and north of England and it would be a great convenience if we had a house there where he could stay rather than going to hotels and inns. One day the house-agent showed me a photograph of Wootton Lodge in Staffordshire. 'How beautiful,' I said.

'It's a white elephant,' said the agent.

M. and I went to have a look at it. We drove down a long avenue of beech trees and after about a mile we saw the house. It is a magically beautiful place, an early seventeenth-century stone house with windows that remind one of Hardwick: 'Hardwick Hall, more glass than wall.' It stands on a rocky eminence surrounded by wooded hills. It belonged to a handsome old sailor, Captain Unwin V.C. We rented it unfurnished, intending to buy it later on, as he was anxious to sell. This was the second time in my life that I had the good fortune to live in a perfectly lovely house; I imagined it was to be my home for good.

Just before I moved in Farve had one of his periodic sales at which I bought quantities of furniture for a song; the market for antiques was still in the depths of slump. I was pleased to have these old familiar things about me at Wootton, which was as perfect inside as out, with splendid early eighteenth-century panelling in almost every room.

The garden was arranged in terraces because the ground descended steeply to lakes far below. Here M. fished for trout on summer evenings. The woods were full of bluebells in spring, there were streams and immensely aged oaks. There were few pheasants and no hunting; we kept a couple of horses for hacking and a pony for the boys. Everybody was happy at

Wootton, it had a delightful atmosphere as well as a noble aspect; each day there was perfection. When snow fell great soft heaps of it weighed down the boughs of an old cedar on the lawn beneath the drawing-room windows, outlined the walls and the two pavilions flanking the entrance, and lit the interior of the house with white reflections. A few miles away the Weaver Hill was the shape of a miniature mountain; it kept its snowy peak for most of the winter. The boys took their toboggans on the steep slopes near the house, the very same toboggans Tom and I had used when I crashed into the electric light house at Batsford. Wootton looked magic, glittering in the snow.

Sometimes in winter and more often in summer an even, dark grey sky made the whole place sombre. The gardeners said it was millions of little flies far away up in the air which hid the sun. Really I suppose it was an encroachment from the black country, from Sheffield, Manchester, Bolton, Derby and the Staffordshire potteries, none of them a great distance from Wootton. The wind changed and soon drove away the swarming flies, or smuts, and then nowhere on earth could be more delicately and brightly coloured than the Wootton garden and woods and lakes. We treasured our days spent in this heavenly place and imagined a long future together there, which was not to be.

Just before I left Eaton Square and went to live at Wootton the Churchills invited me to luncheon at a flat they had near Westminster Cathedral. It was some time since I had seen them, though I remember going down to Chartwell one day and meeting there a wonderfully beautiful girl: she was Angela, Johnny Churchill's wife. At the flat the other guest was Ivor Churchill; Sarah ran in for a moment on her way to a dancing lesson. She was already determined upon a stage career. Out of the unpromising material of a house that was frankly ugly, Clementine with her usual talent had succeeded in creating loveliness.

Cousin Winston wanted to hear about Hitler. There was also talk of Italy and sanctions and the Abyssinian war. Echoing M., I asked if it might not be dangerous for our fleet in the Mediterranean, where home-based Italian aircraft could attack our ships if oil sanctions provoked Italy into war.

'No,' said Churchill. 'An aeroplane cannot sink a battleship. The armour is impenetrably thick.' I remembered his words a few years later, when against the advice of the Admiralty, the *Prince of Wales* and the *Repulse* were sent from Singapore into the China seas with no air cover and were sunk by Japanese torpedo-carrying aircraft. During the war Hans-Ulrich Rudel sank the Soviet battleship *Marat* single-handed in his Stuka, with bombs.

Gerald came back from Rome that year with stories of the fury of the Romans against Mr. Eden and England's policy of sanctions. The Duchess of Sermoneta told him she wished she could open a vein and let out every drop of her English blood.

After settling into Wootton in July I left for Berlin where Unity and I went to the Olympic Games. Hitler gave us tickets and we stayed with the Goebbels at their lake-side villa at Schwanenwerder. I became very fond of Magda Goebbels and her children. She had a handsome son, Harald Quandt, by her first husband, and several Goebbels infants. Dr. Goebbels was intelligent, witty and sarcastic; he had an exceptionally beautiful speaking voice. Magda called him 'Engel'. We taught them to play Analogies. Dr. Goebbels was being questioned: 'What colour does he remind you of?'

'Fiery red!' said Goebbels. He had chosen the Führer for his subject.

Every day we motored to the Games. Fortunately Unity and I had seats far away from our hosts so that we could wander from the stadium from time to time. I have never been a great enthusiast for watching athletics, men throwing discs or tossing cabers and so on. The running and jumping were less dull. There was an American negro, Jesse Owens, who dashed along much faster than anybody else; it was a pleasure to watch him. After Owens came the runners of other countries, bunched together, and far behind them all an Indian with his hair done up in a bun. 'Oh!' cried the Germans near us as Jesse Owens got further ahead and the Indian further behind, 'Oh, der Inder! Der *arme* Inder!', the *poor* Indian!

M. thought it wise to keep our marriage secret, as I was living at Wootton, often alone, and politics were rough. We had meant to be married in Paris, but we discovered that notice of the marriage would have to be posted up on the wall of the consulate so that it was no better than a London registry office as far as journalists were concerned. I asked the advice of the Munich consul and he told me that under a reciprocal arrangement between England and Germany British subjects were married by the ordinary registrar in Germany, and vice versa. Hitler said he would ask the Berlin registrar to keep the marriage quiet, and while we were staying with her Magda helped me with all the form-filling; the wedding was arranged for October.

Unity and I also went to Bayreuth that summer; we had been invited to the Festspiele, an experience as heavenly as the Olympic Games were boring. The Ring, which I knew well from Covent Garden, was splendidly sung and for the first time I heard *Parsifal*. I confessed to Hitler that I liked it least of all Wagner's operas and he said: 'That is because you are young. You will find as you get older that you love *Parsifal* more and more,' a prediction which has come true.

We had supper in the long intervals at Hitler's table in the restaurant near the Festspielhaus, and we made the acquaintance of his great friend Frau Winifred Wagner and of her four children. Wieland, Wolf and Friedelind—Maus, as she was called—looked like Richard Wagner. The youngest and most charming, Verena, was the image of Cosima.

M. and I were married on the 6th October 1936 in the drawing-room of the Goebbels's Berlin house in Hermann Goeringstrasse. I was dressed in a pale gold tunic. Unity and I, standing at the window of an upstairs room, saw Hitler walking through the trees of the park-like garden that separated the house and the Reichskanzlei; the leaves were turning yellow and there was bright sunshine. Behind him came an adjutant carrying a box and some flowers. M. was already downstairs.

The ceremony was short; the Registrar said a few words, we exchanged rings, signed our names and the deed was done. Hitler's gift was a photograph in a silver frame with A.H. and the German eagle.

We all drove out to Schwanenwerder where Magda had arranged a wedding feast. The little girls, Helga and Hilde, came in afterwards to 'gratulieren' and give more flowers.

Magda and Dr. Goebbels gave me a leather-bound edition of
Goethe's works in twenty volumes.

That evening we went to the Sportpalast where Hitler and
Goebbels opened the Winterhilfswerk (a vast organization,
the Winterhilfswerk ensured that everyone had coal, blankets
and so forth). M. at that time understood no German but it
interested him to see the meeting, and the technique of the
speeches. We dined at the Reichskanzlei. This was the second
and last time M. ever saw Hitler. We stayed the night at the
Kaiserhof, and after a quarrel of which, try as I will, I cannot
remember the reason, we went to bed in dudgeon. Next day
we flew home to England.

M. and I were married all over again in 1974. Our marriage
certificate had been in M.'s safe at Grosvenor Road, and had
disappeared into the maw of the Home Office when its officials
burst everything open and removed the contents in 1940.
Years later we needed it, and they appeared unable to find it.
As to Berlin, the Hermann Goeringstrasse must certainly have
been re-named, probably Beriastrasse or something of the
sort, and the whole district blotted out and unrecognizable.
It seemed simpler to re-marry, and we did so at Caxton Hall.

I could now speak and read German. I learnt by listening to
speeches, reading the newspapers, learning poems by heart
and reading trash. Detective novels, which I never cared for
in English, taught one the language of every day. Wagner's
nineteenth-century-archaic style Tom, Unity and I used to one
another, but this was a joke few Germans would share.

I told my parents, and of course Tom, that M. and I were
married, but nobody else. During the next two years journalists,
who strongly suspected the marriage, could not lay their hands
on documentary evidence and therefore did not print the story.
Several times Tom telephoned me from London to say they
had been asking him and other relations about it. One of the
most persistent journalists was Randolph, who pestered Tom
continually on the subject.

Within a few months of my marriage to M. two of my
sisters were married, Pam to Derek Jackson and Decca to
Esmond Romilly. Derek was and is a very remarkable man;
one would say unique, except that he had an identical twin as
brilliant and unusual as himself. Vivian was a great friend of

mine; he often came to Eaton Square and I stayed with him and Stella in the country. The twins were notable physicists (among the best in the world, Prof. Lindemann once told M.). Vivian worked in London, Derek at Oxford. They both loved horses and hunting and steeplechasing, they were as fearless as they were clever. Just at the time of Pam and Derek's marriage Vivian was tragically killed in a sleigh accident at St. Moritz. His loss was a sorrow to Derek that time could never heal; part of himself died with Vivian. It was unbearably sad to think that never again, after the twins had argued everyone else to a standstill, would one hear the triumphant shout: 'I agree with Derek!' and 'I agree with Vivian!'

Decca and our cousin Esmond Romilly, aged nineteen and eighteen, ran off to the Spanish Civil War; Esmond was a communist. As they were under twenty-one they had to get their parents' consent in order to be married. This was reluctantly given and they were married in France with Muv and Nelly Romilly as wedding guests. Soon afterwards they went to live in America.

In 1937 Tom came with us to the Parteitag, and also his old friend Janos von Almasy. Janos had become a great friend of Unity's; she constantly stayed with him at Bernstein, his castle in the Burgenland, and also at nearby Kohfidisch with the Erdödys. She brought Baby to stay with me at Wootton. Every year there were more foreigners at the Parteitag, and the world press waiting for Hitler's speech. Several Paris friends were at Nuremberg that year. We were lodged in an hotel that had been built for guests and was not a bit like the inns of our first visits.

Tom and Janos were very impressed, not only by the extra-ordinary beauty and clockwork precision of the parades but by the speeches giving details of progress in every sphere of the economy. England seemed stagnant by comparison, and shortly after this Tom joined our movement. Janos, a Hungarian whose property had become part of Austria under the peace treaties in 1919, hoped for the Anschluss, which, rightly as it turned out, he thought could not be long delayed. This was my last Parteitag; the following year I was seven months pregnant and the year after that war had begun.

In 1938 Unity had my parents with her at Nuremberg.

Ever since 1934 they had visited her from time to time, and she often took them to see Hitler. She persuaded Farve to send him a present, a life-size, life-like bronze eagle, Japanese. The great bird was alighting on a bronze rock. Did it ever arrive on the Berg? Was it blown up by American soldiers after the war? Or looted? I have no idea. Perhaps it now adorns a garden in Little Rock, Arkansas, or some similarly exotic address. It was heavy for looting purposes, but it is astonishing what Americans managed to put in their knapsacks.

For several years we had seen neither of the Acton brothers. Harold was in China; William with his parents at Florence. In 1938, however, William came to London and painted enormous pictures of all his friends. He painted me in a Wagnerian setting of rocks and stormy sky. He also did a pencil drawing which Muv liked so much that she asked him to make drawings of her entire family. William drew all six sisters; Muv put them in narrow red brocade frames and hung them in her room at Inch Kenneth. Everybody said it looked like Bluebeard's chamber.

When he could spare a few days M. and I went to Paris, and occasionally we motored across France to Provence which we both loved, but Wootton was a place one was reluctant to leave. All seasons there were wonderfully beautiful and perhaps winter supreme. Early in December 1936 Jim Lees-Milne happened to be staying the night and we listened to the King's abdication broadcast with Nanny on the nursery wireless. We felt very sad. Everyone had known for a long time that he was in love with Mrs. Simpson but nobody imagined such a dénouement. If Decca or Debo had mentioned the affair at home Muv had dismissed the whole thing as absurd nonsense and told them they must not speak of the King in such a way. This was the origin of their saying: 'Of course, *Muv* doesn't believe in *love*.'

When I had to go to London I stayed with friends, usually with Gerald at Halkin Street, or with the Dunns near Regents Park. M. left Ebury Street for a house on the river in Grosvenor Road. It had formerly been a night club and it became a restaurant. The Thames washed the walls and at high tide the wide river looked brilliant, at low tide less so; one saw strange horrors imbedded in mud. The enormous room we painted pale blue, with white pillars which held up the roof. In this house my son Alexander was born in 1938; his birth obliged us to announce our marriage. From my bed I could see across the black November water to the wharves on the far bank; they were blanketed in snow. So hard was the winter that birds were famished, flocks of sea gulls swooping down if bread was thrown; there was a wild turmoil of wings and beaks just outside our windows. The nurse terrified me by putting the baby in his basket on the balcony, I thought the great gulls might attack him. She treated my fears as nothing but fevered fancy; she was one of those severe, unbending and stupid puritans who hardly exist now as children's nurses and whose passing no one need regret. The idea that a newborn baby needed 'fresh air' and was better off in the bitter snow-laden wind than he would have been indoors in his cot was a typical puritanical aberration of those days; virtue was equated with spartan treatment of the young.

Early in the new year—1939, fatal year for Europe—we took the baby to Wootton and he was handed over to Nanny Higgs. My happiness was complete.

15

Berlin

EVER SINCE 1932 M. had never ceased, in speech and in articles he wrote for his weekly paper, to demand re-armament for Britain. The disarmament conferences at Geneva and elsewhere had always had the same result; a measure of disarmament was decided upon and the only country which seriously complied with the decision was England. Hitler offered parity; that is, he said that if France and the other countries which together encircled Germany would disarm he would not re-arm. Nobody was prepared to disarm.

In my lifetime, despite League of Nations and United Nations, little has ever come to pass as a result of reasonable men sitting round a table, at least when the strong passion of nationalism is awakened. It is now the Middle East which threatens to become the theatre of war and draw the great powers into its conflict. Who can assert that the slightest attention would have been paid to the problem of the dispossessed Palestinians if they had confined themselves to asking the United Nations to consider the justice of their cause? They tried this for a number of years and the result was zero. Only when they began to behave outrageously did the world listen to them.

The Versailles, Trianon and St. Germain treaties were universally criticized and in many of their provisions almost universally condemned until Hitler came to power, when quite suddenly they became articles of faith to be defended if necessary by throwing our country and Empire into a fight to the death. The Munich settlement whereby the formerly Austrian inhabitants of Bohemia were permitted to join the Reich, thus righting a wrong done in 1919 by those who, hoping to encircle Germany, had listened exclusively to the powerful Czech lobby, was denounced as shameful surrender by warmongers in

England and France. According to them it was so shameful that only the blood of millions would suffice to wipe it out.

When Neville Chamberlain described Czechoslovakia as a faraway country of which we know little he spoke but the bare truth. English politicians are notoriously ignorant of the history and geography of Europe; already at the Congress of Vienna their ignorance surprised everyone. They, and the journalists, are very partial to 'small nations' and quickly build up a chivalrous attitude which can be quite dangerous. To listen to them anyone would have imagined that Czechoslovakia was an historic though small country and nation under threat from a great predatory neighbour, instead of an invention of the peace treaties incorporating not only Czechs and Slovaks, who detested one another, but also a large German-speaking minority, chunks of Hungary and an area where the majority of the inhabitants were Poles. The fact that this rickety country fell apart was no more surprising than that trouble came in Northern Ireland from similar causes.

Europe lurched from crisis to crisis and war seemed possible, yet our dilatory rulers failed to re-arm. It was left to M., and a little later to Winston Churchill, to call for re-armament. Churchill himself was partly responsible for the poor condition of our defences. The 1923 'ten-year rule' under which it was assumed that there would be no war for ten years, was altered by him when he was Chancellor of the Exchequer so that the ten years, instead of dwindling as had been intended in 1923, became a constant, each year the possibility of war officially receding one more year. 'This cunning political device naturally left the Service departments almost helpless in face of a hostile Treasury, which had only to murmur the master formula: "no major war for ten years" to provide an unanswerable counter to any request for an increase in the Service estimates.'* It is one of the ironies of 'history' that Churchill, author of the 'cunning political device' is supposed to have been the far-seeing patriot who could blame the unprepared state of our country upon others.† It must be remembered that at that time Britain was a

---

* Russell Grenfell, *Main Fleet to Singapore*.

† 'Churchill was War Minister and Air Minister combined from 1918 to 1921, the crucial period for the reconstruction of the forces. The Air Staff had evolved a plan under which the post-war RAF was to consist of 154 squadrons of which 40 were for home defence. Under Mr. Churchill's aegis this was whittled down to

'great power' with commitments the world over and that the very extent of these commitments made it uniquely vulnerable. The difference between M. and Churchill was that M. wanted Britain to be strong in order to keep the peace unless any part of our possessions was threatened, while Churchill genuinely hoped for war. As Lloyd George put it: 'Winston likes war. I don't.' The Conservative majority in Parliament included a handful of devoted adherents of Churchill such as Boothby and Bracken, and a number of M.P.s who thought along much the same lines as M. and British Union. In between was every gradation of opinion. Re-armament was expensive and unpopular and Mr. Baldwin admitted that although he knew it was of over-riding importance he did not make it an issue for fear of losing elections. Labour was enthusiastic for war everywhere, provided (as M. said) that the war was not in the interest of Britain, that we had no arms to fight with and that none of the Labour leaders was expected to join the army.

When from time to time I happened to be in Berlin I would telephone the Reichskanzlei to say I was at the Kaiserhof hotel. Occasionally, in the evening, Brückner would ring up. 'Gnädige Frau, wollen Sie zu uns hierüber kommen?' I crossed the Wilhelmplatz and was shown in. Hitler was generally sitting by an open fire; quite a rarity in centrally heated Berlin. Sometimes we saw a film, sometimes we just talked. During these evenings at the Reichskanzlei I got to know him fairly well. In conversation he was quick and clever, and of course very well-informed, and he had that surprising frankness often found in men at the top in contrast with mystery-making nonentities.

It goes without saying that I saw on these occasions a very different Hitler from the man possessed by daemonic energy who had changed the face of Germany in so short a time. Obviously you do not 'get things done' by sitting chatting before a log fire. His Umgebung or little court was always

---

a mere 24 squadrons, with only two for home defence, and the plan for state-aided airways covering the Empire was also discarded. When he moved to a fresh office in 1921 *The Times* had this comment on the fruits of his regime at the Air Ministry: "He leaves the body of British flying well-nigh at that last gasp when a military funeral would be all that would be left for it" ' Liddell Hart, *Encounter*, April 1966. M 's maiden speech in the House of Commons attacked Churchill for this.

concerned not to stir him up. 'Den Führer nicht aufzuregen' was the unwritten law of the Reichskanzlei; no doubt once stirred up he made their life unendurable for a while. He was in Berlin to work; he greatly preferred Munich and the Obersalzberg. Probably my visits, rare enough because I was almost always in England, filled a gap now and again because his cronies were in the south.

It is not easy, in assessing the fascination of his talk, to know how much was due to the interest inevitably aroused by the fact of power, and how much to the intrinsic attraction of his strange personality. Power is a magnet.

Unlike, for example, Stalin who inherited the communist machine of government from Lenin, Hitler had made his own way. He had no money, no influence, not even very good health when he left hospital in 1919, for he had been half blinded by gas on the western front. His triumph, when it came, was peculiarly his own. If Hitler had been anything like the man described in the biographies, how could one explain a whole chapter of history? Could he have attracted the thousands of devoted adherents and the millions of votes which in fact he did attract? The truth is that in private life he was exceptionally charming, clever and original, and that he inspired affection. He also inspired fear, perhaps, but he was essentially one of those rare beings who make people want to please them, want to work for them, eager to sacrifice. He identified himself with Germany and this identification was accepted by his countrymen. In his make-up there was both pride and a modesty, even vulnerability, which aroused chivalrous feelings, a very powerful motive force. His public appearances, his speeches, had this dual effect which must have come from something in his personality; they excited to action while at the same time arousing a deep desire to protect and cherish. He probably appealed in equal measure to women and to exactly the sort of men he needed.

He told me that when he was in prison in Munich after the putsch, on the eve of his trial early in 1924 he had a visit from Frau Bechstein, a rich supporter. She thrust a large bouquet into his arms saying: 'Wolf! Wir stehen immer zu dir!'* When he got back to his cell he found half a bottle of champagne hidden

* We will always stand by you.

among the flowers; he drank it next day before going into court. Later, at Festung Landsberg, gifts showered upon him. In those days his friends called him Wolf; hence Wolfsburg, where the Volkswagen which he designed is manufactured.

Hitler was the most unselfconscious politician I have ever come across. He never sought to impress, he never bothered to act a part. If he felt morose he was morose. If he was in high spirits he talked brilliantly and sometimes did wonderfully comic imitations. Once when I was there he was shown a photograph in a paper of Mussolini. The Duce was on horseback, he had just been presented with a sword, and he lifted it high above his head in a dramatic gesture. Hitler, after 'being' Mussolini, added, 'Of course, if somebody gave me a sword I shouldn't know what to do with it. I should just say, "Here, Schaub, take this sword." ' He admired Mussolini but he saw the comic side of him and he could never quite swallow the histrionics. When Mussolini was reported as having said: 'I offer the world peace resting on a hundred thousand bayonets,' or something of that sort, Hitler read it out and observed: 'Dass ist ja natürlich reines Quatsch.' (That is pure nonsense.)

A German in whom what one might call the chivalrous attitude towards Hitler was very marked was Goering. Hitler admired the brave war hero who had won the highest medal 'Pour le Mérite'; Goering loved Hitler. Unity and I had met him at a reception in the Reichskanzlei and he and Frau Goering invited me to luncheon. There again legend and fact conflicted; the food was quite good but frugal, the wine an unpretentious hock. One day when I visited Goering on a late, foggy afternoon in December he really was in fancy dress. He wore a pale yellow soft leather jerkin over a white silk blouse with voluminous sleeves caught in at the wrist; on his fingers were several rings set with emeralds and sapphires. I believe the jerkin had something to do with his being Reichsforstmeister;* in any case he was an amazing apparition. That evening I could not resist telling a German acquaintance about his astonishing get-up; the only reaction was: 'Yes, he dresses like that because he gets so hot.'

Apart from that one occasion I always saw him in ordinary air force uniform. Although he was much less with Hitler than

* Head forester of the realm.

Dr. Goebbels there was a strong mutual affection between Goering and Hitler. Unity told me that one April Hitler took her to see his birthday presents, arranged in a vast room in the Reichskanzlei. There were hundreds of pairs of hand-knitted socks and jerseys from admirers as well as many rich gifts from all parts of the world. There was an elaborate scale model of the Munich Haus der Kunst and Hitler drew Unity's attention to it: 'Vom General Feld Marschall!' he half whispered, exactly as if it were a marvel that such as he should have been given a birthday present by a famous Field Marshal.

The economic miracle in Germany during the six years of National Socialism up to the outbreak of war is never mentioned now. The myth is that the unemployed were immediately absorbed into the armament factories; otherwise Germany was inhabited by brown-shirted thugs who ran up and down the streets looking for a Jew to bully. Astonishing progress was made and a new prosperity was everywhere apparent. Dr. Schacht managed the financial side of the economy, Hitler himself gave the directives on the political and social fronts. People worked hard and were well rewarded, they supported the régime, and the attacks upon it by emigrants made them xenophobic.

Once when Unity and I were in Berlin a huge crowd assembled on the Wilhelmplatz for some reason I have forgotten. We were at the Kaiserhof, and we went out to see what was happening. Unity always wore a swastika badge, it looked rather like a party badge but without the letters NSDAP on the red circle; she had bought it some years before, subsequently the sale of such badges had been forbidden. Near us on the Wilhelmplatz there were some very tiresome, well-scrubbed and fanatical women. They turned furiously on Unity, pointing to her badge: 'Dazu haben Sie kein Recht! Dass ist ja *betrug*!'* they said, and warming to their work they added, including me in their strictures: 'Schämen Sie sicht nicht, so geschminkt vor dem Hause des Führers zu stehen!'† They kept up a sort of undertone of barracking for quite a while, Unity paying not the slightest attention.

---

* 'You have no right to that! It's cheating!'

† 'Aren't you ashamed, to stand in front of the Führer's house with a painted face!'

Father

Mother

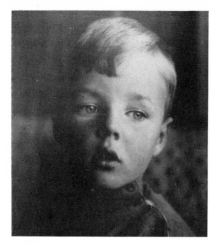

Tom, aged 3

Diana, aged 2

Family group at Asthall, 1922

M. holding the top of a park railing, one of the weapons confiscated from his opponents at the Olympia Meeting, 1934 (Radio Times Hulton Picture Library)

Diana 1934

Lord Berners at Faringdon

Evelyn Waugh (Radio Times Hulton Picture Library)

Barbara Hutchinson, Augustus John and Diana, 1932
(By kind permission of Admiral Sir Caspar John, G.C.B.)

With Jonathan and
Desmond 1937

With Alexander
and Max 1947

Tom and Derek
Jackson, 1944

M. in 1959

Mother at Inch Kenneth, 1960

Mrs. Hammersley, 1960

Nancy

Pam

Unity

Debo

The Gate of
Holloway Prison
(Camera Press)

A "wing" at Brixton Prison (Camera Press)

The drawing room, Temple de la Gloire
(Photograph: Connaissance des Arts)

Temple de la Gloire (Nicolas Uriburu)

Next day we were invited to luncheon at the Reichskanzlei. We were four, Hitler, Goebbels, Unity and I. We told about the cross women on the Wilhelmplatz. 'Why did you stay out there? You should have come in here to us,' said Hitler. Unity and I marvelled at his ignorance of what went on below stairs in his own palace. The idea that on a day when the Wilhelmplatz was packed with crowds clamouring for him to show himself on the balcony one could have walked past the police and the guards and uninvited into the Reichskanzlei was wildly unimaginable.

We had a cheerful luncheon with many jokes from the Doktor. A few weeks after this incident Unity saw Hitler at the Osteria Bavaria and he took a little parcel out of his pocket. 'Next time anyone complains about your badge just take it off and let them see the back,' he said.

His gift was a swastika badge, identical with the party badge except that it had no lettering, and on the reverse side his signature was engraved. She thanked him, but when we talked it over we agreed that to show the signature to the cross women would have been almost to invite a lynching. In their eyes it would have been an additional outrage, for they would never have believed that Hitler himself had had it done. As to the lipstick, Hitler's supposed antipathy to make-up seems to have been a myth.

Was Unity 'in love' with Hitler? This is a question frequently asked. In my opinion, and nobody knew her better than I did, she was not. Her admiration and even affection for him were boundless, but she was not 'in love'. On his side, he was certainly very fond of her and she amused him greatly; most of the women he met were desperately shy and over-awed in his company. There were exceptions like Frau Wagner and Magda Goebbels, but anyone meeting him for the first time after he became Führer of Germany hardly spoke in his presence except to say 'Ja, mein Führer' or 'Eben, mein Führer' or 'Selbstverständlich, mein Führer', as the case might be. Unity was never awed in her entire life. She said what came into her head.

Once there was some talk about clerics and she asked him: 'Have you been excommunicated?' The Umgebung looked startled, but Hitler laughed.

6

'Excommunicated? Never! Why, if I were to go into the Frauenkirche this minute the whole place would soon be black with priests come to greet me.'

'Don't go then,' said Unity.

Another time he told us: 'Last week I was driving in Munich and I saw a car coming the wrong way down a one-way street. I told Kempka to slow down and I said, why, it's a woman driver! And then I saw, of course, it was *die Unity*!'

She knew about Eva Braun. At a Parteitag we were given seats next to Fräulein Braun, and thought her pretty and charming. There again, if Unity had been in love she would have been jealous of Eva Braun, and this she quite obviously was not. She herself had a boy friend in Munich called Erich; his surname, if I ever heard it, I have forgotten. She also had innumerable friends, and was constantly on the move.

There was a book about Hitler after the war called something like *I was Hitler's maid*; it was made fun of by Beachcomber in the *Daily Express* who invented another book *I was Himmler's Aunt*. Hitler's 'maid' described thrilling orgies with Hitler flagellating his housemaids and parlourmaids on the Berg. The 'maid' rather gave herself away by saying that when Unity stayed on the Obersalzberg she used to unpack her lovely silk underclothes. In fact, Unity went up there a few times for luncheon or tea, and once took my parents, but she was not invited to stay. The lovely underclothes were just one more figment of the 'maid's' imagination.

In 1938, as I was pregnant, I travelled less than usual and spent most of my time at Wootton. Unity rushed to Austria to witness the arrival of Hitler in Vienna. English newspapers pretended to think the Anschluss was a 'rape'. More seriously they announced that German tanks and armoured cars had broken down *en route* and that half the tanks were made of cardboard. Such reports were probably not believed by the well-informed, but they may have been partly responsible eighteen months later for embarrassing songs about hanging washing on the Siegfried Line, during the phoney war.

That summer, the summer of the Munich crisis, Unity got pneumonia at Bayreuth; she was very ill and Muv travelled from England to be with her. Hitler heard of her illness and he sent his own doctor, the swarthy Dr. Morell, to see her at the clinic. Later on he asked: 'What did you think when you saw Dr. Morell at your bedside?'

'I thought it was the Aga Khan.'

'Sie denkt weltweit,' ('She thinks in world-wide terms,') said Hitler, laughing.

While she was in the Bayreuth clinic, at a time when war seemed a possibility, Unity made up her mind that if it came she herself would disappear from the scene. Her love of Germany was deep, but it was equalled by her love of England. Rather than see these two countries tear each other to pieces she preferred to die.

Whether or not Unity was 'in love' is a purely private matter which, should it interest them, people may speculate about. There is another question of more general interest. Did Unity 'influence' Hitler? Did he get from her a one-sided or untrue picture of her native land? Did she, for example, give him to understand that the English would in no circumstances fight; did she prevent him from seeing the 'red light' which would have stopped him in his tracks? Is she therefore partly responsible for the 1939 war? To ask these questions is to demonstrate their absurdity. Any well-informed person would answer no, in every instance. Imagine the situation reversed. Imagine Chamberlain, or Churchill, as prime minister making friends with a German girl. He would question her about Germany, and about any German politicians she happened to know. If she was intelligent he would be interested to hear what she had to say. But he would have hundreds of other sources of information, beginning with his ambassador and a large staff at the embassy and ranging from commercial information to translations of newspapers and magazines and the speeches of politicians. It is inconceivable that he would ignore all this and believe only this German girl I have imagined.

If Unity had come from what Chamberlain once called a faraway country of which we know little, it is just possible that she might have influenced Hitler's attitude to the place. But England, Great Britain, the British Empire, a neighbouring great power with which Germany had innumerable links, where it kept a large embassy and of which it had vast experience in both war and peace, in trade, at the League of Nations, at international conferences and so forth, to imagine the German dictator setting aside the information gathered by these various agencies and deciding to rely instead upon what Unity told him at luncheon is inconceivable. To believe such a thing of the silliest hereditary prince, or king of the cannibal islands, would be to stretch credulity. In the case of an astute self-made politician and leader of a great European power it is quite simply impossible.

Unity adopted the whole creed of the National Socialists, including their anti-Semitism, with uncritical enthusiasm. She had many gifts and was a perfect companion, with dozens of devoted friends. She was clever, funny, quick-witted, intelligent and affectionate. She had the seeing eye, her *collages* were imaginative and skilfully executed.

As to courage, she was one of the bravest people I have ever known, but she was not rash. She was to have motored Mrs. Hammersley up to stay with me at Wootton, but she put off the journey because of snow, ice and fog. Mrs. Hammersley, who had no idea how disagreeable, if not dangerous, the drive would have been, was quite cross. She telephoned me saying: 'But surely, with *Unity*, one could go to *Spitzbergen?*' a remark which tells much about both of them.

When I say she adopted anti-semitism, it was in the sense that 'the enemy of my friend is my enemy'. With her, it was theory; in practice she often liked Jews, and did a whole Munich *Fasching* (carnival) with Brian Howard.

16

War

I was not particularly in favour of what came to be called appeasement as practised by the unfortunate Neville Chamberlain. Naturally everyone with a grain of sense prefers peace to war, but flying to and from Germany and waving little bits of paper 'signed by Herr Hitler' was no way to achieve lasting peace. The Munich settlement was not a settlement, it left almost as many loose ends and injustices as there had been before.

In order to strengthen his hand at home, Chamberlain should have dissolved parliament and had an election on the issue of peace or war. In this way he could have trounced the Churchills and Edens. A conference of all the countries involved should have followed, and plebiscites in disputed territories. Ever since the Saar had voted by over ninety per cent to become part of the Reich, plebiscites, formerly so well regarded, had been unpopular with politicians in the democracies. Yet they were probably the only way whereby war could have been avoided, and where ethnic groups were mixed the losing group should have been offered rich inducements to move into its own mother country. Those who refused would do so with their eyes open.

The same should have been done for the Jews, if they had so desired, not only in Germany but throughout central Europe. The millions spent in re-settling them would have saved their lives and endless suffering. In his book *Peace Making at Paris* published in 1919 Sisley Huddleston, a well-known journalist on the *Westminster Gazette*, writes: 'Throughout the proceedings one had perpetually news of pogroms in Rumania or in the Ukraine or in Czecho Slovakia. The Jewish problem was not the least difficult.' It is interesting to note that he does not mention Germany as one of the countries where there were perpetually pogroms. Thousands of Jews poured into Germany at that time from the east, and made an acute Jewish problem there. Nothing much was done, either by the League of Nations or by world Jewry, and they were left to their fate.

'Munich' was a watershed. Although at first many people and most conservatives were delighted with Chamberlain (a newsreel film of the cabinet greeting him at the airport upon his return from Germany showed his colleagues shouting with joy, one could even see Lord Halifax's tonsils) they began to have second thoughts, and no wonder. Given the premise that Britain had a duty and a right to interfere in central Europe, what had happened was unsatisfactory. We, of course, did not accept the premise; our slogan at that time was *Mind Britain's Business*, the very last thing politicians of either party intended to do. The Munich 'settlement' had been quick and easy, and hard conundrums involving nations, sovereignties, transfers of population cannot be solved in this slap-dash style.

In England re-armament went apace at last; plans were made for the evacuation of women and children from the big cities and it became more and more obvious that the politicians were preparing for war. When, predictably in the circumstances, Czechoslovakia fell apart Hitler was said to have 'broken his word'. Shortly afterwards a guarantee was given to Poland, another far-away country of which they knew little, though there was one thing about it they might have remembered. In 1919 Lloyd George had pointed on the map to the Polish corridor, saying: 'Here is where the next war will start.' At Versailles he had been strongly opposed to the arbitrary arrangement which divided Germany and put millions of Germans within Polish frontiers. As there was nothing Britain could do directly to help Poland, the guarantee was practically a declaration of England's determination to fight for the status quo. It encouraged the wilder spirits in Poland to be intransigent and to resist even moderate adjustments; it encouraged the wilder spirits in Germany in their belief that since Britain was determined to fight sooner or later it might as well be sooner, and it delighted the war party in Britain itself. So much has been written about this period of our history that there is little left to say. Apparently not one of Britain's 'statesmen' sat down to think what the result of the war with Germany would be for us. Win or lose it was bound to diminish not only England and France and Germany, but Europe itself. As to the British Empire, it was all very well to sing 'Wider still and wider shall thy bounds be set; God who made thee mighty make thee mightier yet'. In sober fact it was wide but not mighty. It was vulnerable, and the way to preserve it was not by weakening the mother country. The British Empire was a great potential, according to M.'s ideas an almost totally neglected potential; the war dealt it a blow so that it fell to pieces. M.'s speeches for peace in the summer of 1939 emphasized that whoever won the war, Britain was bound to lose it.

As to 'evil things' in Germany which we were fighting against, the very same evil things were the rule in Soviet Russia in infinitely greater degree. If one is to fight a war against evil things wherever they are to be found in the world there would never be peace. There were evil things in England too, including the most disgusting slums in all Europe and widespread undernourishment.

The idea that one can 'learn from history' does not obtain with regard to what happened in 1939. Fatally weakened by the war, there can no longer be any question of interfering or intervening in central Europe. When Russian tanks drove into Budapest in 1956, and when Russian tanks occupied Prague in 1968, our rulers lifted their hands in shocked surprise but nothing was done because there was nothing that could be done. Russia could not stand idly by while Czechoslovakia joined the West; Bohemia is still, as it always has been, the key to power in central Europe.

In July 1939 M. had an immense meeting and demonstration for peace in the Exhibition Hall at Earl's Court. It was the culmination of several months' campaign all over the country. Tom, hoping for peace but seeing that war was probable, had joined a territorial regiment, the Queen's Westminsters. He gave the fascist salute as M. marched up the hall, and this was reported in one of the newspapers with a comment implying that an officer in the army could not at the same time be a follower of Sir Oswald Mosley. Tom's Colonel strongly upheld him and said he was not going to be deprived of one of his best officers; no more was heard of this nonsense.

Soon afterwards Unity and I went once again to Bayreuth as Hitler's guests. As before, we sat with him in the restaurant during the long dinner intervals. On the last day he invited us for luncheon in the Wahnfried annexe where he always lived during the Festspiele. Afterwards he spoke to us alone. He said that as far as he could see, England was determined upon war, and that war was therefore inevitable. I said I thought M. would continue his campaign for peace for as long as such a campaign was legal. Hitler said: 'If he does, he may be assassinated like Jaurès in 1914.'

When we left him, Unity said once again that she would not live to see the impending tragedy. That evening we heard *Götterdämmerung*. Never had the glorious music seemed to me so doom-laden. I had a strong feeling, almost a conviction, that I should never see Hitler again, that a whole world was crumbling, that the future held only tragedy and war. I had no illusions that there might be anything in the nature of the Peace of Amiens, the truce during the Napoleonic wars during which the Whigs went over to Paris to dine with the Emperor. This time all would be bitterness and cruelty. I knew well what Unity, sitting beside me, was thinking. I left her next day, death in my heart.

After flying to London I got the last train to Derby where M. met me at about 1 a.m. As we drove through the summer night to Wootton I told him Hitler's words, and what Unity had said. During the short time that remained we moved between Wootton and London. I was pregnant again. In case a miracle happened, I made plans to go to Unity in Munich, but it was not to be. The mad drive to war accelerated, the men on both sides behaving in such a way as to make it inevitable. Towards the end of August it became obviously impossible for me to make any more journeys because war was imminent.

M.'s sister-in-law Irene Ravensdale came to Wootton with Micky and his nurse. She and the two nannies made enormous black curtains to cover the huge windows. M. and I went back to London; we listened on the wireless to Chamberlain announcing that England and Germany were at war. It was a hot and cloudless September morning; a minute or two later the sirens blew an air raid warning. Everyone knew what the noise meant, it had frequently been tried out and practised. We went on to our river balcony but nothing appeared in the serene blue sky.

For a few days I could think only of Unity, but when no news came I began to hope. News of a death travels fast, and there were neutral journalists in Germany, Americans and Italians. It seemed just possible that she had done nothing, since hitherto the only fighting was taking place in Poland; England was not involved.

Everyone knows that war is foul and terrible and that it brings frightful sufferings and injustices and horrors with it. Yet there is undeniably something about a great war which grips the heart. There is a heightened awareness of the beauty of the peaceful countryside, of love of family and of love for one's country because of the threat that hangs over them all. The threat that hung over Unity was immediate, but there was nothing to be done. She and I had talked it over and over; I dreaded her iron resolve.

Céline, in his *Voyage au bout de la nuit*, describes how a man is caught by the thrill of a military band marching past the café where he is sitting with his drink. He rushes to join the colours and spends the rest of the war regretting his precipitate gesture. On various levels all manner of men are caught by the attraction of war and a great many of them actually enjoy it. It is not hard to imagine that a clerk with a really dull job, a nagging wife and a fortnight's holiday a year might prefer the comradeship of an officers' mess, leaving behind the petty worries of his humdrum life and buoyed up by the exhilarating feeling that he is helping his country in its hour of need. Yet in 1939 there was certainly no war fever and not much enthusiasm for the war.

All that autumn M. made speeches demanding 'peace with the British Empire intact'. He was astonished by the reception he got from the crowds who went to hear him. They listened in silence to what he had to say, and then they applauded. There is a film of one of these meetings, typical of many at that time. The street is packed with people, and at the end of his speech M. asks them to lift up their arms 'for peace'. A forest of arms goes up. All this was very different from what we had expected, and very different for example from the experience of Ramsay MacDonald when he spoke for peace during the First World War. MacDonald's meetings had been violently attacked, as had Lloyd George's during the Boer War. During our campaign the communists, for obvious reasons, kept quiet, but the interesting thing to note is that the type of patriot who had attacked Ramsay MacDonald, and before him Lloyd George, was not much in favour of the Second World War. Many such men probably saw that England had nothing to gain and everything to lose by fighting Germany on behalf of Poland, or for any other reason except in order to defend our country or our Empire, and hence their enthusiasm for the war was non-existent and they were prepared to listen to M.

One Sunday afternoon M. hired the Stoll Theatre in Kingsway, for a meeting. Alone on the stage as always, he held an audience of three thousand. It was far and away the most moving speech I ever heard him make. The applause went on for several minutes. As I went out through the foyer someone touched me on the arm; it was an American called Odom who lived in England; he had a lovely Nash house full of treasures overlooking Regents Park where we had visited him once or twice. He now pressed £5 upon me 'for the cause'. He was the very last person I should have expected to see at one of M.'s meetings, but this was typical of the attitude of quantities of men and women who came to us at this time.

Meanwhile Poland had been divided, as so often before in its history, between Germany and Russia. Hitler made a speech offering peace in the West, but anything so rational was out of the question for the politicians who had taken us into the war, and they would certainly have looked foolish if after so much beating of the breast they had taken us out again before firing a shot. The fatal drift to disaster went on, though at a snail's pace. Keeping people's spirits up the newspapers pretended to believe that we were winning the war by doing nothing at all. According to them Germany would soon abandon the unequal struggle because it had no rubber or oil, and in any case the German generals were just about to murder Hitler in order to make peace. I cannot remember whether the cardboard tanks were mentioned again; the Polish campaign may have finished them off, but as there was no oil the German armour was immobilized.

On the 2nd of October my parents got a letter from Janos's brother, Teddy von Almasy, saying that Unity was ill in hospital. Farve sent him a telegram to Budapest and he replied: 'Continual improvement. No fever.' Another cable came on the

17th: 'Further progress. Your letters forwarded.' (They had written through Janos in Hungary.) No mention was made of what her illness was; I guessed the truth. The relief and joy of knowing that she was alive were great, but the second cable with its reference to 'improvement' after six weeks in hospital was not reassuring, to me at least, and it was dreadful not to be able to rush to her side. Weeks of silence followed. Muv was awakened once in the middle of the night by a *Sunday Pictorial* reporter telling her that Unity had died in hospital. She did not tell me at the time; she said afterwards that she never believed it for a moment: 'It was just the *Sunday Pictorial*,' scornfully. Early in November a letter came from the American Embassy through the Foreign Office to say she was progressing well, but still no details.

General Fuller often came to see us at Grosvenor Road that autumn. He was stopped near our house by an A.R.P. warden who asked: 'Where is your gas mask?'

'I've left it at home with my bow and arrows,' said the General. He knew Germany well; his books on tank warfare, like Liddell Hart's, had been translated and they were widely read by the German High Command. He was sarcastic about the real or assumed optimism of Fleet Street, and he said our own generals were preparing to fight the 1914 war over again.

General Fuller was easily moved to sarcasm. He had joined the B.U. after the row about the Olympia meeting, a typical gesture combining courage and the fun of giving a backhander to the hysterical and silly Left in English politics. He had the charm of brilliant intelligence as well as imagination. Hitler, who saw him several times and admired his beautifully precise and logical mind as much as I did, said to me about him once that he felt sure he would be an 'unbequemer' (an awkward colleague) in any organization, an observation which seemed to me to sum him up exactly, though to M. he was a loyal and valued collaborator.

We decided that we must leave Wootton. It was too big and too far from any railway station. The house at Denham was near London, in metroland, and the whole family would live there. As this arrangement was by way of being semi-permanent I put my own furniture in one of the rooms and had curtains made out of the grey silk of the vast Wootton curtains, all of which as it turned out was a complete waste. Grosvenor Road was also unpractical for a wartime house; it was big, and difficult to heat. We moved across the street to Dolphin Square.

We spent a last Christmas holiday at Wootton; it was a hard winter and the boys skated on the lakes. On Christmas Eve my parents had a telephone call from Berne; first Janos spoke, and then Unity herself. As soon as was possible Muv and Debo set out for Switzerland to bring her home. I longed to go with them, but as M.'s wife I should have been a hindrance, apart from the fact that I was pregnant. The sorrow of packing up Wootton was completely overshadowed by anxiety about Unity.

We gradually pieced together the history of the last four months. She had shot herself on the 3rd of September at the moment when England declared war on Germany, in the Englischer Garten at Munich, a park near the River Isar. A day or two before she had been to see Gauleiter Wagner about a licence for her little pistol. She seemed distraught, and he felt so worried about her that he told two men to keep a discreet eye upon her. The result was that no sooner was a shot heard than Wagner's men, who were at a little distance, ran to Unity and picked her up. They thought she was dead, but they took her to a clinic where she lay unconscious. Hitler was told, and during the campaign in Poland he telephoned the clinic several times for news. When, after weeks, she regained consciousness he went to see her, it must have been on the 8th of November when he was in Munich for the usual meeting at the Bürger-bräukeller commemorating the 1923 putsch. He asked Unity what she wished to do: stay in Germany or go back to England? She chose England. When she was considered well enough to travel Hitler sent her in an ambulance train to Switzerland, accompanied by a doctor and a nurse. The faithful Janos tra-velled with Unity in the ambulance train, so that she should not be alone in a strange land, and they arrived on Christmas Eve and telephoned my parents.

Farve went to see Oliver Stanley, the Minister for War. He told him that, gravely ill as she was, he hoped there was to be no question of arresting her for 'intelligence with the enemy' or on some similar charge. Oliver Stanley gave him his word that

she could come home without any danger of that sort. Muv and
Debo set forth. All this happened during the 'phoney war'; a
few months later it would not have been possible.

Perhaps Muv realized how desperately sad the end of their
journey was going to be, but Debo did not. When they arrived
at Berne, after sitting up all night in an unheated train, Janos
was on the platform with a man from the Swiss Foreign Office.
They went straight to the clinic. Muv could hardly bring herself
to open the door of Unity's room, dreading the unknown. She
wrote: 'There she was, half sitting up, her hair all spread out,
her face all eyes. Very thin she was, but looking beautiful. What
a wonderful meeting it was. We were all three so happy.'

Janos left them and went back to Munich on his way to
Bernstein. He was a wonderful friend. But for him and his
brother months would have gone by after Unity shot herself,
with no news. His kindness in going with her to Switzerland,
and staying until Muv and Debo arrived, showed he truly loved
her. It must have been the gloomiest week of his life, for one
could not look at her without pain, remembering what she had
been only four months before.

Debo's description is not the same as Muv's; it is an illustration of how differently two people can report the same
scene. She says: 'I remember the grey cold in the town, and
being taken to the clinic, and the fearful shock of seeing her
propped up in bed, two enormous dark blue eyes in her face
which had shrunk and become almost unrecognizable because
it was totally different from *her*, short matted hair and yellow
teeth neither of which had been touched since the 3rd of September when the bullet had gone through her brain. She couldn't
bear her head to be touched and it was only very gradually that
this became a little better. Her hair never got right again and
had a sort of brittle, hard look. Her sunken cheeks made the
teeth seem bigger and more horrible and yellow and her skin
was dry and yellow too. She had an odd vacant smile and was
terribly thin and seemed so small. She was pleased to see us,
but the shock of finding a completely *different* person was great
—it was like getting to know a sort of child one had known
ages ago.

'I think we stayed two or three days till an ambulance
carriage was attached to a train. The journey to the French

coast was a nightmare because every time the train lurched it was agony for her, and it seemed almost to do it on purpose and heaved and jigged about even more than usual. I suppose it was specially long. It was certainly specially dark and cold and seemed endless. She was taken on a stretcher to the boat and off again at Folkestone where Farve met us with an ambulance. We went to an hotel, the Press were everywhere. Then back to the ambulance for the journey to High Wycombe. Having pretty well avoided talking to the Press we wondered if they had somehow arranged that the ambulance should break down after a few miles, as that is what happened, and all the journalists who were following crowded round to get pictures as she was transferred after a long wait to another ambulance. When we arrived at Wycombe we had police protection. I think that went on for some months.

'I suppose Muv and Farve realized then that she would never get better and become her old self. Her whole nature changed and she even looked completely different and yet there was a shadow of her old self, a most strange mixture of what she had been and a new person. She was never beautiful again. When she started to walk she was clumsy.'

So Muv and Debo brought Unity across France by train as far as Calais, they had missed the boat and had to wait two days for another. At Folkestone they had to go to an hotel because Unity was exhausted. In both ports they were besieged by journalists, falling over each other to cash in on tragedy as is their custom. They bid each other up, offering Muv ever larger sums to be allowed to interview Unity just for one minute. Naturally she refused. Tripping over pressmen the whole way, they finally got the exhausted and half-paralysed Unity to Old Mill Cottage at High Wycombe. There was nowhere else to go. Swinbrook had been sold and Farve had bought an island in the Inner Hebrides, Inch Kenneth. There was quite a big house on the island, but the journey there would have been utterly impossible, apart from the fact that it was in a Defence Area. The High Wycombe cottage was vulnerable to a Press siege; soon Muv and Unity moved to the Mill Cottage at Swinbrook where they stayed until the end of the war. Farve went to Inch Kenneth; there was no room for him in the tiny cottage.

Lord Nuffield, an old friend of my father's, suggested that

Unity should go to the Nuffield Hospital in Oxford where the great brain surgeon, Professor Sir Hugh Cairns, worked. After keeping her under observation for some weeks, Cairns said he agreed with the German doctors, who had advised against an operation to remove the bullet. He told Muv that if, with all his skill, he had put an instrument through a head in the same way as the violent bullet had gone, the patient would have died.

Unity looked deathly ill. She was emaciated and half-paralysed, she had to be fed as she could not lift a spoon. It was heart-rending to see the terrible change in her. She had been cared for in Germany by devoted nuns; they had brought her painfully back to life when all she desired was death. They had also, as good Christians, tried to persuade her that she had committed a grave sin by taking her own life. She questioned me over and over again: did I think it very wicked to die by one's own hand? She probably knew my answer. To that small extent man must be the master of his fate. He did not ask to be born; if his life becomes too tragic or unbearable he has the right to die. I told her this was my opinion, but that as she had been saved all her energy must now be summoned up and concentrated on recovering her health.

All this time there was still no fighting. After the partition of Poland there were months of rather ominous silence. The Allies were dug in along the Maginot Line and beyond. During the long cold winter only small inconveniences like the blackout, or bossy men and women asking one another about gas masks, showed that we were at war. The evacuated mothers and babies drifted back to the towns. We had a few of them at Wootton but by Christmas they were already gone.

The day I left Wootton was one of those frosty sunny mornings when everything sparkles and glitters. Though M. said we would return there after the war I knew in my heart that a happy time in my life had come to an end. The remaining months of my pregnancy we spent in London, and on the 13th of April my fourth son, Max, was born.

The war was just about to begin in earnest. The Allies, in order to cut supplies of iron ore to Germany, mined neutral waters south of Sweden. The riposte was swift. The Germans occupied Norway and drove out our small expeditionary force. Then quiet descended upon Europe once again.

The baby and I went to Denham at the end of the month, with a nurse as kind and gentle as my nurse of the year before had been abrasive. If the first weeks of life are important, as the psychologists believe, it is interesting for me to remember the different treatment these two brothers received, the one born in bitter November, the other in an unusually balmy spring, with nurses to match the weather. With a new baby and the country in its early May heavenliness an unreasoned optimism kept welling up. It was still just possible to hope that there would be no fighting war; perhaps Unity would completely recover: any miracle seemed as if it might happen, so perfectly happy were my own private circumstances, so perfectly beautiful the world. These irrational illusions were remote from reality and I suppose I hardly believed in them. It was just that the dreary winter and my dreary pregnancy were over and done with.

A few days later German armies invaded the Low Countries and France. M., when this seemed imminent, had issued a statement:

'According to the Press, stories concerning the invasion of Britain are being circulated . . . In such an event every member of British Union would be at the disposal of the nation. Every one of us would resist the foreign invader with all that is in us. However rotten the existing government, and however much we detested its policies, we would throw ourselves into the effort of a united nation until the foreigner was driven from our soil. In such a situation no doubt exists concerning the attitude of British Union.'

This was printed in *Action* (9 May 1940). The following day Churchill took over from Chamberlain; the phoney war was at an end.

17

Prison

ON THE 23RD of May 1940 M. and I spent the morning at Denham and motored to London after luncheon. As we turned into the road leading to the entrance of our Dolphin Square block of flats I immediately saw that four or five men were standing about on the pavement near the doorway. They were not talking, as a group of friends might, but were aimlessly staring into space.

'Look. Coppers,' I said to M.

We got out of the car and one of them stepped forward and said he had a warrant for M.'s arrest. We went up in the lift with the policemen; on the landing of the seventh floor there were a couple more. All of them were in plain clothes. We went into M.'s flat and he asked to see the warrant. They said he was to go to Brixton prison and that I could visit him the following day. M. and I said goodbye. We went down in the lift and they drove him away. A cold fury possessed me, I can feel it now as I write.

Several hours before everyone, men and women, who worked at the B.U. headquarters had been arrested, as I soon discovered. As I drove back to Denham alone there were posters on the streets: 'M.P. arrested,' and in the evening paper a description of what had happened that morning. They must have waited for M., guessing that he would come up to London, which he did every day. It was pure chance that I happened to be with him. The M.P. was Captain Archibald Maule Ramsay, leader of a group called the Right Club which, as its name implies, was to the right of the Conservative Party.

A couple of hours later my step-daughter Viv and I were having dinner when from the dining-room window we saw the big wooden gate the other end of the garden pushed open and policemen poured across the lawn. We let them in; they said they had come to search the house.

'In that case you'll have to stay at least a week,' I said. There were not only many rooms and attics in the rambling old house but also tithe barns used as store rooms stuffed with miscellaneous objects. I went into the library; two policemen were taking the books out of the shelves. At about five past nine the telephone rang. It was Muv, who had heard on the nine o'clock news of M.'s arrest.

'What is the charge?' she asked.

'Oh, no charge,' I replied.

'*Disgraceful*,' said Muv, and I repeated, for the benefit of the policemen, 'Yes, it is disgraceful.'

In fact, although Habeas Corpus had been suspended, it had required an Order in Council passed late the previous evening and framed in suitably vague terms to give a semblance of legality to these arbitrary arrests.

I then telephoned to Mr. Butterwick, Nicky's housemaster at Eton. He told me not to worry. Nicky was seventeen and had his friends and would not be much affected. Mr. Butterwick added: 'I should be more worried myself about your boy at his private school.'

The search was far from thorough; one got the impression that it was only a matter of form and that the men had no idea what they were supposed to be looking for. They searched my room in a desultory way; Max was there, asleep in his cot. He was almost five weeks old. They soon pushed off and left us to our thoughts. Next morning Vivien, Micky and the nurse left Denham; they were never to return. Nanny and I remained with the two babies. I drove up to London and went to Brixton prison. M. appeared, unshaven; I gave him a parcel of washing things and change of linen. M. told me to try and get hold of a solicitor as soon as possible. Seeing him thus filled me with rage but outwardly I was calm, and I am thankful to say that in the years I am about to describe I, who cry easily, never shed a tear when anyone could see it. My feelings, best described as contemptuous anger, precluded tears.

Finding a solicitor to act for us was easier said than done. The firm which had dealt with B.U. affairs refused at once. M.'s family lawyer, a man called Sweet, turned out to be most unlike his name. He was almost rude. There had been no thought of asking him to do anything himself, I saw him about household bills, but I had imagined he would have advised me what to do next. There was an indescribable atmosphere of panic, barely suppressed, and wherever I went I was met with glances not so much hostile as terrified. My own lawyer, a kind but elderly man, explained that he could not leave his office and go and wait about at Brixton prison; all his clerks had been called up and there was nobody to answer the telephone but him. He gave me precious advice: to go to Oswald Hickson, an old radical who, he said, would care not in the very least what 'people might think'. Indifference to public opinion is an essentially aristocratic virtue; it is rarer than one might imagine, as I discovered in those difficult days. I was very worried. If lawyers who knew M. and who therefore must have realized that his imprisonment was a great wrong were unwilling to act for him, how should I ever find a stranger who would do so? Mr. Hickson questioned me closely. He agreed to go to Brixton next day; he behaved perfectly. He acted for us for years, until his place was taken by our wise friend and counsellor Mr. Lane.

I was allowed to visit M. once a week. He always had a list of things he wanted: books, and his oldest and most degraded country clothes. He insisted that he was perfectly all right, and although I knew this was to comfort me I never guessed that he and his companions were lodged in verminous cells. Lice and bugs infested the wood frames of the beds.

Three times after M. was arrested I had visitors at Denham. Muv and Unity came over from Swinbrook. Unity was recovering. She could now walk, rather slowly. She was touching, pathetic, and not in the least like her old self. Another day Gerald struggled over by bus. He was living in Oxford at the time, and he said that various dons of his acquaintance had earnestly tried to dissuade him; they told him that to spend a day with me was to put himself in jeopardy. That was the popular view. I was untouchable. I could see that Gerald felt extremely bold to have disregarded the dons' advice, and I was grateful for his courage and his friendship.

Gerald told me that day of his two fears. The lesser of these was that he would be cut off from all his friends. He imagined no telephone, no post, no petrol. In the event this never happened, post and telephone were not even rationed. His other dread was that he would be hurt but not killed; he was thinking of air raids. He did not fear death, but he greatly dreaded the idea that he might agonize untended, and he wished for a pill which would kill instantly. There had been so much talk in the newspapers about total war that in his imagination Gerald lived through a total breakdown which in fact never happened in England, though elsewhere it did. As at that time nobody could know what war would bring and the news from across the Channel got worse every day, it was impossible to dismiss his gloomy thoughts as unrealistic. All the same we had a lovely day; I walked with him to his bus and he promised to come again. My other visitors were Pam and Derek. Derek is one of those people referred to above with a complete disdain for public opinion, or what is called public opinion: the views put forward by politicians, Press and BBC.

When I went to London for prison visits I also saw one or two faithful friends. On my thirtieth birthday I lunched with the Fullers. The General said he imagined 'at this moment the French are asking for an armistice'. It seemed unbelievable. The most powerful army in Europe, beaten in a matter of weeks. We discussed his own position as an outspoken critic of the government.

'They'll never arrest Boney,' said Mrs. Fuller. 'He knows too much.' And sure enough they never did.

Once Lady Downe came to see me at Dolphin Square, and on yet another day I ran into William Acton in Piccadilly. 'I'm going to Brixton prison,' I told him, and he came with me part of the way in a bus, so that we could have a few minutes together.

'What are you doing now?'

'I'm learning Urdu,' was the reply. I was never to see him again; he joined the army, and died towards the end of the war.

No words can tell how much I loved and admired the handful of friends who cheered me during the first five weeks of M.'s imprisonment. I grieved and worried about him night and day, and wondered about my future, and my babies, and Jonathan and Desmond, defenceless in a hostile world. Making every allowance for the panic of the government at a time when disaster was overtaking the Allied armies, it still seemed unbelievable that Englishmen could be held in prison indefinitely, without charge (because no charge could be made) and without trial. They were of course held silent. Our paper *Action* had been banned, and in any case all the men who ran it were in prison. Prisoners were not allowed to write to *The Times*. On the old principle of 'there's seldom smoke without fire' the general public got the impression that the prisoners must have 'done' something. In England (the theory goes) people are not put in prison for no reason, and if the reason could not be told in open court, that in itself must be a very bad sign. The number of those who knew enough about politics to guess the squalid reasons behind the arrest of M. and his companions was severely limited.

A few weeks after M.'s arrest the War Office commandeered Savehay Farm. This was a tremendous blow; I had no idea where I could live with my children within reach of Brixton prison. The man from the War Office said that in any case Denham would soon be 'unhealthy' for us. Asked what he meant by this he indicated that it would be a target which was likely to be bombed to smithereens. (It survived the war, undamaged.) The gardeners' cottages also had to be evacuated on orders from the War Office, which found accommodation for them not too far away. I consulted Muv about what I should do, and Pam nobly said we could all go to Rignell for the time being. Nanny and I packed the trunks. We planned to leave on Monday the 1st of July.

The beautiful hot summer weather went on and on; the garden at Denham was full of flowers. On Saturday afternoon I fed the baby and put him in his pram. I took my book into the garden. A maid appeared.

'There are some people at the door who want to speak to you,' she said.

'What sort of people?'

'Three men and a woman.'

I knew at once they must be police. Journalists sometimes hunt in couples, and one or two had come since M.'s arrest asking rude and irrelevant questions, but three men and a woman sounded more like police. I went to the door, and a warrant for my arrest was produced. The woman came with me while I put a few things in a small box; 'enough for a weekend,' she said. I was thinking about the baby and the bombing of London which, since France had fallen, was expected hourly.

He was eleven weeks old that day. I asked where I was to be imprisoned; I had heard of a women's prison at Aylesbury; but it was to be Holloway, therefore I decided, much as I longed to take him, that I must leave him with Nanny, who would take both babies to Rignell where they would be as safe as it was possible to be. Since, however, the policewoman had said 'a week-end', I thought I should do my best to be able to continue nursing the baby when it was over, and then wean him in the usual way. It was supposed to be bad for a baby to have a complete change of diet. I hugged the babies, and Nanny who was in tears, and was driven away.

The police motored me to London along empty roads; we were there in no time. Hoping to be able to nurse the baby again I asked my escort to stop at Bell and Croydon in Wigmore Street, the policewoman came with me and I bought a contraption called a breast pump. I should have been wiser to have got the salts and bandages which women use who do not intend to nurse their babies; I should have had far less pain. At Holloway prison the great gate opened and the car deposited me the other side of a yard.

Then came the strange procedure called in prison language 'reception'. I was locked into a wooden box like a broom cupboard. It had a seat fixed opposite the door; if you sat on it your knees touched the door. There was no window but light came in from the wire netting roof of the box. Here I remained for four hours. This was in the nature of a practical joke on the part of the prison authorities, for there was no reason why I should not have been taken straight to my cell after the usual formalities. There was nobody else arrested under Regulation 18B that day.

I collected my thoughts. My ideas about prison came from American films, and I envisaged cells of which one side would be made of iron bars, all giving on to a landing, like a zoo. The walls of my cupboard, painted a dirty cream colour, had been scribbled on by former denizens; there were a few swear words and cryptic sentences. 'Fraser is a cow,' was one. I tried to read the book I had brought with me, a pocket edition of Lytton Strachey's *Elizabeth and Essex*. It was not an ideal choice but I had snatched it up as I left my room.

After a couple of hours the door was unlocked for a moment

and I was given a chipped enamel plate with a vast sandwich upon it, also an immense mug of thick china made in the shape of a bobbin with a waist but no handle, containing a hot brown liquid which I guessed was supposed to be tea though it looked more like soup. I was thirsty but dared not drink. I missed the baby in an almost unbearable way. I left the sandwich untouched. After a while I heard other prisoners arrive and being locked into the adjacent boxes, and for the first time I heard the odd noise made by women prisoners, particularly prostitutes. They shout to one another in a sort of wail that is more like song than speech. It was to become a familiar sound over the years; also the accompanying shouts of the wardresses: 'Be quiet, you women.'

After about four and a half hours in my box I was taken out to see the doctor, an unprepossessing female with dyed hair and long finger nails, varnished dark red. I told her that I had been nursing my baby but that I could look after myself, and when a bath was mentioned I said I had had one that morning which seemed to satisfy her. Then a wardress took me to F Wing.

She made me go first, an act of apparent courtesy which, like so much in prison, is not quite what it seems. Wardresses must always have their prisoners in front of them; if they were following there's no knowing what they might take it into their heads to do: run away, for example.

As she unlocked the door and we stood in the entrance to F Wing a babel of voices suddenly fell silent and a sort of gasp went up. Dozens of women, many of them in dressing gowns, were standing about in groups, most had mugs in their hands. I did not know it, but it was ten minutes before they were due to be locked in their cells for the night and for this reason they were all on the landings. They crowded round me with kind expressions of sympathy; they knew I had left a little baby and were furious on my behalf. I knew very few of them, though they were members of B.U. Since Cimmie's death M. had been haunted by the idea that she had worn herself out by political activities beyond her strength. My work for him had been entirely connected with business and not at all with propaganda; I was quite incapable of making a speech. Thus I hardly knew any of them even by sight; one and all were to be kindness itself; there was nothing they would not do for me, they idolized M. and it was for his sake.

During the long time I was locked up with them I got to know these women and girls very well indeed. They were all ages from eighteen to sixty-five, from all classes, from every part of England; some intelligent, others less so, but they had without exception one thing in common: love of country. The idea that they could in any circumstances have betrayed our country was quite simply incredible. It was an idea which came from the political Left which has itself so often harboured traitors, and the people whom Churchill once called 'the race of degenerate intellectuals of whom our island has produced during several generations an unfailing succession—those very high intellectual persons who, when they wake up every morning, have looked around upon the British inheritance, whatever it was, to see what they could find to demolish, to undermine or to cast away.'* In 1940 Churchill was in coalition with these people, and although he had the decency to say in parliament that he doubted whether there had ever been a fifth column in England he was apparently obliged to keep us in prison in order to placate them.

I shall mention no names of my fellow-prisoners. Even at this late date, it might injure them in some way.

There was discussion about a cell; there was an empty one on the top floor and to this I was taken. After some whispering between wardresses I was told that after all I must have a cell in the basement. It had not been used because the tiny barred window was completely covered by sandbags; the cell was below ground level and the window, high in its wall, was in the middle of an immense pile of rotting sandbags so that no air could penetrate. The floor was awash; someone had emptied a pail in a primitive attempt to remove some of the encrusted dirt. On the wet floor a thin and lumpy mattress was put; there was no bed. A moment later came the crashes of cell doors being banged shut, then silence fell. I was in pain and the mattress was not very attractive, being both damp and hard. I sat on it and leant against the wall, making no attempt to undress. I could not sleep. I thought of my two babies, and my boys, and M. I wondered if he knew about my arrest. Probably not;

* House of Commons 28/10 1948.

probably he had gone to sleep in his bug-infested cell imagining me in my four-post bed at Denham, air scented with honeysuckle coming through the open windows.

There is a frightening look about the metal door of a prison cell because it has no handle on the inside. A small hole enables a wardress to peep in at will. In the wall there is a bit of painted metal about three inches long hanging down; this is the bell; and in the ceiling a naked electric bulb of feeble wattage. A couple of hours later the light was turned off from outside.

After what seemed an eternity, for though daylight came early none filtered through the sandbags, there was a clatter of cell doors being unlocked. The wardress shouted into each cell the words, 'Are you all right?' and hurried on her way. I discovered later that this was the only moment of the day when it was in order to ask to see a doctor, or the governor. If one was not 'all right' one had to watch the door lynx-eyed in order to capture this fleeting second when the wardress and her notebook were available. A groan from the bed would pass completely unnoticed because of the tearing hurry of the wardress, longing to rush off for her cup of tea.

A crowd of kind B.U. women came to my cell and offered me all manner of delicacies such as biscuits and cocoa, all of which I refused. I was afraid to drink and was not hungry. I ached all over. The great worry was the filth and grime. I washed my hands but they did not seem clean. One had so often been warned by doctors and nurses about the danger of infection and fever in my condition. Nevertheless, and despite the misery of not having the sweet baby, I was profoundly thankful that I had not brought him with me. It was a surprise that the prison should be so dirty; a sort of hospital-like bleak cleanliness was what I had vaguely envisaged. Unlike the Brixton cells, our cells were not infested with vermin, but the whole place was foul beyond words and efforts by the 18B prisoners to clean it had been only partly successful. The lavatories were disgusting and there were queues for them.

A wardress appeared and told me I was to be moved; I was taken to E Wing. In F Wing there were English women, the vast majority being members of B.U. with a few of Captain Ramsay's Right Club members. E Wing was fairly empty; there were Germans and Italians imprisoned under Regulation

18B rather than as enemy aliens because they had English pass-ports; most of them were the wives of British subjects. I was given a cell upstairs; it was light but dirty. A wardress came with a filthy grey rag and told me to clean the landing. This I refused to do because I was in pain and could not stoop; to move my arms hurt very much. She did not insist; it must have been a little private enterprise on her part because the ward-dresses never interfered with the prisoners' arrangements for cleaning or not cleaning their cells and the landings. She knew who I was and probably hoped to annoy.

After a time a wardress accompanied by a convict came to my cell with my 'dinner'. I was given a pat of margarine, some sugar in a pot and a bit of bread; also a revolting greasy metal container in two parts. The upper part had some small black potatoes with traces of earth upon their wrinkled skins and some yellowish straw-like strings which had probably once been a very old cabbage. When one lifted this tray and looked beneath, the gorge rose; oily greyish water in which swam a few bits of darker grey gristle and meat. The margarine had an excep-tionally disgusting taste, as I quickly discovered. I ate the bread and some sugar on it. The wardress and the convict came and collected the tin and its untouched contents and I went and stood on the landing and looked about me. I had almost finished my book and wanted to save a few pages. I became aware that somebody on the landing below was trying to catch my atten-tion; she held up a newspaper for me to see, the *Sunday Express*. The banner headline read LADY MOSLEY ARRESTED AT LAST. My thoughts flew to Jonathan; how would it be with him at his unloved school? Would he be bullied on my account? He was only ten. Long afterwards I discovered that Gerald Berners, with rare and sensitive kindness, had been to Summer Fields and taken him out for a treat. Oxford was full of posters about my arrest; Gerald tried to divert his attention and they spent the afternoon in a tea shop.

I soon realized that the policewoman's 'week-end' was fantasy, and that I was in Holloway to stay. After a couple of days I began to feel better and soon after that almost well. I was no longer confined to my cell and the landing but was allowed to mix freely with my fellow prisoners and to read what the Sunday papers had to say about my arrest: 'Goering's ideal woman' and similar rubbish, carefully designed to engender the maximum prejudice and dislike in its readers.

E Wing led on to a sort of apology for a garden. It was very dungeon-like and in fact, though I only discovered this later, it contained what journalists call 'the hanging shed'. I had imagined this as a separate building within the precincts. The condemned cell, which comprised two cells, led straight into a third cell with a trap door in the floor, the 'drop' through which the hanged woman fell. There was a sinister empty cell below. Once when E Wing was being used as a parcel depot the door of the condemned cell stood open and I had a quick look inside before a hurrying wardress banged it shut. The furniture was not the regulation chair, table and bed. It looked more like a very cheap lodging house furnished from the Caledonian Market. This was probably the doing of some well-meaning Prison Commissioner; the only result was that its comic appearance seemed to make it even more sickeningly tragic.

The ground floor cells were really basements and in the ditch outside ivy and laurels grew in profusion. This was the only part of the prison I rather liked; the dark green leaves and the old grey stones were lovely and reminded one of parts of the Forum; I used to imagine myself back in Rome in happier days.

As the status of prisoners held under Regulation 18B was that of prisoners on remand we not only wore our own clothes but could have parcels and food sent into the prison. Everything had to be searched, and a combination of too few censors and a good dose of spite meant that the parcels took a long time to reach the prisoner; this was particularly tiresome in the case of some book one was impatiently waiting for. During these early days in E Wing I was invited to partake of food cooked by a brilliant German cook. She and several others had been there for months and they were well-organized. Rationing was not strict in 1940. One could get eggs, olive oil, charcuterie, almost everything except meat and butter.

The Home Office allowed us to send and receive two letters a week. I asked that I should have one from M. and one from Nanny; I was frantic to know how the babies were faring, and Nanny would also send news of Jonathan and Desmond. So it was that for several months I had no letters from friends or from sisters; I had no idea which of them had written. When at last the rule about receiving two letters was relaxed, I was given a heap which had languished in the censors' lair unread except by them. The friends whose letters were post-marked the day my arrest was reported were Henry Yorke, Robert Heber-Percy, Mary Dunn, Gerald Berners. It was brave of them to write. Gerald's letter had evidently been read and re-read; it was dirty and full of pin-holes. One soon saw why. 'What can I send you?' he wrote. 'Would you like a little file concealed in a peach?'

After a time I was taken back to F Wing. I was given a corner cell on the third floor. It had a tiny gothic window instead of the usual square window with shallow Roman arch. Like them it was high up near the ceiling, one had to climb on the table in order to see out and then there was nothing but a prison view. Two small leaded panes could be opened for air; this never worried me because the prison was so cold, even in summer, that my requests to my faithful visitors—usually Muv, sometimes Pam—were for woollen clothes and hot water bottles. Somehow this became known, and Driberg put a sarcastic paragraph in his Hickey column. As it was in August I suppose it ranked as a joke. Long afterwards the governor admitted that many hot water bottles had arrived at the prison; none of them reached me, but the news of them warmed my heart.

Some old House of Commons friends visited M. in Brixton: James Maxton the I.L.P. leader, Bob Boothby and Walter Monckton. The latter also come to Holloway to see me. To my first question, how did he find M., Walter replied, 'Oh, all the old brilliance.'

The cells were six feet by nine; each contained a hard bed, a hard chair and a small heavy table. Under the bed was a chipped enamel chamber pot with a lid upon which in dark blue was a crown and the royal cipher. There was a battered jug and basin and a small three-cornered shelf. The sheets were made of canvas, painful if it touched one's chin.

Before I arrived the 18Bs had decided to eat together at trestle tables set up in the space between the cells on the ground floor. They took it in turns to fetch the food in huge metal containers from the prison kitchen, and to wash up. Washing up was a nasty affair, the plates were battered enamel, the forks bent and old, there was no soap and very little hot water. As soon as I decently could I abandoned this communal style of living. I got a china plate of my own and avoided the dreadful enamel. In any case I could not eat the prison food, except for the delicious bully beef; I made my ration of this last several days, otherwise I lived on prison bread and Stilton cheese sent me by M. We all shared our parcels from friends and relations. On my bread and cheese diet I became very thin though I was quite well; however it was partly to blame for something I afterwards regretted.

Although there was no trial for 18Bs since they had committed no offence and could be charged with no crime, there was an Advisory Committee which heard each prisoner and advised the Home Secretary as to whether he or she should be released. He was not bound to take the advice of the Committee; the Home Secretary was a little autocrat whose word, or whim, was law. Dozens of B.U. women were released as the autumn of 1940 wore on; they had been arrested during the panic in May and June. I fully expected to be released myself. I imagined that when the authorities had had a good hunt among all our belongings, and had broken open our safes and looked at what they contained, and had searched our bank accounts (which they had frozen) and everything connected with our private lives as well as studying M.'s speeches, articles and books, that they would certainly release us. I supposed that there would be a rule against free speech for the remainder of the war.

The Advisory Committee was presided over by Norman Birkett, a lawyer who had been readily scored off by M. a few years before when he appeared for the *Star* in a libel action brought by M., who had won the case and had been awarded £5,000 damages and costs against the newspaper. The Committee sat in a house in Burlington Gardens, which was destroyed by a bomb. For this reason I did not appear before it until the autumn. By then, with M. still in prison after a hearing of several days the previous July, I could not take it seriously. It seemed to me then, as it seems to me now, that our politicians behaved in a totally dishonest way, first of all in arresting us and later, far more dishonestly yet, in holding us silent in prison after the panic about invasion had died down. British Union was a patriotic, possibly too nationalistic movement; we thought the war a tragic mistake, but nothing could ever have induced any of us to harm our own country; it would have run counter to our deepest feelings and beliefs. I was convinced that Churchill knew this perfectly well; he was the prisoner of his coalition with M.'s old enemies in the Labour Party. As to Birkett, a mealy-mouthed Nonconformist, he was in my opinion the paid creature of these unprincipled men.

Therefore when I heard I was to be taken to Ascot, where the Committee was now installed, I looked upon it as a delightful outing. I had been told that the hearing was to be in a requisitioned hotel, and that one could have luncheon there. When I set off with my escort on a heavenly morning in October I felt I was on pleasure bent. I thought more about the menu than the Committee. A low diet generates fantasies about feasting.

The Advisory Committee consisted of Birkett, who was chairman, Sir Arthur Hazlerigg and Sir George Clerk. I had not seen Sir George Clerk since lunching with him ten years before at our embassy in Constantinople where he was Ambassador. Hazlerigg was a dear old boy who blinked in friendly fashion.

Birkett's line was to ask silly questions about Hitler, Goering, Goebbels and other National Socialists among my acquaintance. Why had we been married in Berlin? Because we wanted to keep the marriage secret for a while. Why had Hitler arranged this for us? Because I asked him to. Birkett pounced. 'This friend of yours is now bombing London.' I said that since Britain had declared war on Germany and we had bombed Berlin it was rather obvious that the Germans would bomb London. Birkett asked me when I had last seen Hitler. In Bayreuth in August 1939, I replied. And what had I said to him about Britain? Had I said that Britain would not fight? I replied that Hitler told me that he was certain Britain would declare war; he was convinced of it. There was a theory current at that time, which even now crops up, to the effect that Hitler had been deceived by Ribbentrop into imagining that England was decadent, or at any rate not prepared to fight. I have naturally no idea what Ribbentrop may have told Hitler; all I know is that Hitler saw what was perfectly obvious to everyone, that the English guarantee to Poland, even if it was not much help to the Poles, had made war practically inevitable. Birkett seemed rather put out; possibly he was one of those who preferred to believe a myth.

The whole thing lasted about an hour. At the end Birkett said: 'Your husband was very worried about your health when we saw him in July.' I said: 'Thank you, I am perfectly well now.' I regretted this subsequently. It is a fault of our upbringing that it should be considered unthinkable to allow the enemy to see that he has crushed one, or to admit to weakness, misery or despair. This should have been my cue. Instead of thinking about driving out of London and seeing woods and fields and ordering luncheon in an hotel, I ought to have prepared a devastating indictment of the unprincipled politicians and their disgraceful behaviour with an unvarnished description of the foulness of the prison. I ought to have enlarged upon the monstrosity of a system which could imprison innocent people and hold indefinitely the mother of four young children. From these dishonest politicians and this monstrous system no court in the land could protect one. It was the triumph of rumour, gossip, spite and lying tongues, and it was done in the dark, underhand, where the light of reason and truth could not penetrate.

I do not suppose for one moment that my words would have moved Mr. Birkett, but Sir Arthur Hazlerigg and Sir George Clerk would at least have been made to feel uncomfortable, and they might even have put in a plea for me and my companions. As it was, they did perhaps have a glimmer of something like remorse. When the moment came for the famous luncheon, brought on a tray to the stables where my wardress had taken me, I was touched by being given a bottle of claret 'with the compliments of Sir Arthur Hazlerigg'. The food was mediocre, as was inevitable. How could I have ever dreamed it would be otherwise?

While we were held silent in gaol the gutter press hit upon a new way to whip up popular prejudice against us. There were articles saying that at a time when the entire population was cheerfully putting up with wartime austerity, we were living in idle luxury. M. in Brixton 'called for alternate bottles of red and white wine', while the Holloway prison dustbins were choked with empty champagne bottles after our orgies.

Prisoners on remand, which was our status, are allowed a bottle of beer or half a bottle of wine a day, if they care to pay for it. Spirits are forbidden. I ordered some half bottles of port, which were doled out one by one. A glass of grocer's port and a bit of Stilton cheese helped me through many a sad evening, locked in my cell and sitting on my hard bed freezing with cold and straining my eyes to read by the tiny dim ceiling light. In M.'s next letter after these newspaper stories he said he had had no wine or beer at Brixton and that we should bring a joint action for libel. Fortunately my port did not wreck his plans. The hearing of the libel action provided another delightful outing, more wonderful by far than the visit to Ascot because for the first time since my arrest I was to see my beloved.

We met, with the lawyers and accompanied by our prison escorts, in the law courts. After giving evidence we were allowed a few minutes together in the robing-room, with our counsel Khaki Roberts. Looking forward to this meeting and thinking about it afterwards kept me happy for several days. M. was very thin; he had grown a beard because the shaving arrangements at Brixton were so revolting. The newspapers paid costs and an agreed sum of damages. With my share Muv bought me a shaggy fur coat, it was not very elegant but it was warm. I looked like Fafner and Fasolt rolled into one, I wore it all day and it covered my bed at night. I often felt grateful to the journalist who had invented the orgies.

There were air raids almost every night that winter. The Home Office had given orders that our cells were to be unlocked when the sirens sounded; apparently it was thought that we might become hysterical if we were locked up when bombs were falling. Only the wardresses had torches; the lights were put off at the mains and one crept about in pitch dark. I generally went and sat with Mrs. D. whose cell was on the ground floor. We used to sit and laugh; despite the misery of our situation cheerfulness broke through and there were certainly plenty of things to laugh at in the prison. One night she had struck a match to light her cigarette when a wardress passing the cell saw the glimmer through the open door. 'D.!' she cried in terrified tones, 'put out that light!'

'There's a black curtain on the window,' said Mrs. D.

'Yes, I know. But if an *incendiary* came in you might *set it off*!'

As the months passed the attitude of the wardresses towards us changed completely. Probably at the beginning they had thought we must be traitors, or near-traitors, because otherwise how was it that we had been locked up by the good and noble men who were leading the nation? After a while they came to know us fairly well and most of them were very kind and friendly. I was fond of several of them and they told delightful prison stories.

The prison words never ceased to amuse. Reception, for example, which in the ordinary world means a rather dull and formal sort of party, was the broom cupboard already described. Court was a police court, not Buckingham Palace. Wing, such a beautiful word, meant a section of the vile prison. Garden Party was a group of bedraggled prisoners who, directed by an ignorant wardress, dug for victory in the prison yard. To a wardress, the word 'woman' means a convicted prisoner. One of them told me: 'I took my woman to court and we were waiting for our case to come on when one of the policemen called down to us: "Would any of you women like a cup of tea?" Well! I didn't know *what* to say. He meant us officers! Of course I suppose we *are* women, but *women*! you *women*! Wasn't it *rude*, it was *ever* so rude, I felt like saying *no*.' But to wardresses, who are like nurses in this respect, tea is the elixir of life. 'She's been to the reception' and 'Come along for the garden party' were added to after the Advisory Committee changed its venue; one heard: 'Are you going to Ascot?'

Just occasionally concerts were given for the prisoners by well-meaning and philanthropic visiting musicians. They took place in the chapel. Compared with the dirty, smelly, dark old prison the chapel was rather pleasant, it was clean, well-polished and brightly lit. At one of these concerts there was a man who sang folk songs and at the end of each line of verse he raised himself on tiptoe and poked his head out first to the right and then to the left. I began to laugh and could not stop, something that had never happened to me since childhood. I buried my face in my hands and tears of laughter ran through my

7

fingers. Terrified that he might see me and be deeply hurt, I bit my tongue; but still I shook with laughter which became more painful with every Hey nonny no from the singer, who had so kindly come to Holloway to amuse the prisoners but had not meant to amuse them quite as much as that. It was agony; back in my cell I was overcome with extreme exhaustion. I hoped he had not noticed, or that perhaps he thought I was like Mme Verdurin, who demonstrated her sensibility by listening to music with her face in her hands.

The cold weather came and the prison was icier than ever. A wardress appeared with a convict carrying a pile of blankets. I went to get one. Never have I seen a more disgusting sight than these old hard blankets; without going into details every variety of human filth had left its unmistakable marks upon them. I turned away.

'Don't you want one, dear?' said the wardress.

'Not really,' I replied.

'Here's a lovely clean one,' she said. But it was only less foul than the others. As I had asked my visitors for a china plate, a glass, a pillow, so I now asked for a blanket. I read nearly all day long, books that were sent in for me and a few from the prison library. The wardresses said that the convicts generally chose a book with a red cover from the tray that came round 'because they lick their fingers and get a bit of the red dye to put on their lips'. The pathos of this attempt at beautifying themselves on the part of women sentenced to sleep under filthy blankets and to wear coarse and stained underclothes that had been worn by countless prisoners before them, and the scratchy black stockings and painful clumping old shoes in which they were arrayed at the 'reception', quite haunted me. Few convicted women remained at Holloway, most had been removed to Aylesbury at the outbreak of war and probably the best prison gear had gone with them, leaving the worst dregs behind. A majority of those one saw had pathetic piebald heads, the ends of their hair being brilliant peroxide while the remainder was either black or grey.

I read Carlyle's *French Revolution* at this time. I thought if, like the prisoners he describes, I had to stay many months in gaol, I would prefer to die. As we had not been sentenced one could not count the days, uncertainty was our lot. It was lucky for me that I could not peer into the future, for had I known that only during the fourth bitter winter would I be set free I should have been near to despair.

One night a bomb fell hard by the prison. It broke the water mains. In the dark early morning there was the sound of lavatory plugs being pulled in vain. The lavatories, always foul, became frightful. Floors awash with urine, everything choked, an appalling smell. We were all grey with grime because the bomb had shaken the old prison and a thick layer of dust and soot covered everything. We were given half a pint of water each, I drank a sip and tried to wash in the remainder but it only streaked the dirt. It so happened that I was to see Mr. Hickson that day. When he came I said that the prison had become uninhabitable and unless something was done about the lavatories the Home Office would have hundreds of sick women on its hands. Mr. Hickson made sympathetic noises.

'Don't you know anyone in the government I could appeal to for you?' he said.

'*Know* anyone in the government? I know *all* the Tories beginning with Churchill,' I cried.

This was an exaggeration, but I did know several of them and heartily despised them for their hypocrisy; always mouthing platitudes about freedom, free speech and the rule of law. 'The whole lot deserve to be shot,' I added.

Unlike murderers or burglars we were never allowed to see our lawyer alone; the little wardress in the corner must have reported my intemperate words, for 'Cousin Winston' knew what I had said, as I discovered years later.

When we were taken to the yard for exercise that day there was a rush for the row of outdoor lavatories. Mine was fairly clean, but when I emerged I was surrounded by horrified cries of, 'You *shouldn't* have gone in there!'

'Why not?'

'Didn't you see the V on the door?'

I had noticed that a red V was painted on the door, and thought it was for Victory. The papers were full of tales about Vs which apparently were to be seen here, there and everywhere; the prison was unlikely to be behindhand in this patriotic demonstration.

'That lavatory is only for women with venereal disease,' I was told.

One of our number was a French girl who had made her way to London in some unexplained manner from occupied France. When we asked why she had been arrested she said she had been closely interrogated and one of the questions was about the Vs which were supposed to be chalked up all over Paris as a gesture of defiance to the German occupying forces. When she said she had never herself seen a V anywhere in Paris her interrogators were so disgusted that they sent her to Holloway, at any rate she could think of no other reason. This girl was quite badly hurt when a bomb fell on the prison. It tore away the landing and she stepped out of her cell in the dark and fell on to the stone floor far below, breaking her leg.

It was two days before the water flowed once more, and during the second night I was in bed in the dark with the cell door open because an air raid was in progress when I heard horrible sounds of people being sick. Thirteen women were violently ill, all had eaten prison food. Nothing had been washed up in the prison kitchen and no doubt as foul stews succeeded each other in the same dirty vessels poisons were secreted.

Doubtless water mains in other parts of London were broken in air raids with similar results to people's lavatories; what made our situation uniquely horrible was that we were locked in and there was absolutely nothing we could do about it.

The governor of Holloway was a sandy-haired Scotchman, Dr. Mathieson, who had lost an eye and a leg in the first war. He received one accompanied by a grim-looking hatchet-faced wardress, Miss Manley; she was unpopular with her underlings who called her Chiefy. One day he sent for me and said: 'There's a message from the government: Lady Mosley is to have a bath every day.' I looked at him. He knew, and I knew, that it was not possible. There were two degraded bathrooms in the wing, and enough water for four baths; we took turns and got a bath roughly once a week. It had been a kindly thought of Winston's, who had I suppose been told that this was one of the hardships I minded.

A musical German lady among the prisoners was given permission to bring a gramophone into Holloway. She arranged concerts in a room across the yard and asked me what records I should like. She seemed to be quite rich and ordered dozens. We had Beethoven quartets, the second and the sixth symphonies, Schubert, Bach, Händel, Debussy, Wagner. Despite the tiresome pauses while the gramophone was wound up these concerts were heavenly. There is nothing like music for transporting one a thousand miles from hateful surroundings into realms of bliss.

This lady was very pretty and she had amazing jewels which she carried around in a fish basket. When I suggested that she might be well advised to give them into the care of the prison authorities she obviously thought I was quite mad. How could one trust one's jewels to the lying swine who put an innocent woman in a vile prison, she asked.

Thus day followed day, the level waste, the rounding grey. The weekly visit was lovely but a quarter of an hour went in a flash. I was ashamed that Muv should make the long journey from Swinbrook, and back again in the black-out, in order to sit for ages in the drear prison waiting-room before being admitted to the miserably brief visit. In the holidays she brought the boys; I shall never forget their dear anxious faces as they stared at me, and the relief when they saw I had not much changed, and that I laughed as usual. Alexander was brought up by Nanny; he looked beautiful beyond words with huge dark eyes. He was now two years old and began to talk. A large proportion of B.U. members were released before Christmas, including all those who had small children with the exception of me. There was more room all round, and as a result of M.'s and Mr. Hickson's ceaseless complaints, backed up by a couple of brave M.P.s in the House of Commons, R. R. Stokes and Sir Irving Albery, various small improvements were made in our conditions.

The best of these was a fortnightly visit from M. in the spring of 1941. Admiral Sir Barry Domvile came with him to visit his wife. He was a delightful and very clever man who had been Director of Naval Intelligence during the first war. In the 1930s he started an organization called The Link, with the object of encouraging friendship between Englishmen and Germans, and for this grave sin he was imprisoned. M. and Sir Barry were always in tearing spirits for the spree and from the police car which brought them across London from their prison to ours the Admiral used to shout to the astonished passers-by. One day they saw a red-headed girl. 'Ginger for sport!' cried the Admiral. M. and I talked without drawing breath; so much to hear, so much to tell. These visits gave my spirits a lift; I never felt cold on the day M. came, I was excited and happy. The visit over, one counted fourteen long and tedious days until the next.

A Christian Scientist fellow-prisoner who told me when I was perishing with cold that it was 'nur anscheinend—*seemingly* Lady Mosley', was delighted when I was forced to admit that I never felt cold on visiting days. Although she believed that to feel cold was simply 'error' this German lady had a clever way of warming her cell. She collected waxed paper containers, tore them in strips and burned them in the enamel chamber pot. This made a delicious though transitory warmth, rather like when Hans Andersen's little match girl burned all her matches. We then began to add eau de cologne to the flames. It burnt beautifully. We ordered large flagons of eau de cologne of the cheapest variety for our fire (paraffin was of course forbidden), and we read plays. Goethe, Schiller and Racine lasted us through the miserable winter, and like the gramophone concerts our play readings transported us far away from our sordid surroundings. My Christian Scientist friend broke all the prison rules and once she was carted off to the punishment cell. While she waited in this cheerless hole she wrote on the wall: 'Father, forgive them for they know not what they do.' In the end they did nothing, but it caused me intense amusement. I was very fond of her and she never minded being teased. Her favourite saying was culled from Mrs. Eddy: 'In jedem Moment gibt Ihnen der liebe Gott *alles* was Sie brauchen.'* Once for several wretched days no parcels came so that we ran out of everything, not a scrap of cheese nor a drop of eau de cologne was left and I was reduced to my bread and sugar diet. Suddenly the welcome cry of 'Parcels!' was heard. My Christian friend flew down and reappeared half an hour later with her arms full.

'Lady Mosley! Ist es nicht rührend!' she said, adding the inevitable 'In jedem Moment'. When I pointed out that the benefactor was Harrods, where she had an account, she said I should never make a Scientist.

* God gives you everything you need.

Apart from physical discomfort everyone in the prison had dreadful anxieties and worries. When the docks burned in the air raids those whose homes were in the East End were frantic about their mothers and sisters and brothers; it was agony for them not being able to telephone and discover whether they were wounded, homeless, or even dead. One poor woman had a little boy aged eighteen months who was dragged away from her to a 'home' by the police when she and her husband were arrested. For many days nobody would tell her where he was. I was lucky, with Nanny and Muv and my sisters and the fact that my four children were out of London during the bombing. All the same a terrible worry half killed me. This was a message delivered by the Governor that Jonathan had had an emergency operation for acute appendicitis at school. I asked permission to go to him. It was refused by the Home Office. Day and night I could not rest, I walked to and fro in my cell and could not bear company. The girl in the cell under mine told me afterwards she heard me walking all night long. To think of my beloved boy lying between life and death and probably looking for me was almost unbearable. He was indeed very ill, but he recovered. The Governor sent for me and told me he had 'turned the corner'. I said I supposed if he had died they would have allowed me to go, when it was too late. He did not answer; he knew very well that was exactly what would have happened. Many of the prisoners had sons or brothers in the forces; Lady Domvile's elder son was killed in Crete that summer. Poor woman, she *knew* it even before she was told.

I was not frightened of the air raids. This had nothing to do with courage; it was simply that I hardly cared whether I lived or died. The prison had the same effect that the hardships of war have upon soldiers: if you make people miserable enough they become very brave.

The raids stopped during the spring of 1941 and at last I felt it was safe to have Max up for a visit. They allowed me an hour, and he was brought to a room in another part of the prison. He was completely changed from the little baby I had left ten months before. He sat up and gazed about him with solemn expression. The wardresses thought him wonderful, but then they always took a great interest in my visitors, and the younger the better. Alexander was also surrounded by admirers when he was a prison visitor.

So the months passed and in June Germany attacked Russia. The war seemed as if it would never end. I no longer believed in release. Tom visited me whenever he had leave, and that autumn he had time one day to go to see M. at Brixton and then come on to me.

'I am dining at Downing Street tonight,' he told me. 'Is there anything you want me to say?'

'Only the same as always. That if we have to stay in prison couldn't we at least be together?' This was exactly what M. had said to him and he promised to do his best. I had no hope about it; the Governor and a Prison Commissioner I asked had both said that such a thing was out of the question. It was an administrative impossibility, according to them. However, Cousin Winston was a noted cutter of red tape and after his conversation with Tom during dinner he ordered the prison to find a way. So it was that our circumstances altered dramatically. After a separation of a year and a half we were re-united. Our joy was such that, unlikely as it might seem, one of the happiest days of my life was spent in Holloway prison.

We were lodged in a house in the prison grounds called the Preventive Detention Block. It was hard by the mighty prison wall and set in a yard which had once had a lawn; this had been dug for victory and contained a few mouldering cabbages. Three other married couples were put there as our stable companions, but two of them were quickly released, and we settled down with Major and Mrs. de Laessoe. The men took it in turns to stoke the boiler; on M.'s day the water was stone cold and the kitchen ankle deep in coke. Major de Laessoe was a wonderful stoker and we gratefully allowed him to perform upon the boiler. He was altogether an admirable person who in the first war had won the M.C. and D.S.O. Brave, intelligent and very kind, he was the salt of the earth. They put him in prison because he was a prominent member of B.U. and, like us, was against going to war unless to defend Britain or the Empire.

We were given our rations raw, so that one could make quite eatable food. As to the cabbage patch, the men transformed it into a productive kitchen garden. We grew exotic delicacies like the Jersey pea-bean, and fraises des bois. M. got dozens of books on gardening and in one of them he read that weeds, far from being noxious, are an excellent help and make the pea-beans grow. As he did not care for weeding he adopted this theory with enthusiasm; his end of the garden was wildly untidy, but Major de Laessoe's was like the photographs in a seedsman's catalogue. I think Major de Laessoe suffered slightly; he loved order and neatness and he worked in his garden for hours and probably wished M. had not come across his unorthodox book, but he was far too loyal to say so.

Into this place we were locked for a further two years. We saw the seasons come and go. We walked round and round our yard, sometimes in snow or fog, sometimes in rain and wind or in the airless heat of a London summer. There was a single tree; the leaves and the pattern they made against the sky were the one beauty. We read enormously; M. had learnt German. He loved the German neo-Hellenists and the English neo-Hellenists, and he read history, economics, poetry, psychology and plays. He loved *Faust* and *Wallenstein* and learnt passages by heart. In Bernard Shaw's opinion prison is less horrible than school, because in prison they do not torture your mind by obliging you to read books written by the Governor or the warders. There is a good deal in his theory. The high thinking we were able to indulge in compensated in some measure for the low living. To have had to read the collected works of our gaolers, Dr. Mathieson, Miss Manley, Herbert Morrison, and Sir John Anderson would have been no joke. All the same, at school there are holidays.

We both pined for freedom, and I pined for my children, more and more as years went by. M. was very thin and he got painful phlebitis. He was far from well.

Needless to say, our new circumstances had not passed unnoticed. The yellow press managed to make it sound once again as if we were living in unimaginable luxury, and (to annoy the readers further) at the taxpayers' expense. A favourite newspaper word is 'suite'; it conveys a vision of glamour and comfort, Noël Coward-like dressing-gowns, lace-encrusted négligés. Therefore our cells were described as a suite. Muv, coming to see us on a bus, was amused by the conductor's calling:

'Holloway gaol! Lady Mosley's suite! All change here.' She was less amused by a huge poster not far from the prison gate: 'YOUR FREEDOM IS IN DANGER. Lend to defend the right to be free.'

During one bitter winter I became so ill with persistent diarrhœa that M. asked the Home Office to allow my doctor to see me. When permission came I could think of no one except Dr. Bevan; he had been Lady Evelyn's doctor. He was quite hopeless. The Governor had given him a good brain-washing before he got to me. In my cell the thermometer stood at freezing point; we had heat in our sitting-room but the block was unheated as a war-time economy. Dr. Bevan said, 'You need a milk diet and warmth. You should go to the prison hospital, it's warmer there, and they can't allow you milk unless you do.' Our ration was a quarter of a pint; the old days of milk from a shop in waxed cardboard were long past; everything was now rationed. I had heard grim tales about the prison hospital where the dyed female doctor held sway. I determined on no account to go; and in any case if I did who was to look after M.? I dreaded being released without him, he was ill and the thought of him going back to Brixton terrified me. After poor silly useless Dr. Bevan had gone I told Miss Davis, a wardress I was fond of, what had happened.

'Can you imagine,' I said. 'The Governor managed to make Dr. Bevan believe that there's a lovely hospital here.'

'It's not so much the *hospital*,' said Miss Davis meaningfully. 'It's the people in it.'

One evening I was so exhausted by diarrhœa and in so much pain that M. went down to consult Major de Laessoe. After the first war in which he had served with such distinction Major de Laessoe had made his life in Angola. He had recently been given permission to bring a trunk containing all his worldly goods into the prison from a store; he and Mrs. de Laessoe wished to save what clothes they had from being eaten by moths. Among other things this trunk contained Major de Laessoe's medicine chest from his days in Africa. He said to M. 'I've got the very thing, a pill I used to take if I got dysentery travelling in the bush.'

M. gave me Major de Laessoe's pill and I got into bed. It was as if I had been hit on the head; semi-unconscious I never moved all night long. M. slept peacefully until quite late. When he awoke he was frightened by what he saw. I was lying in exactly the position I had been in after I swallowed the pill. He spoke to me, touched me, but I did not wake. He flew for a wardress and asked for a doctor. A woman doctor came, not the one with the long red nails but a nice, clever, sensible young woman; I believe she is now a life peeress. M. showed her the bottle from which the pill had come; she questioned Major de Laessoe. The pills were opium, and very old. The doctor said some drugs change over the years, becoming either weaker or more potent. This opium pill was strong; a little more and it would have been the end of me. I was suffering from opium poisoning. Disagreeable though it was it nevertheless gave me a couple of days' respite from my other misery. My perfect digestion was almost ruined in prison; for many years afterwards I suffered intermittently from it. When this happened I followed the régime prescribed by Mme de Sévigné for M. de Grignan in like case three hundred years ago: nothing but plain boiled rice. As she truly said, it was 'adoucissant'. But during the war rice was unobtainable.

A wardress and two convicts came to clean the block; we were not supposed to talk to the convicts but naturally I always did. 'Don't worry about them,' Miss Davis had said. 'You don't want petty pilfering so I'm sending sex offenders; they are always clean and honest.' One of them, a pretty woman of about thirty-five, told me she was a bigamist. It had happened by mistake she said and she had been sentenced to nine months. She said something very true:

'Prison is not the same punishment for everyone. There are women here who are glad to have something to eat and a bed to sleep in.' To her, it was clearly a terrible punishment, the wearing of the stained clothes and in every other way. But I told her she was lucky to be able to count the days until her release. 'We seem to be here for life,' I said.

Visiting rules were now relaxed. Nicky, who had left Eton and joined the Rifle Brigade, was allowed to come for the day every time he got leave. M. loved talking with him about his new passion, neo-Hellenism. Nicky, whose mind is unlike M.'s, was clever and receptive enough to be an ideal companion at that time. Jonathan and Desmond came in the holidays; they stayed with Nancy who was working at Heywood Hill's bookshop. Their visits were unalloyed joy. Nancy sent me books; Cherry Garrard's *The Worst Journey in the World* still conjures up prison days for me. People sent me their books when they were published; Evelyn Waugh sent *Work Suspended*, Gerald Berners *Far from the Madding War*. Such small attentions made me feel not quite forgotten in our living tomb. Another benefactor was Derek Hill who sent me drawings of Jonathan and Desmond. I had them framed and they gave me great pleasure.

A visiting pass marked 'Lady Andrews' was for Debo, now married to Andrew Cavendish. She ran across the yard with two graceful whippets. Nancy, Pam, Unity, all came; and Tom whenever he was in England. Also a few friends: Henry and Dig Yorke, Gerald Berners.

In 1943 the Home Office gave permission for Alexander and Max, now aged four and three, to come and stay with us in the prison for two nights. Adorable though exhausting, the little boys rushed up and down stairs and trampled on Major de Laessoe's neat garden. Mrs. de Laessoe gave them her whole ration of sweets. The second time they came they did not want to leave. Alexander clung, and when he had been torn away there were tears where he had pressed his face against my skirt. I decided—a terrible decision for me—not to allow any more of these visits, which seemed to do more harm than good. Before many weeks went by fate intervened.

As M.'s health was visibly failing, and since Tom was abroad with his regiment, I asked Muv if she would go and see Clementine Churchill just to make certain that the facts about M.'s illness should be known. We knew, because Randolph had said it to Tom many times, that Churchill himself wanted to release us. I was afraid for M. that winter.

Muv was extremely reluctant; she hated to seem to be asking a favour of people whom she regarded in a very poor light. She looked upon Churchill as one of the architects of the war itself, quite apart from his disgraceful complicity in our imprisonment. However, she did go. Needless to say, Clementine irritated her beyond measure, first by remarking: 'Winston has always been so fond of Diana,' and then by saying that we were better off in prison, because if we were released the furious populace would be after us. Muv replied that we were perfectly willing to risk that. I can picture her cold and proud demeanour. The two had known each other for a long time; Clementine had been one of my mother's bridesmaids nearly forty years before.

Whether this démarche had any result I do not know, what is certain is that the report of Dr. Geoffrey Evans who came to the prison to examine M. gave the Home Office a fright. He said that if M. got a chill, or influenza, in his present condition he would not answer for the consequences.

On a dark, cold morning in November 1943 I was standing by the kitchen stove making porridge when Miss Baxter rushed in, threw her arms round me and said: 'You're released!' She was in tears.

'How do you know?'

'I heard it just now on the wireless,' said Miss Baxter. I flew to M. and told him. It was like coming to the end of a dark tunnel and seeing a glimmer of sunshine. I was filled with inexpressible joy; M. was saved, our own particular nightmare was over, life was to start again with the family re-united, even though the war dragged on.

The Governor came and told us details. There were many restrictions; we must not be in London but must go to the country, somewhere approved by the Home Office, and there we should be under house arrest and not permitted to travel. We were not to see any of our former political associates. No motor car was allowed. We were not to give interviews to the press. Denham was occupied by the War Office, our flat was in London, Muv was living in a minute cottage with Unity, Nancy was in London, Debo was following the drum. We asked Pam and Derek. In their usual splendid way they immediately said yes. The Home Office agreed.

Meanwhile outside the main gate of the prison a crowd of reporters and photographers had gathered. They erected a scaffold which was manned night and day, waiting for us to appear. Communists began to organize protest marches (Nancy said that in order to get into an underground station she had to chant: 'Put him back, put him back.'). Only on the third day, before it was light, did two police cars drive us away; we were led in pitch darkness across the whole prison compound to a little door in the wall outside which the motors were waiting with their engines running. We were driven fast through the dark, sleeping city; the police kept looking behind them but we had given the journalists the slip. As day broke and revealed the frosty country landscape M. and I thought that nothing so beautiful was ever seen by human eye.

At Rignell a wonderful welcome awaited us. Derek had got leave, Muv used her month's allowance of petrol and came over with Debo. We had delicious food, beautiful wine, talk, laughter, perfect happiness. Then, for the first time for three and a half years, we slept in soft, fine linen in soft, warm beds.

With disgraceful cynicism the Home Office gave Major and Mrs. de Laessoe an order of release the very day we were freed. Nothing could have been more obvious: they were released in order that the P.D. Block could be emptied and shut. Penniless, and with nowhere to go, or possibility of getting a job (they were in their sixties) they must have been desperately worried. However a kind former 18B, Iris Ryder, took them in. All this I discovered later; no contact between us and them was allowed.

Bernard Shaw was the only public figure who openly mocked our adversaries. Asked: 'Would you think it too strong to say that the Home Secretary's decision . . . is calculated to cause alarm and despondency among the masses of the people who responded to his exhortation to "go to it"? he replied: "I do not think it is a strong proposition at all. It makes me suspect that you are mentally defective. I think this Mosley panic shameful. . . . Even if Mosley were in rude health, it was high time to release him with apologies for having let him frighten us into scrapping the Habeas Corpus Act. Mr. Morrison has not justified the outrageous conditions—the gag in Mosley's mouth and the seven-mile leg-iron. We are still afraid to let Mosley defend himself and have produced the ridiculous situation in which we may buy Hitler's *Mein Kampf* in any bookshop in Britain, but may not buy ten lines written by Mosley." '

I never went back to Holloway to see my friends Miss Andrews, Miss Baxter and Miss Davis, but many years later a prison visitor, Anne Tree, told me Miss Davis had said to her: 'We've never had such laughs since Lady Mosley left.'

18

Crux Easton

AT RIGNELL WE made M. stay in bed. He was weak and desperately thin. The newspapers took various points of view about our release, all more or less hostile. The *Daily Worker* had an article saying I should be put back in prison at once because I was 'in rude and vigorous health'. This was illustrated with a photograph; I recognized it as having appeared some years before in a magazine, of me and Randolph at the Derby. The *Daily Worker* had cut Randolph out. I certainly looked blooming with health in the photograph.

It was not long before the journalists discovered our whereabouts. They laid siege to Rignell; every laurel, shrub and hedge or ditch concealed some unfortunate half-frozen reporter. They got little change from the near-by villages because nobody had seen us arrive. They made up thrilling stories about a mansion, and baying hounds. The baying hounds were the Jacksons' dachshunds, Wüde and Hamelin. Finally they chucked it and went away. M. stayed in bed, partly in order to cheat the journalists of their prey and partly because he was very weak.

I was able to see Alexander on his fifth birthday a day or two later; Muv had a little party for him at the cottage. Nanny had dressed him and Max in party clothes that had belonged to the older boys in palmier days; plum coloured moiré with white chiffon jabots. They looked happy; they knew there were to be no more heartrending partings.

We had not been many days at Rignell when the Home Office moved us in a hurry. Derek was doing secret scientific work for the Air Ministry, and according to their mythology we had been 'directed' to the wrong house. Derek, who had won several medals for gallantry as a rear-gunner in the R.A.F., was sarcastic to the Home Secretary, Herbert Morrison, and told him he required no lessons in patriotism from a man who had spent the first war dodging about in an apple orchard. However, we had to go.

We found an inn at Shipton-under-Wychwood, the innkeeper used the bar but the rest was empty. Into the Shaven Crown we moved, with Nanny, Alexander and Max, and when the holidays began we were joined by Jonathan and Desmond, and there we spent Christmas, our first free Christmas since 1939. For the feast on Christmas Day we all squeezed into the Swinbrook cottage with Muv and Unity.

The newspapers went on with their absurd tales, and one day a photographer who had been hiding in some nettles jumped out and got a picture of M. carrying coal across a yard. They said we were living in an immense hotel, they made it sound rich and luxurious. But they also said that nobody would work for us so that I was obliged to do all the work myself. It was quite one of their best efforts. It conjured up a vision of me living in a country Ritz with my large family, keeping the enormous place clean all by myself as well as cooking and shopping and minding the children. The result of these newspaper stories was a flood of letters from people who wanted to come as cooks and butlers and housemaids. At breakfast each morning I read the letters aloud; the applicants gave themselves glowing references. Nanny was scornful: 'H'm. *She* sounds pleased with herself,' she said. Among the dross there was one golden letter, it came from a former cook of Gerald's, Mrs. Nelson. She had been his London housekeeper and when I stayed at Halkin Street she used to chat when she brought my breakfast tray. She and her husband came; they only stayed a few months but they saw us into our next house.

All the boys got whooping cough at the Shaven Crown; Alexander was really ill. The Burford doctor of our childhood days, Dr. Cheatle, came. He brought us gifts of eggs as well as medical advice, and he told us news of a petition which the local communist was trying to organize, objecting to our presence at Shipton. 'None of the village people have signed,' said Dr. Cheatle.

Gerald came to stay. I said, 'Are you frightened of germs? The boys have got whooping cough.' 'No, I'm not frightened of germs I'm frightened of bombs,' was the answer. I loved his visit except that I knew we were not making him comfortable.

We laughed and talked and went for little walks. I was not allowed to go to him at Faringdon, it was miles out of bounds.

One morning Muv telephoned. I went back to the sitting-room and said: 'Bad news.'

Jonathan looked up from his book. 'Bad news! No sausages at Hammett's?' in anguished tones. Sausages, the only un-rationed 'meat', were infinitely precious.

'Worse than that I'm afraid. Jakie has drowned in the mill pond.' Jakie was Unity's dog. Apparently he had been found near the bank, it was sad and mysterious. Unity said she must have him buried in the churchyard, but the clergyman refused. 'Don't you think it's *awful* of Mr. Wells?' she said. She ordered his tombstone; on it was to be engraved:

JAKIE

BLESSED ARE THE PURE IN HEART.

'You see, he *was* pure in heart. *Much* purer than Mr. Wells.'

Desmond went back to Summer Fields and Jonathan to Eton; late, because of their whooping cough. Jonathan had got a scholarship and went into College. He was clever but bad at games, and we thought he would be happier in College than in the house he had been going to. He wrote once, from Summer Fields, 'I am the lowest jumper in the school'; it reminded me of our own family; none of us was much good at such things. Of course I could visit neither of them, both schools were far out of bounds. During those years when I was living under house arrest Nancy often went down to Eton to take Jonathan out. She reckoned to pay her journey and the luncheon from the profit she made by buying old books in Windsor and selling them at Heywood Hill.

Eton boys, never smart, became increasingly degraded as the war went on. Clothes were rationed, therefore they bought old and worn overcoats and morning coats from boys who were leaving. Jonathan's overcoat, which had once been black, had a greenish hue; it was also stained. Nancy said to him: 'You know, do forgive my saying it, but one would imagine there was *soup* on the front of your overcoat.'

'Oh,' said Jonathan, unconcerned, 'there *is*. You see it's so cold that we always wear our overcoats at supper.'

Wartime austerity had not improved the menu in College. A few years later, when Cyril Connolly took André Gide, at his request, to see Eton on their way back from Oxford where Gide had received an honorary degree, they arrived just as the Tugs were about to eat their supper. Gide was quite upset by what he saw. 'Cela me coupe l'appétit,' he said to Cyril.

Not long ago I went to Eton to see my grandson Valentine act the name part in Anouilh's *Pauvre Bitos*, translated into English. His mother took me down with my grand-daughter, Catherine, and Harold Acton, who had not been back to the school since he left it more than fifty years ago. I asked him: 'What is the biggest change here? Is it the boys' long hair?'

'Oh no,' said Harold, 'we always had long hair. The Dames were always telling us to go and have our hair cut. No, the great change is in the boys' accents.'

Scotland Yard had sent a detective called Mr. Jones to Shipton to keep an eye on us; he told us thrilling crime stories. One starry frosty night I walked through the village to the church where Händel's *Messiah* was sung. As I sat wrapped in my Fafner and Fasolt coat in the dimly-lit gothic church listening to the divine music I noticed Mr. Jones in a nearby pew; he was a musical Welshman.

We could not stay indefinitely at the Shaven Crown so we got in touch with a house agent. There was a house near Newbury on his books and I told the Chief Constable I must see it. He sent me in a motor with two policemen, and on the way over I stopped at Faringdon for luncheon. I was in the seventh heaven, to visit the charming house once more and eat Gerald's delicious food and listen to his jokes was like being transported back in time to happy days before the war. As he saw me off with my two policemen sitting in front Gerald said: 'You are the only person who still has a driver *and* a footman on the box.'

The house, Crux Easton, was exactly right and I bought it on the spot. We got our Wootton furniture from store and moved in at once. We bought a cow, Max named her Wellson; from then on we lived well and she gave us butter and milk and cream in abundance. In the yard there was a gardener's cottage with a crowd of children; they became bosom friends with

Alexander and Max and in a matter of days had taught them every swear word in the calendar. They quickly discovered the electric effect these words had upon Nanny and they used them freely. Our new detective, Mr. Buswell, a nice and helpful man, told us one day: 'The boys always say here comes that battleship Buswell when they see me.' Fortunately he had not understood, owing to the Berkshire accent they already affected, that what they were calling him was bugger-shit.

Tom was home again from the Middle East and he spent the summer of 1944 at the Staff College. He came to us nearly every week-end; we were intensely happy to see one another. He asked the little boys about the words Nanny forbade them to use. Max, now aged four, told him:

'Nanny doesn't like sod. Or bugger. Or yourn.'

'*Yawn?*' said Tom. 'Why, what's wrong with yawn?'

'She doesn't *like* it. She doesn't like it when we say One o' yourn.'

Randolph telephoned to ask if he could come down but we said no. He complained loudly to Nancy: 'Why can't I see them if Berners can?' M. said that as long as he was forbidden to see his political friends, some of whom were still in gaol, he refused to see political opponents. Although Randolph fought many elections he never got into Parliament except during the war when he was given a seat under the party truce. The reason always advanced for his failure to be elected was that he was rude to one and all. In the many years I knew him, Randolph was never rude to me, or to M. whose qualities he admired. He was often tiresomely argumentative, but always affectionate and even flattering.

Crux Easton was a delightful old house, it faced south with an immense view over Berkshire and Hampshire. The garden was stocked with fruit and we gave the gardener seeds for every vegetable under the sun; food had almost disappeared from the shops by the summer of 1944. This gardener could not be called up for war work because he had flat feet, he shuffled slowly along and managed fairly well. One morning M. was chatting to me in my bedroom and said: 'I must go now and chase up Cleverley.' Alexander, who was having his reading lesson, became very agitated and his eyes were huge and anxious.

'Please don't let Dad chase Mr. Cleverley,' he said. 'You see, poor Mr. Cleverley can't run.' I explained that M. only meant that he wanted to find Cleverley and tell him something about the pea-beans.

I taught both boys to read, write and do simple sums. They were very quick and learnt in no time. Apart from swear words they knew no slang. Alexander told me of his great friend in the cottage: 'Bernard has got a kid coming to stay. I asked him where he was going to put it, and he's going to be allowed to have it *in his room*!'

'Are you sure it's not another little boy?'

'Oh, quite sure. He said a kid.'

Gerald came over to stay with us at Crux Easton. I managed to buy a lobster in Newbury. With Wellson's cream and some brandy it was going to be a treat. Gerald was with me in the kitchen, chatting while I prepared. I went up to change, and told him to watch the clock and at ten past eight to take the lobster out of the oven. At ten past eight I heard agonized screams coming from the direction of the kitchen and flew downstairs. Poor Gerald had used one of those cloths made of knitted string, he was terribly burnt but had bravely not dropped the dish. It spoilt the evening, huge blisters appeared on his hands.

'Martyrs went to the stake for their faith,' said Gerald, 'and I went to the stake for Diana's lobster.'

During the war our first gaoler, Sir John Anderson, had married Ava Wigram, who had a comfortable little house in Lord North Street and an excellent cook. According to Gerald a friend called to congratulate: 'Oh, Ava, what thrilling news! Was it the coup de foudre?' Ava replied crossly: 'Nothing *whatever* to do with food.' Gerald loved this story which he had doubtless invented, and he gave his sneeze-like laugh.

Among our guests were Debo's babies aged two and one. I loved them and their presence partly compensated me for my loss, all the years when Alexander and Max had been babies. When Diddy, their nurse, said 'Emma has got a crush on her Aunt Honks' I was as pleased and proud as possible.

All my sisters came to stay at Crux Easton, and Muv and Viv and Micky. Nicky was with his regiment in Italy; he won the M.C. which delighted us.

The quaint notion expressed by Cousin Clementine to Muv, that if we were set free we should have a bad time from our fellow-citizens, was proved to be the purest fantasy. The reason is not far to seek. For seven years before the war M. had made speeches up and down the country; in all, he had been heard by several million people. It was impossible for them to believe that M., with his impassioned advocacy of 'greater Britain' and 'Britain awake!' and parity of armaments, could suddenly have turned into a traitor who desired the defeat of his country, or that if it was defeated he would be prepared to collaborate with its conqueror. It was just too unlikely, and they did not believe it, despite the fact that we had been held silent in gaol for many years.

The Churchills lived in a world of their own. They believed that Churchill would win the election to be held the moment the war ended, thus paralleling Lloyd George's massive win at the end of the first war. In 1944 Stalin was still Uncle Joe (a nickname which, when he heard of it, enraged him), the great statesman of whom Churchill said, toasting him at one of their banquets: 'It is no exaggeration or compliment of a florid kind when I say that we regard Marshall Stalin's life as most precious to the hopes and hearts of us all,' and again, 'We feel we have a friend whom we can trust.'

At the Yalta conference Poland, as usual, was on the agenda, and Churchill announced: 'Honour was the sole reason why we had drawn the sword to help Poland against Hitler's brutal onslaught, and we could never accept any settlement which did not leave her free, independent and sovereign.' It goes without saying that neither Stalin nor Roosevelt paid the smallest attention to Mr. Churchill's hopes, or his heart, or his honour. It slowly dawned upon him—a painful, tardy awakening—that Stalin's aims were incompatible with our own, which had to include freedom for Poland, the ostensible reason why we had gone to war in the first place. At this time communism was fashionable; once at Crux Easton somebody came with a collecting box and was met by Muv who was staying with us. 'Mrs. Churchill's fund for *what*?' I heard her ask; she was already getting deaf.

'For China.'

'Oh no,' said Muv. 'China's *too big*.'

In November 1944 Walter Moyne, who was Minister of State in Cairo, was murdered by Jewish terrorists. The assassins were executed. Thirty years later their remains were taken to Israel and given a state funeral attended by the Israeli cabinet and a deputation from the United Nations, which demonstrates once again that one man's terrorist is another man's freedom fighter, though this hardly explains why the United Nations joined in the Israeli beano.

Lord Moyne was a very charming and an exceptionally brave man. Either he hardly knew what fear meant, or, more likely, for he was clever and sensitive, he willed himself to ignore it. Anthony Eden, in his book about the first war, *Another World*, describes walking down a road with him; about 200 yards ahead the Germans were shelling heavily. 'We continued to walk, Walter to expound and I to listen . . . Walter made no sign, but I could bear it no longer and stopped in my tracks with the comment: "I don't know, Walter, whether you intend walking into that barrage, but I am against it," ' and Walter fell in with a suggestion that they should go round another way. Raymond Greene once told me that out hunting Walter's courage amounted to rashness. I was very sorry that my elder sons, just getting to the age when they could have appreciated him, were never to know their clever grandfather.

The war was now going entirely in the Allies' favour, and the English and Americans had landed in Normandy. It was the beginning of the end. Tom decided that the imminent invasion of Germany was something he would prefer not to take part in; we often spoke of it. He volunteered for the Far East and after Christmas he was sent to Burma. Rather unexpectedly, he loved soldiering, and he said he would stay in the army after the war.

In March 1945 a telegram came to say Tom was wounded. I knew instantly that he had died, and so it proved. Near in age, we had always been more like twins than brother and sister. A day never passes when I do not think of him and mourn my loss. He was clever, wise and beautiful; he loved women, and music, and his family.

M. telephoned the Home Office to get permission for me to go to London, for we were still living under house arrest. I should have gone whether it was given or not. Muv, Farve and Nancy were at the Mews; we consoled each other as best we could, but Muv was never comforted. For our generation the losses were heavy; four of our first cousins, Debo's brother-in-law, Decca's husband, had all been killed; and now Tom.

The end of the war came with the Americans encouraging the Russians to march ever further west until they occupied half Europe. The Americans dropped their two atom bombs on Japan. Churchill, according to the newspapers' myth had 'won' the war, but he was defeated in the General Election; this was a surprise to no one who took an interest in politics, though it undoubtedly amazed him and his cronies who had come to believe that he was the most popular man in England, the indispensable man.

Everything turned out according to M.'s predictions. He had always said that if outside powers were drawn into Europe's quarrels they would end the war paramount in our continent. England counted for nothing at Yalta or at Potsdam. Russia, with the complaisance of ignorant America, drew new frontiers. The cruelties and persecutions of which every European must feel deeply ashamed did not end with the war.

With the enthusiastic connivance of America the British Empire began to be liquidated as M. had also predicted. Not only was half Europe occupied by Russia and subjected to compulsory communism but England was gradually shrunk from a great power to its present little measure. True, it has been badly governed for half a century; but the biggest single factor in its decline was the last war.

Early in 1945 M. had a letter from Osbert Sitwell, who wrote:

'To have been deprived, as you have been, of a period of time, is beyond bearing. The only comfort for you must be, that it is impossible to blame *you* for anything that happened in those years.'

Surveying the disasters, great and small, I knew that Osbert was right. It was a comfort, albeit a cold one.

For me the chief tragedy of the war was the loss of Tom and Unity, hers on the first day, his almost the last. They were closer to me in age and in every other way than anyone else in our family at that time. Most of my friends in Germany were dead, including Magda Goebbels and all her children except Harald. That the politicians who had lost the war should take their own lives seemed to me inevitable; as Voltaire says:

Quand on a tout perdu, que l'on a plus d'éspoir
La vie est une opprobre et la mort un devoir.

It was only later when I saw how the living were treated by the Allies that I came to realize that Magda had also been right in her resolve to die with her children.

The Nuremberg trials I shall not comment upon. Everything I think about them was perfectly expressed by M. in *The Alternative*. The great and unforgivable crime of the German leaders was the killing of helpless prisoners. It may be thought that Britain's leaders committed a comparable crime by driving a million Cossacks, men, women and children to be murdered by the Russians, having first induced the men to lay down their arms by lying to them. This crime only recently came to light when Solzhenitsyn wrote of it in *Gulag*. It goes without saying that apart from the politicians who gave the orders, and the unfortunates who obeyed them, nobody in Germany or in Britain knew anything about what was happening.

At the time of the trials I was surprised that the Allies should not have thrown in a few war-crimes of their own, in order to make the whole thing seem more like even-handed justice and less an isolated act of vengeance. The Russians would not have participated, but one would have thought Anglo-Saxon hypocrisy could hardly stretch as far as it did. Bernard Shaw, writing about the trials of Nurse Cavell and Sir Roger Casement in the first war, said that for them to *seem* fair it would have been necessary to have neutral judges. However true, this is not practical politics.

Cruelty and violence and tragedy, all are inseparable from war. Men who wage war give cruel orders which are executed with violence and provoke tragedy. This applies to them all, Hitler, Stalin, Roosevelt and even Churchill in so far as he had the power. It was the same further down the scale. Prof. Lindemann with his memorandum advocating the bombing of working-class districts as more disruptive to the German war effort than the bombing of 'military objectives' achieved a ghastly result in which countless thousands of men, women and children were burned to death in Dresden, Hamburg and elsewhere. No wonder Prof.'s memorandum 'gained him a reputation of ruthlessness'.*

* Roy Harrod, *The Prof.*

19

Crowood

M., WHO SAW that food shortages would continue for a long time, decided the most useful thing he could do for the present would be to farm. As Crux Easton had only eight acres he bought Crowood. With its usual senseless spite the Home Office refused us permission to go over and see it, we therefore bought it unseen. There were several hundred acres in hand.

With the end of the war Regulation 18B was lifted at once, we got hold of our car and drove to see Crowood. We had to move there. It was not practical to farm it from Crux Easton so we packed up and left, with Wellson, and our books, and the people we had gathered round us. I was sorry to go, but everyone except me preferred Crowood. We were to live there for five and a half years, and it was there M. wrote his books *My Answer* and *The Alternative*.

Harassment of various kinds by no means ended with the war. Things were always more difficult for us than for other people; it was harder to get paper, or a printer. We set up a publishing house, Euphorion Books, and published a few classics that were unobtainable at that time; in this way M.'s books could appear in a 'list' along with Virgil's *Georgics*, a couple of short Balzac novels and Webster's *Duchess of Malfi* and *The White Devil*. M. wrote a preface to *Faust*, and for Goethe's bicentenary we published it with an old, not too inadequate translation. I fully realized that *Faust* is untranslatable, and that anyone who is interested in Goethe's ideas must take the trouble to learn German. His novels are another matter. *Werther* is quite easy to translate, and as everyone knows Napoleon took it with him on his campaigns. But *Die Wahlverwandtschaften*, a perfect book, one of the novels I have lived in, is unavailable in English. I boldly decided to have a shot at it myself; we put it in the Euphorion autumn list. The total orders amounted to three copies; I therefore abandoned the idea. I already had cold feet and a strong feeling of inadequacy faced with this masterpiece. Goethe is simply a name to nearly all English people, and even those who know German prefer Thomas Mann, a sort of Galsworthy (one can readily imagine a *Buddenbrooks Saga* on television), while Goethe is neglected.

Goethe tells in his memoirs, *Dichtung und Wahrheit*, that the French officers who were billeted in his parents' house in Frankfurt during the Seven Years' War used to take him to the Comédie Française, which had taken over a theatre to entertain the troops. The whole of the eighteenth century is in this episode; compared with our own time the change has been notable. First there is the difference between the Comédie Française and Ensa, Racine and Corneille in place of Joyce Grenfell and Vera Lynn. Then when the war was over, if one transposes to the Second World War, Goethe's parents would most likely have been accused of wicked collaboration if their boy had been taken by German officers in Paris to hear Weber or Mozart or Wagner sung in German. Yet the importance of what happened cannot be overrated; it awoke in Goethe, who was seven when the war began and fourteen when it ended, his passion for the theatre, and for the theatre as a civilizing influence, in which he believed all his life.

I visited Frankfurt for the first time in 1974 for the Book Fair when M.'s book *My Life* was published in German. (M. made a splendid speech about his European ideas, speaking to a large and crowded hall, in German, without a note, on the same occasion.) I went to see Goethe's old home, which has been lovingly reconstructed since the bombs. A thousand details from *Dichtung und Wahrheit* came into my mind in that house. Who can be certain that we do not owe *Faust* to those French officers? Goethe was always torn between science and art, and devoted an enormous amount of his time to his Farbenlehre (theory of the colours of the spectrum) and his idea of the Urpflanze, the sort of Adam and Eve of all vegetation.

Nancy translated *La Princesse de Clèves* for Euphorion Books and wrote a long preface, and we published Desmond

Stewart's first novel, *Leopard in the Grass*. The greatest success Euphorion had was with Hans-Ulrich Rudel's *Stuka Pilot*. Rudel had performed extraordinary feats with his dive-bomber. He had destroyed more than five hundred Russian tanks, and he had sunk the Russian battleship *Marat*. Having won all the medals for gallantry a special medal was invented of which he was the unique possessor. Rudel was admired for his skill and bravery by airmen of every country; our edition of *Stuka Pilot* had a foreword by the English hero Douglas Bader, and the French had a preface by Pierre Clostermann.

M. had his secretaries at Crowood; he was very busy with his writing and the farm. But naturally his chief concern was politics. The day the war ended he said the future of England lay in Europe, united Europe, it must become a great power to match America and Russia. His pre-war vision of a powerful and prosperous British Empire having been thrown to the winds by the politicians, the new vision must take its place.

Ramsbury and the other villages near Crowood were picturesque and country neighbours abounded, but owing to our circumstances we were completely immune from this pest of country life. We had our friends—Gerald at Faringdon, Daisy Fellowes at Donnington, the Betjemans at Wantage. Gerald and Daisy had guests every week-end and there was constant coming and going. Daisy, the daughter of a French duke and an American mother, had bought Donnington at the end of the war. It was a lovely eighteenth-century gothic house; she made it luxuriously comfortable and very pretty. There were strict rules about how much one was allowed to spend on decorating a house.

'Daisy has been so clever with her £10,' said Gerald. She even had a cinema in the basement for Monsieur, as she called Reggie Fellowes, who was in a bath chair and unable to dash about as she did.

At the end of the war and for a couple of years afterwards Duff Cooper was British Ambassador in Paris. It was a time when austerity was only tempered by black market, and the embassy must have been an oasis of comfort and fun where friends met and life seemed to have gone back to normal. The moment came when Duff Cooper retired; he and his beautiful wife went away to live at Chantilly and their place in the Faubourg St. Honoré was taken by a duller pair called Harvey. A pro-Cooper faction, of which Nancy was a keen member, never tired of contrasting the brilliant yesterday with the drear today. Daisy, although she was a great friend of both Coopers, evidently thought all this had gone far enough; in any case it gave her an opportunity to tease. One night at Donnington when she had several Paris friends staying and we were dining, she exploded her little bomb. 'Moi, je trouve que Maudie Harvey est une femme *délicieuse*.' Nobody spoke. Daisy fixed Christian Bérard with a beady eye. 'N'est-ce pas, Bébé? Elle est charmante?' Bébé wriggled and breathed loudly into his beard. 'Oui, oui. Tout à fait charmante,' he said. I could not resist describing this scene in my next letter to Nancy. She was incensed by Daisy's appalling disloyalty. She reproached Bébé, who was by way of being strongly pro-Cooper. 'Ah!' he said sadly, 'c'est que vous ne connaissez pas le coté punitif de Daisy!'

Not only at Faringdon and Donnington was the company scintillating and the food delicious, we ourselves had a wonderful cook who stayed with us the whole five years we were at Crowood and then went to Debo for another five. Perhaps I speak too often about food in these memoirs of my past life; my excuse is that for so long I was deprived of the joy of 'eating anything savoury' as Churchill put it. Ages ago, Eddie Marsh had told me that he and Winston found themselves in a very poor district of Liverpool, and that Winston, looking around at the misery, had said: 'Imagine how terrible it would be, never to see anything beautiful, never to eat anything savoury, never to say anything clever.' These words often came back to me when I was in gaol. Prison is a slum from which there is no escape. One cannot, as even the poorest Londoner can, walk on grass in a park, visit a picture gallery, wander by the river, feast the eyes upon the Jones collection at the Victoria and Albert, read in a public library, or worship the scent of lilacs and roses with the sun on them. The best things in life are free, but they are not available to a prisoner.

As to saying anything clever, there is nothing intrinsically impossible about that whatever one's circumstances, but there is no doubt that wit and good talk flourish best at a good table. Gerald provided all these joys, so did Daisy and her guests, and so, I think, did we at Crowood.

The boys were growing up; on Saturdays Max often left Nanny and went to Swindon to watch football. He was a fan of Swindon Town. One day he came back very silent and glum. He had taken his autograph album hoping for the signature of his hero, Tommy Lawton, but had not been able to get near enough to ask. Bob Boothby was staying with us and good naturedly suggested that he might sign the book. 'I'm very well known,' he said. M. also offered to sign, saying: 'I'm famous. Surely Tommy Mosley is just as good as Tommy Lawton?' Max gave them a withering glance as he put his autograph book in a drawer. 'No thank you,' he said.

At the end of the war Nancy wrote her first really successful novel, *The Pursuit of Love*. She gave it to me to read in typescript and I knew at once that it would be a best-seller. It was romantic and sad but wonderfully funny, all Nancy's comic genius is in that book and its successor, *Love in a Cold Climate*. She made Farve into one of the great comic characters of fiction, Uncle Matthew. Soon after *The Pursuit of Love* came out, when Nancy was still working at Heywood Hill's bookshop, one of her regular customers, an old Jew from eastern Europe, came to tell her how much he had enjoyed it:

'Onkel Matthew!' he cried. ''E eez my father!'

Nancy told Evelyn Waugh of this unexpected compliment, and Evelyn said: 'Yes, Uncle Matthew is *everyone's* father.' Farve himself liked being Uncle Matthew, he even went so far as to read the book.

Now that she had made some money Nancy had left the bookshop and gone to live in Paris. In France she was both happy and successful; all her books were best-sellers. Her life had taken a wonderful turn for the better, as she richly deserved that it should. Her cleverness and wit were rewarded financially as well as by the devotion of her friends. She often came to stay at Crowood, dressed by Dior, the glass of fashion. At a meet of the local hounds we heard a little girl say: 'Look! There's a lady come out in her dressing-gown!'; so long and voluminous did the new clothes seem after years of wartime parsimony.

In 1945 Nancy told everyone she had voted Labour. When the result of the election was declared, belatedly because of the soldiers' votes, some of Nancy's friends pretended to think that she, alone and unaided, had brought socialism to Britain. Osbert Sitwell ran into the bookshop and seized the till crying 'Labour has begun!' as he carried it into the street.

When Nancy left Blighty, as she called it, for Paris, Evelyn Waugh felt betrayed. Not content with voting socialist, he complained, she had left him to live with the fruit of her folly.

The Betjemans were not very far from Crowood. Gerald Berners was devoted to them, and it is John Betjeman who has best described him, choosing exactly the right things to say, so that those who never knew him can get some idea of this original, gifted, charming man, and understand why he was so beloved by his friends. This is not at all easy, for some reason; his personality is curiously elusive.

Penelope Betjeman organized a mystery play in her village church for which Gerald composed the music; he played the organ during the performance. I asked him about it afterwards, he said it had been a great success. 'Penelope in her nightgown was God the Father and she chased the children out of the church.'

'*Out* of the church?'

'Yes. You see they were Adam and Eve, and the church was the garden of Eden,' said Gerald.

Farve practically lived at Inch Kenneth during the war; he and Muv now preferred to live apart. During the war Unity was not allowed to go to the island which was in a defence area, but as soon as restrictions were lifted she and Muv went back there in the summer. Farve, who had become accustomed to being on his own, left for his cottage at Redesdale where he lived for the rest of his days.

As the years went by Unity had reached a certain degree of recovery which was no doubt the maximum possible given the brain damage she had suffered. She was able to drive her car again, and she travelled about and visited friends and sisters. She was apt to forget things; one day on the boat to Oban she found she had left her bag and tickets behind at Inch Kenneth. She went up to the first man she saw and asked him for £10 which he immediately gave her. When she arrived in London she had already lost the address of her benefactor; Muv managed with difficulty to discover him and repay.

Her great amusement during those years was to go from one Christian sect to another, from church to chapel, striking up acquaintances among Catholic priests, Protestant clergymen, Christian Science Readers and so forth, half promising her adherence to each and every one in turn. She never quite settled which to prefer above all others, probably because she knew she could not resist the temptation of change and variety. I am not suggesting that the clergy she frequented were proselytisers who hoped to convert; on the contrary she was doubtless rather a time-waster for them. They were generally patient and often kind. If one asked which she was favouring at the moment she laughed, but it was only half a joke. She was genuinely seeking something or other.

In the spring of 1948 I went with her and Muv to see them off at the station on the night train for Scotland. Unity would have preferred to stay in London; her hobbies were the cinema and church-going and neither was available on the island. Inch Kenneth must have been very dull for her.

I was never to see her again. A few weeks later the old wound in her head began to hurt terribly. Poor Muv took her on a nightmare journey to Oban hospital. She could never bear to speak of it, ever. She telephoned me at Crowood and told me on no account to come, it was too late, Unity was unconscious. An hour or two later she died.

Muv and my sisters all came to Crowood and from there, on one of those brilliant days which mock sorrow, we went to Swinbrook for Unity's funeral. It was the saddest day of my life. Brave, original and beloved, she had died by her own hand when England declared war on Germany. Great skill and devoted care had inexorably brought her back to life after many weeks, but only to a half-life. She certainly had happy moments, but the main-spring was broken.

After the first grief I think Muv felt a profound relief. Her agonizing worry had always been the thought that when she died there would be nobody to look after Unity. We often spoke of it, and however much I said we would all share it she felt she alone was the right person. Unity had the qualities Muv most admired: fearlessness, generosity, independence, a total absence of deviousness. She was perhaps my mother's favourite child. 'Say not the struggle nought availeth' were the words she had carved on the tomb.

A few weeks later M.'s mother died. She had often stayed with us at Crowood and for her last years she too had lived in the country, near her son John in Norfolk. Thus for both M. and me the summer of 1948 was a time of mourning.

20

Alianora

HAVING BEEN INCARCERATED for so long we craved the
Mediterranean, the feel of hot sun, the taste of French food
and a sight of Paris. A spiteful Labour government refused
us passports. We applied over and over again, always with
the same result. In its little way the Labour government
was just as determined to keep us in England as East Germany
is to keep its citizens behind the Berlin wall, or as Soviet
Russia is to prevent the Jews from leaving. Not allowing
free travel is one of the typical features of socialism everywhere.

M. wrote to Brendan Bracken, who replied that the Tories
would give us passports when they got back; but in 1947
we could look forward to several years more of Mr. Attlee and
his colleagues. An old friend, Hugh Sherwood, raised the
matter for us in the House of Lords. Jowitt, the Lord Chancellor,
reminded the House that we had never been charged with any
offence, let alone convicted of one. Nevertheless the passports
were refused.

Daisy Fellowes wrote offering to lend us Les Zoraïdes,
her villa on Cap Martin, but we could not accept this kind
invitation. Daisy herself often went to the south of France
and when she was there she sometimes saw Churchill, who
was Reggie Fellowes's cousin and who stayed with his pub-
lisher near Monte Carlo. Apparently one day they were
talking about me and Churchill said bitterly: 'During the war
Diana said I ought to be shot.' Daisy told me this; at first I
denied it, then I remembered my outburst to Mr. Hickson the
solicitor when everything in the prison had broken down and
I was cold and grimy and there was no water and the lavatories
were choked and we were locked in with all this so that our
circumstances were unbelievably foul. It all came back to me.
Yes, I had said it.

Daisy begged me to write to Churchill. She was so insistent that I did so. No sooner had I posted the letter than I regretted it. However a few days later I got a telegram thanking me signed Winston, and then a letter. Fatal as I thought Churchill the politician had been for our country I never ceased to feel something approaching love for Churchill the man. How admirable, for example, was his loyalty to some of his children however eccentric their behaviour and however distressing to him the publicity inevitably surrounding it. He had a great heart.

We spent the month of August 1947 with Muv at Inch Kenneth. We, and my four boys and Nanny, our cook and his wife and two children, she welcomed us all. It chanced to be a hot summer and we even swam in the cold Scotch sea. After dinner it was still day and we used to climb up the Humpies to a height from which, seated on the short and scented grass, one could look out to a sea bathed in the yellow light of sunset upon which floated the other islands of the Inner Hebrides. They seemed to hang between sea and sky. In such weather the Hebrides are beautiful as the Aegean islands, but it seldom lasts and most of the time, clad in oilskins and gumboots, one is battling against wind and driving rain.

The following summer we bought a motor boat and went to the Channel Islands. We made various small journeys in the boat; Daisy stayed with us on board, and Robert Heber-Percy, and Muv, at various times.

M. had an idea. He discovered that under Magna Carta a British subject has the right in peacetime to leave his country at will and return to it at will. Nobody has the power to stop him, it is a right enshrined in ancient law; it has nothing to do with the rather absurd Atlantic Charter cooked up by Churchill and Roosevelt. Despite this right, however, no aeroplane or ship will carry you away from the British Isles unless you have a passport issued by the Foreign Office. As all the world knows, the Foreign Office at that time harboured a nest of communists, some of whom were Soviet agents: Maclean, Burgess and Philby among them.

The only answer to our dilemma was to buy a boat of our own and simply sail away. M. bought a sixty-ton ketch, the *Alianora*, whose owner had built her to withstand the storms

of the Atlantic west of Ireland. He engaged a skipper and
an engineer and explained our circumstances to them, that we
should have to slip away quietly. He sent a man to Portugal
and Spain to ask whether we should be allowed ashore if we
arrived with no passports, and the Portuguese and Spaniards
said certainly we could come. We stocked the yacht with
tinned food and supplies, and prepared to set forth in the
early summer of 1949.

A few days before we were due to sail the Foreign Office
suddenly told our solicitor, Mr. Lane, that we could have
passports after all. We had made no secret of our plans, and
presumably the politicians had been informed by their lawyers
that we were fully entitled to make fools of them in this way
and frustrate their knavish tricks. We were delighted to have
the passports, denied us for four years after the war ended,
because now we could land anywhere we wished.

We set sail in June, with Alexander and Max, aged ten
and nine; Max, who had just had his tonsils out, looked white
and ill. Unlike Muv, I am no sailor and rather hate being
at sea; our journey was rough to begin with. After the rigours
of the Bay of Biscay we turned into the calm estuary of the
Gironde, and guided by a pilot, for there were wrecks here
and there left over from the war, we sat on deck gazing at
the historic vineyards which have given so much innocent
pleasure to mankind in general and the English in particular.

Bordeaux is a delightful city of noble aspect and with
some of the best restaurants in France. It was a disappointment that the boys did not enjoy the fare. The only compliment
from either of them was when Max said at the end of a superb
dinner: 'This plain ice is almost as good as them I gets down
the village.' He spoke with purest Wiltshire accent.

As to M. and me, our happiness was boundless. A boat of
one's own gives an intense feeling of complete freedom provided by no other form of travel. We were in our beloved
France surrounded by every possible beauty and perfection;
the sun shone; we were on our way to the Mediterranean.
Our next port of call was Corunna, then Lisbon. We hoisted
our sails and stopped the engines. A following wind sent us
rushing silently through the sea: a new sensation; the ship
seemed to come alive.

The yacht basin at Lisbon is unique, just near the monastery and great church of Belem. As at Bordeaux we lived on board and spent our days sight-seeing ashore. We went over to Estoril for a swim; there were severe rules about bathing clothes. As M. only possessed pants, which were forbidden, I walked into the sea with him and whisked away his dressing-gown as he slipped into the water. That evening we dined with Portuguese friends and I asked what would have happened if he had been caught bathing topless by the beach guards. Their reply made my blood run cold: 'Une forte amende.' We were very short of foreign currency; I cannot remember how much one was allowed that year, but in any case a heavy fine at Estoril would have been a body blow.

Outside Tangier we ran into a wild storm. We were all sea-sick except Alexander. I could hear him, when for an instant there was a lull, pattering about over my head on deck. I dragged myself out of bed and managed to warn him to look out for himself. Waves were breaking over the deck and if he was swept overboard he could never be picked up in the dark in such a rough sea. He reassured me; he was strong and agile. He was as happy in the storm as the rest of us were miserable.

In Tangier harbour the wind still blew and the boat danced about; there is no shelter and it is easy to understand that when Catherine of Braganza brought Tangier to England as part of her dowry English sailors valued it lightly. Gibraltar is a very different matter; deep and calm. In Gibraltar there were some repairs to be done after the storm. It is a dreary place, and the food in the restaurants of the strong tea and Brown Windsor variety. M. and I took a train to Madrid.

We were received with the utmost kindness by Serrano Suñer and his beautiful wife Zita. Madrid was baking hot and one night they gave a dinner for us in the country, up in the hills. On the way we stopped at the Escurial; our host had the church opened. The menacing gloom of Philip II's edifice was enhanced by the mysterious darkness as we stood by the grave of José Antonio.

Spanish hours are so late that by the time we got back to Madrid it was past three. To my astonishment children were playing in the street near our hotel. 'Their parents let them out because it is the coolest hour,' we were told.

I had never been to Madrid before and was therefore seeing the Prado in all its glorious splendour for the first time in my life. I decided to go back there as soon as I possibly could, and I have often been since to see our Spanish friends, and eat at Horcher's superb restaurant, and re-visit the Prado.

We found *Alianora* and the boys once more at Formentor in Majorca. The coast, the silvery sand on the beaches, and the rich, fertile interior made the place in those days a paradise on earth. I have no desire to see this island smothered in villas and hotels, preferring the memory of what it was.

After a week we sailed away, this time for France. We landed at Cassis. Nancy was staying with the Tvedes at Monredon; she and Mogens came to greet us. Mogens's wife Dolly was dreadfully worried because Nancy had told her that every communist in nearby Marseilles would be on the alert for our arrival, and that if it became known that we had been so much as to tea with her the cottage would instantly be burnt down. Nancy's love of teasing had not diminished with the years, and she had every reason to be pleased by the effect she produced upon her hostess. She told me with delighted shrieks how she had succeeded in frightening the unfortunate Dolly.

However Dolly bravely invited us, and we had a swim from the rather dirty beach the other side of the main Marseilles road. At the cottage Nancy had got some tree frogs in a glass box, she fed them with mosquitoes. At night the mosquitoes avenged the death of their fellows by stinging. D.D.T. had been invented and every evening after dinner, according to Mogens, Nancy said: 'Spray Mogens, spray!' and he sprayed the bedrooms. We used similar sprays in our cabins, but the smell was so foul that I preferred the mosquitoes.

Nancy was completely happy with the Tvedes at Monredon. She never noticed the busy main road or the paper blowing about on the stony beach; she was living in a flowery meadow by the blue sea. Such was the power of her imagination, of which numerous other examples could be cited.

Mogens also loved Monredon, but when Daisy Fellowes appeared in *Sister Anne* he could not resist her invitation to come on board. She had kept her promise to us, that wherever we landed in France she would come along the coast in her yacht and greet us. Unlike Dolly, one felt she half hoped there would be trouble of some sort; there was nothing she enjoyed more than a row, or a situation fraught with difficulty and risk. As *Alianora* followed *Sister Anne* from port to port along the Riviera and all was peace and joy Daisy may have been slightly disappointed. Later on, as will be seen, she found a way to ginger things up.

Alexander and Max left us to spend the rest of the summer at Inch Kenneth. I begged them not to fight too much, as it worried their grandmother. Alexander said firmly: 'Granny Muv is so lovely and *deaf* she never knows whether we are fighting or not.' Both boys looked splendidly well and strong after their weeks at sea as I saw them off on the train.

Nancy stayed with us for a while on *Alianora*, and after her Hugh Cruddas, a perfect guest. The only fly in the ointment was our English crew. It turned out that they hated the 'Med' as they called it; they felt much too hot and never seemed to enjoy a swim or indeed anything else. One heard them grumbling quietly on deck just above the cabins; their grumbles drifted in through the open port holes. Nancy heard one say: 'If only we were at Burnham on Crouch!'

Most of the time we were at Antibes or Monte Carlo, ideal harbours for yachts. The coast was noisy and crowded, but nothing like the sea-slum it was subsequently to become. Such is the man-made pollution that the Mediterranean is now said to have lost its sparkle, but in those days it sparkled brilliantly.

One evening Hugh, M. and I were sitting in a small restaurant in Cannes when a figure from the past, Brian Howard, appeared. He was accompanied by a giant Indian. He immediately spotted us. 'Can we sit with you, my dear?', and to M., 'Of course *you*, my dear, are the wickedest man in the world.' We talked for a while and it became apparent that Brian, formerly wonderfully amusing especially when he was at his most outrageous, had turned into a repetitive bore. He soon rounded on his Indian friend and said: 'As to *you*, my dear, you are nothing but a great big black booby.' Whereupon we thought we had had enough and got up to go. Brian insisted on walking with us to where the boat was moored.

He insulted us all in a fairly genial way, reserving his more
spiteful barbed attacks for the Indian. We were determined
not to let him come on board, and said a firm goodbye. He
went off into the night with his unfortunate companion; I
never saw him again. Hugh told us it was well known that
his rudeness was a deliberate attempt to induce someone to
hit him, but that nobody ever did so because Brian had become
frail and thin and quite unable to hit back.

Daisy had a villa at Cap Martin where we often spent our
days by the sea-water pool, she had bought it years before
from Kenneth Clark's father. In his memoirs Lord Clark
says his father sold Les Zoraïdes to a character out of *Les
Liaisons Dangereuses*, without mentioning Daisy's name.
Gerald, who loved and admired her, also compared her to
Mme de Merteuil. While admitting the partial truth of this
analogy I am bound to say that Daisy was a very good friend
to me and to M. and to all my four boys. She showered kind-
nesses upon us, whether at Donnington, Cap Martin or at
her house in the rue de Lille in Paris. She was a life-enhancer
and she had a real talent, denied to many rich people, for
surrounding herself with beauty and the delights of the senses.
She had a rather false-sounding laugh and her society was not
reposeful; one never knew what she might do next.

When Desmond came to stay with us Daisy suggested we
should all go to St. Tropez, then a mecca of the young. He
quickly transferred himself from *Alianora* to the infinitely
more comfortable *Sister Anne*; Daisy became his heroine. He
was seventeen. One evening at St. Tropez Daisy and Desmond
got themselves up to match. They wore black trousers, she
had a leopard patterned chiffon blouse and he a wisp of the
same chiffon, and round his neck a massive diamond necklace
lent by Daisy. When they appeared thus arrayed at the
restaurant where we were having dinner and began to dance,
there was an angry murmur of intense disapproval from the
French at the other tables. It was not long after a much
publicized robbery of the Begum Aga Khan's jewels and one
man shouted at them, 'A bas la Begum!' The murmur became
quite embarrassing. Mogens and M. tried to look as though
they did not belong to us; Hugh, Emmeline de Castèja and I
wondered how it would end. When Daisy judged she had

caused enough sensation and enough annoyance to us, she left. Desmond escorted her to the yacht and then came back wearing an ordinary white shirt which mollified everyone. Mogens afterwards painted a brilliant little picture of the scene in the restaurant which he gave me and which I treasure. Nowadays it would be no use trying to create a sensation at St. Tropez, or anywhere else for that matter, by dressing in an unorthodox way; fancy dress is the norm. In Daisy, Desmond had found a twin soul. His books and his lectures on Irish and American eighteenth-century architecture have made him a serious reputation but he has never lost a positively Daisy-like predilection for doing the unexpected and giving everyone a surprise; not always a pleasant one. Like her, he does it for his own amusement; it is so to speak art for art's sake.

We realized that Daisy had been angelic for so long that in the very nature of things there was bound to be a reaction. As M. was having his first real holiday for twelve years and was deeply averse to rows in private life we said goodbye and went for a few weeks to Italy accompanied by Hugh.

We stayed for some time in the pretty but noisy little harbour of Portofino where we found several friends, and we went on down the coast to Ostia and Rome.

Back at Antibes, our last guest came, Debo. The summer was almost over and we planned to motor home through France. Once we had left the yacht Debo insisted that we should share expenses, francs being in short supply. The first day of this new régime we went to a delicious but very expensive place where we had an enormous luncheon lasting well into the afternoon. When M. was given the bill Debo snatched it away saying it was her turn. Before the astonished eyes of the waiter, Mademoiselle (as he had called her throughout, for she looked about sixteen in her cotton shorts) pulled huge sums out of her purse. The waiter looked at her, and then at M. 'C'est Monsieur qui a la chance!' he said in admiring tones.

Debo drove us to Paris along the road we knew so well. Eleven years, war, occupation and near-civil war had left no visible traces. The food was wonderful, M. Point of the Pyramide at Vienne still supreme.

When we got to Paris we found Nancy in the charming flat at 7 rue Monsieur which was to be her home for twenty years. She had the ground floor of the eighteenth-century house, between courtyard and garden. Her garden was dark and full of ivy and old trees; green reflections from it made the rooms seem cool and countryfied. The courtyard, where we sat among her pots of geraniums, was sunny on those early October days. Paris seemed almost too good to be true, but we had to go back to an England still gripped in austerity.

Near Crowood there were islands of resistance to the encircling gloom, Donnington and Faringdon among them. At Faringdon I found Gerald far from well. He had a bad heart, a condition which notoriously makes its victims pessimistic and miserable. He often came to stay with us for quite long visits; he liked the change of scene and I loved his companionship.

In the afternoons we used to take carriage exercise, I drove him about the neighbourhood and once far from home we had a puncture. In the back of the car were Jonathan and an Eton friend, Christopher Shuldham. Both boys were in uniform doing their national service. None of us had the slightest idea of how to change a wheel. I made them all hide behind a hedge and finally managed to induce a saintly motorist to stop and do it for me. It took some time, finding the tools and so forth. Just as he was screwing the last of the screws, kneeling in the dirt, he was astonished to see two able-bodied young soldiers and an elderly man in a long black overcoat get silently into the car. My shame was deep; all I could do as I drove away was to call 'Thank you, *thank* you'.

I reproached them all bitterly for not hiding until the saint had gone on his way. There was a long silence, then Christopher said: 'Well, you see, Lord Berners says it's teatime.'

Once when Gerald was staying with us I had to go up to London for the day. When I returned he was on the doorstep. 'What did you do? Who did you see?' He was always avid for news. I said I had lunched with Evelyn Waugh. 'He says he prays for me every day,' I added. Gerald looked quite put out. 'God doesn't pay any attention to Evelyn,' he said crossly.

During the early spring of 1950 he more or less took to

his bed. When he could no longer come to us I constantly went over to Faringdon and tried my best to think of stories to amuse him. Robert Heber-Percy and Hugh Cruddas performed wonders; they kept the house alive and prevented Gerald from falling into too deep a depression.

Mogens Tvede, who had done a charming little painting of Nancy, came over to England and painted Debo at Edensor and me in the Crowood drawing-room. We took him to see Gerald, who was in bed and very depressed. Gerald turned his back on Mogens and simply said: 'Tell me something amusing.' Mogens has never forgotten this difficult moment. 'Oh my God! What can one say? Something *amusing*! My God!'

In April dear Gerald died. I miss him always. He was a perfect friend through thick and thin and we had many a laugh. He had always said he wanted no religious service at his funeral. This is not easy to arrange, but Robert had the minimum of ceremony. One of Gerald's great preoccupations had been to try and make sure Robert could continue to live at Faringdon. He would have been happy to know he is still there a quarter of a century later, and that Faringdon has become if possible lovelier than ever in his imaginative care.

After our four months away we had felt ready to face the winter and the myriad trivial annoyances inseparable from life in England under a Labour government. M. redoubled his political activity, writing and speaking. There were the usual barriers to free speech, but whenever he did get a hall there was always a full house and an enthusiastic audience, in Manchester and Birmingham as well as London. His political ideas of those days are worth studying; everything he predicted then has happened since, though often it took longer than he imagined it would. At each turn of events he advanced a constructive policy, but he was unheeded.

We were still the object of special treatment, and not only with regard to halls for M. to speak in. After a complicated tax case when the verdict was given against him, M.'s counsel said: 'I should have won that case for anyone in the country except you.' Never in the least bitter, because our opinion of our political opponents was not very high and therefore their behaviour caused little surprise, M. nevertheless began to think there was something to be said for living outside England. As he put it, referring to the politicians: 'If you are trying to shift a load of manure you don't start by putting yourself underneath it.' There was no hurry, but he determined to have a look round.

The day the war ended he had said: 'Now we must work for United Europe.' He guessed rightly that the Empire was irrevocably lost as a result of the war; his old dream could never now become reality. For my part, I was entirely in sympathy with his new ideas. The loss of the Empire was a great blow to M. and his supporters, and also to Churchill and many Conservatives. My own predilection had always been for Europe. Beyond any personal consideration M.'s European ideas decided us to leave England and live in France, whence it is easy to travel all over the Continent. He wanted, he said, to become a European, in a way that is hardly possible for somebody living in England. He always kept in close touch with England and innumerable English friends and supporters, speaking at public meetings wherever he could get a hall, and spending almost three months every year there. When the BBC ban was finally lifted in 1968 at the time his autobiography, *My Life*, was published, and a whole Panorama programme with James Mossman was devoted to him, the fact that the 'ratings' showed M. to have had a record audience made it obvious that public interest in him and his ideas was as alive as ever. He was a Cassandra, predicting crisis, which he said was inevitable unless the politicians who had administered our country since the war completely changed their economic policies.

We spent one more summer on board *Alianora*, then we sold the boat. Venice is the place we love best for holidays, and a small yacht is far from the ideal lodging there. *Alianora* had given us freedom of movement; we were now to leave England with all our worldly goods. Only one sister remained there: Debo. Nancy lived in France, Pam in Ireland, Decca in America. Derek and Pam had left Rignell and gone to live at Tullamaine Castle in County Tipperary where Derek hunted with the 'noble Tips'. He had fought with great gallantry in a war he was convinced Britain should never have been engaged in.

Now he did not feel disposed to stay in England while it went downhill under an inefficient Labour government, and be slowly ruined himself in the process. Later on he worked for the French government, in a laboratory near Paris.

Early in 1951 we left Crowood.

21

Le Temple de la Gloire

IN DECEMBER 1950 we were in Paris, and one day, lunching
with Gaston and Bettina Bergery and speaking vaguely about
getting a Paris flat, Bettina said: 'Would you like to live in a
tiny Directoire temple? We know of one, it's for sale.' We
motored down to Orsay and there on a cold, dark and foggy
afternoon we first set eyes upon the Temple de la Gloire.* It
was as shabby as a house can be that has stood empty for many
years; only the small but magnificent shell was unravaged by
damp and neglect. It looked older than its one hundred and
fifty years. For me, it was love at first sight, and the following
March it was ours.

Leaving Crowood was painful. Although less sad for me than
leaving Wootton had been, I minded terribly for the boys,
whose first real home it was. We had to leave all our kind
village friends, among them Mr. Watson, a clever old Scotch
hermit who had taught Alexander, and then both boys, in his
tiny cottage on the hill. He had recently been ill and they now
had a tutor, Mr. Leigh Williams, but Mr. Watson was a wonderful friend to Alexander. Packing up Crowood was a nightmare, partly because M. had used rooms there as an office and
there were myriads of files and old papers as well as relics of
all our former dwellings, Denham and Grosvenor Road and
Wootton. We planned to get a house in Ireland and everything
was sent to Cork; meanwhile the Temple was not yet habitable.
We took a little flat in Paris from Jean de Baglion, who was to
become one of our dearest friends, and from there we supervised
the work at the Temple. In June we moved in. It was the third
time in my life that I had had the luck to live in a beautiful
house, and this time it lasted.

---

* The temple was built in 1800 for General Moreau by his wife and his mother-
in-law, to celebrate his victory at Hohenlinden. These enthusiastic ladies gave it
its rather high-sounding name. The architect was Vignon.

Thus our move to Ireland and our move to France were simultaneous, but the circumstances were not the same. Our furniture arrived in Ireland battered, scratched and broken. Even the heavy marble tops of two large sideboards appear to have been thrown from the ship on to the quay and were shattered. It took months to get everything mended and polished. M. used to say that I wandered through County Galway in search of an ébéniste; it was only too true; I did.

At the Temple on the other hand we had no furniture at all. For months we had to take our chairs with us from drawing-room to dining-room; and we had five forks, which severely limited the number of guests. I haunted the Hôtel Drouot, the Paris salerooms. It is very easy to become a saleroom addict, absorbed by the thrill of bargain-hunting. The old Hôtel Drouot was like Christie's and Sotheby's and Bonhams and salerooms in darkest Fulham and the Caledonian market all rolled into one. It had twelve rooms, in some of which lovely and precious things were sold while in others one found the lowest of the low, degraded rexine chairs with horsehair stuffing falling out of them on the dusty floor, filthy old carpets full of holes, broken and chipped gas stoves. Many, probably most of the crowds of people who came were not buyers at all, but liked the warmth and amusement of the place. I had to be very careful in my purchases because our francs were strictly limited, also the Temple is so small that there is nowhere to put anything inessential.

One saw incredible bargains. A perfectly nice sham Louis XVI canapé in grey painted wood went for twenty francs: in modern money twenty centîmes, that is to say less than the price of the stamp on a letter to England. The auctioneers got very impatient when nobody bid. A monstrous carved and highly coloured group of heavy panels, vaguely Burmese in style, were being propped up by several strong porters for the public to admire but nobody made a move. 'Voyons, voyons,' said the auctioneer; 'combien pour le petit cosy-corner Chinois?' As well as the hôtel des ventes I went to dozens of antique shops hunting for suitable objects for the lovely little Temple, and we also brought favourite possessions from England.

No sooner had we got some chairs and spoons and forks than we began asking friends down to the Temple. Both of us had old friends in Paris from before the war whom we were pleased to find again. The Foreign Office forbade English diplomats to see us; just occasionally when a friend or a relation happened to be en poste in Paris I was sorry about this, but as a rule it mattered not at all, though possibly it resulted in us seeing more French and less English people than, for example, Nancy. She used to complain loudly about the number of our compatriots who, as she put it, ambled into the courtyard of the rue Monsieur wanting to be fed and generally hoping to borrow a few francs for their shopping. She was at their mercy, because she often sat sunning herself among her potted geraniums and one only had to push open the heavy porte cochère in order to discover what Debo called 'the French lady writer'. To escape from importunate countrymen she was obliged to leave rue Monsieur when she was writing a book. She took a room in a pension at Versailles and hid the address from everyone except her great friend Gaston Palewski and me. Between books she earned her living by journalism, writing a column in *The Sunday Times* which often made people apoplectic with rage. Her teases were usually directed towards England, but from time to time even her beloved French were at the receiving end.

For the bicentenary of the birth of Marie Antoinette an exhibition was arranged at Versailles. Beginning with her childhood at Schönbrunn one saw the whole life of the tragic Queen in room after room, through her years of luxury, grandeur, fun and riches to the poverty and suffering in the prisons of the Temple and the Conciergerie and ending with David's cruel drawing of her with her prematurely grey hair cut short as she sat in the tumbril on her way to the guillotine. It brought tears to the eyes.

Nancy chose this moment to publish her deep thoughts about Marie Antoinette. I think what set her off was a letter from Maria Theresa to her daughter when she was Dauphine, in which the Empress enjoins her never for one moment to forget 'que vous êtes Allemande'. That word, *allemande*, was too much for Nancy. She wrote that Marie Antoinette was a traitress to France who tried to persuade her brother and the other German monarchs to invade France on her behalf. There was just enough truth in it to annoy, for the French idolize Marie Antoinette, the martyred queen, in much the same way but multiplied a thousand-fold as the English idolize Mary Queen of Scots.

During the ensuing storm we were lunching one day with Princess Natty de Lucinge. When we arrived she took me aside and whispered: 'I'm afraid I've made a terrible gaffe. Van der Kemp is here!' M. Van der Kemp, curator at Versailles, had arranged the exhibition.

'Does it matter?' I asked.

'Oh yes. Your sister's article,' said Princess Natty.

However, he rose above it, and a few years later Van der Kemp became one of Nancy's great friends; during her illness he used to arrive at her house with armfuls of flowers for her.

A friend we were fond of at that time was the Marquis de Lasteyrie, an old gentleman who was descended from Lafayette and who lived at Lafayette's country house, La Grange. He invited us to tea and raspberries in summer. Although he was very poor he never dreamed of selling any of the priceless documents at La Grange; priceless, because Americans would pay anything for the slightest scratch from the pen of Lafayette. He allowed his guests to look at everything but he himself was unimpressed, and he avoided his famous ancestor as far as possible. When M. de Lasteyrie died and his cousin René de Chambrun inherited La Grange he was astonished at the chaotic way in which these Franco-American treasures were stored and disposed about the house. 'C'est que Monsieur le Marquis n'aimait pas le Marquis,' explained his butler, Delphin.

This dislike was the result of his deep love and veneration for Marie Antoinette. When Lafayette was supposed to be in charge of the safety of the King and Queen at Versailles the mob burst in and killed the Swiss guards. The Queen only escaped by using a secret passage which connected her room with the King's. 'Monsieur de Lafayette dort bien!' she was heard to say.

Once at the Folies Bergères they did a comic sketch in which Louis XVI and Marie Antoinette were made fun of. M. de Lasteyrie heard about it; he bought a ticket and sat in the front row of the stalls. When the rude sketch got under way he stood up and waved his arms shouting in his quavery voice: 'Ce n'est pas vrai! Notre reine Marie Antoinette était une sainte!' There was a moment of shocked silence and then the whole audience began to laugh. There was a sort of riot of laughter. According to Josée de Chambrun, as dear, brave old M. de Lasteyrie left the theatre someone from the management rushed up to him and asked what he would charge to do the same turn every evening.

At the end of the war when the American army arrived in France some American officers were billeted on M. de Lasteyrie at La Grange. One day they asked their host whether he would care to accompany them to Paris, and M. de Lasteyrie, who had been marooned with no petrol for long enough, jumped at the chance. They walked across the Tuileries gardens; he described the scene: 'I told them, this is where the palace of our kings and queens stood.'

'Aw!' said the Americans, 'so this is where the orgies took place.'

'*Orgies!*' said M. de Lasteyrie. 'My dear Sir, I can assure you there were no orgies here. *All* my grandmothers were ladies in waiting to our queens. I can promise you there were no orgies.'

Lunching with us one day M. de Lasteyrie was performing what M. called the ceremonial dance at the dining-room door. Charles de Noailles was there and neither would move, M. de Lasteyrie saying: 'Ah non! Je ne peux pas passer devant M. de Noailles;' whereupon an American boy marched out, showing them the way into the new world of the twentieth century.

During our first months at the Temple Farve came to Paris for a last visit. We showed him the Temple; he loved it, and sent me £500 'to buy a pair of curtains'. Nancy invited M. de Lasteyrie to meet him. There was talk of a recent election and someone asked M. de Lasteyrie whether he was pleased with the result.

'My dear lady,' he replied, 'when it is not the guillotine I am *always* pleased.' Then, turning to Farve, he explained.' You see, my dear Sir, five of my grandmothers died on the guillotine during the revolution.' After he had left, Farve said: 'I liked that old relation of Joan of Arc.'

22

Clonfert

THE SAME YEAR, 1951, as we went to live in France at the Orsay Temple we bought an old house, formerly a bishop's palace, at Clonfert in Co. Galway. It was less than a mile west of the Shannon, a broad river which regularly overflowed its banks in winter causing widespread floods. The name Clonfert means 'an island' in Gaelic, and the house itself was never flooded. It stood in flat country on the edge of the bog. In the garden there were great beech trees and an avenue of age-old yews called the Nun's Walk which had been used by our predecessor for exercising his hunters when there was frost. There was a carpet of needles under the yews that remained soft in even the hardest winter.

It was George McVeagh who told us about Clonfert. He was our Dublin solicitor to whom we had been introduced by Derek and Pam, a delightful man, whose passion was snipe shooting. He often shot over the bog near Clonfert, so he knew it was for sale.

We put in bathrooms and electric light and central heating, and while the work was going on at Clonfert the boys and Mr. Leigh Williams and I stayed with Pam at Tullamaine. The drive over, which I did every day, was never easy. Either there was frost and I slithered on black ice, or else there were deluges of rain; once for a week there was snow. It was lovely to get back after a dreary cold day standing about in rubble to Tullamaine and Pam's delicious dinner. Clonfert Palace was in parts so ancient and its walls were so thick that piercing them for heating pipes was a far harder job than anyone had anticipated. It seemed to take forever. There was hardly a single window of which the sash cord was not broken. The French call sash windows fenêtres guillotines and these really were guillotines; one might very well have been beheaded by a Clonfert window. While Harry Conniffe and his son Paddy put the garden in order I measured the windows for curtains and tried to decide where the electric light points must go. Of all the many houses I have done up in my life the hardest work was Clonfert. Fortunately I could not peer into the future and see how vain our labours were to prove. Our furniture and books had been stored in Cork, and had arrived in very poor shape. We got curtains and covers made in Dublin and by degrees the house became comfortable and pretty. We did not install a telephone; it seemed to us wonderfully peaceful to be without, but we lived to regret it.

The house faced south and just across the lawn was Clonfert Cathedral, a large and ancient church with a curiously-carved Norman west doorway. As is usual in Ireland, this old church was the place of worship of a small handful of Protestants. The vast majority of the people were Catholics and they filled their little modern church to the brim. To any outsider it seemed crazy that of the two sects of Christians it should be the few belonging to the reformed church who made up the tiny congregation in the old cathedral, built centuries before reform was ever dreamed of. Not only few in numbers, they were also lax in attendance compared with the Catholics. They could easily have fitted into a minuscule chapel.

To a newcomer Clonfert did not at first sight give the impression of being a village at all, but in fact there were dozens of people living here and there in well-hidden little old cottages. One realized how numerous they were when they came out of church on a Sunday or a saint's day, or when there was a hunt on the bog.

The East Galway hounds hunted a big country and there were always a couple of meets a week within reach of Clonfert. Max adored hunting. We had brought our Crowood ponies to Ireland and it so happened that Max's pony, Johnny, was a star. He enjoyed hunting every bit as much as did Max himself. When they were standing while a covert was drawn and the huntsman blew 'gone away' on his horn, Johnny in his excitement before galloping off to the first fence would give a great sigh. 'He sounds just like a train when it leaves a station in the Paris metro,' said Max. He could jump fences and walls bigger than himself.

The hunt could never cross the bog, which was treacherous

and dangerous for the horses, therefore sometimes on winter Sundays after church the village men and boys would hunt there on foot. Everyone brought his dog, one saw mongrel, puppy, whelp and hound and curs of low degree just as in Goldsmith's day. One Sunday they were out and Max was feeding Johnny in his stable and just preparing to run off and join the hunt when a man was heard to holla quite near at hand. Max told me: 'There was a great thumping noise; it was Johnny's heart beating.' The pony knew that a holla meant someone had seen the fox and he was dying to be off. As Max ran out of the stable without him he heard Johnny give a furious squeal. The holla at Clonfert also reminded one of how little Ireland had changed since the eighteenth century, for the bog echoed with wild cries of 'Ya-hoo'. Jonathan Swift, 'the great dane' as the Irish call him, had stayed with the Bishop in our house, which was old even in his day. Max thought it must have been here that he conceived his idea of Houyhnhnms and Yahoos.

When we went to Ireland Max was eleven and Alexander twelve. They took their tutor with them; there was no hateful boarding school to interfere with their lives, but Alexander bitterly regretted Crowood and Ramsbury and the old familiar faces. He suffered as we had when we left Asthall, and as Debo had when Farve sold Swinbrook. Like us, he gets deeply attached to places. He never cared for hunting; he buried himself in books. At gymkhanas in the summer he was to be seen kindly holding two horses for Max, the reins hitched over his arms, reading, oblivious of his surroundings.

There is no doubt that round Clonfert the people were exceptionally kind and welcoming. We quickly became very fond of the place. My room looked over the bog, and through the open windows delicious scents wafted in from the sweet smelling wild flowers which covered it in spring, and sounds of curlews, snipe and water-fowl of all kinds. Sometimes one heard the curious dry sound of wild geese flying in formation to Norway or wherever it is they go. At Clonfert I regretted knowing so little about birds.

It was at Clonfert I first realized Muv had got Parkinson's disease. Jean de Baglion was staying with us and he pointed out that when she was reading the paper her hand continually trembled so that the newspaper gave a sort of rhythmic rustle.

Jean's father had died of it and therefore he knew the symptoms. At that stage it did not seem to inconvenience her, and it certainly never stopped her making journeys to visit all of us, even Decca in distant California. She often came to Ireland and to France, and I went every year to Inch Kenneth where she spent her summers.

During these years my elder boys were at Oxford. While he was still an undergraduate Jonathan married beautiful Ingrid Wyndham. Desmond was at Christ Church and it was in Christ Church cathedral that he married a lovely girl, Mariga von Urach. One Sunday a week or two before my forty-second birthday in early June, M. and I were lunching at Groussay with Charlie Beistegui and when we got back to the Temple there was a telegram from Jonathan; my first grand-child, Catherine, was born.

We have always loved Paris at Christmas time, though on the whole we spent our winters in Ireland and our summers in France. Dolly and Mogens Tvede gave a reveillon party one New Year's Eve. Mogens telephoned to say that Randolph had turned up in Paris; was it all right for us all to meet, he asked? I said it was. We had no sooner arrived than Randolph rushed across the room to sit near M. and began quoting passages from M.'s pre-war speeches; they talked half the night about days gone by. He came down to the Temple for luncheon next day and stayed till 7.30 when we were obliged to go to Paris for a dinner. He reminded M. of stories he had told him years before, he talked about Tom, he was at his gentlest and kindest. I was shocked by his appearance; he had become prematurely old, he looked puffy and ill and drank quantities of brandy and whisky hour after hour. We never saw him again, and when he died I regretted not having been to visit him in Suffolk. Occasionally he telephoned, generally at unearthly hours, two or three in the morning. If he was awake himself he saw no reason why anyone else should be asleep.

In London a few years later we sometimes dined with Diana Sandys, who lived in Gerald Road with her beautiful daughters surrounded by her father's cheerful daubs. A good hostess, she seemed happy and amused, but she was often frightfully depressed and on the verge of suicide and finally she killed herself.

Evidently life was too much for her; she lacked robustness, she was quite unlike Randolph and her sisters.

Tom, Randolph, Diana C. and I had been very devoted to one another when we were young, but I remembered with remorse that as children we used to run off and hide from Diana. She would wander about looking for us, singing out of tune. Her favourite ditty, a quite exceptionally irritating song, was 'Yes! We have no bananas.'

After Christmas Max always rushed back to Ireland as soon as he possibly could, and one winter M. let him off lessons altogether so that he could hunt to his heart's content. The tutor had left and Alexander had gone to school at Pontoise. The head master was Father Superior of Oratorians, a teaching order, at St. Martin de France. At first he refused my written request for Alexander to go to his school and I went to see him to ask why. He said: 'I see you are English which changes everything. I cannot take American boys, they are too far behind our boys in their work.' After his winter spent hunting Max went to school in Germany, at Stein an der Traun.

We had only been at Clonfert for two and a half years when a disaster happened. M. and I were in London and about to return to Ireland, but I put off my journey for a day because Farve was coming south and it was a good chance to see him. I dined with him and flew to Dublin next morning. When I got through the customs I was surprised to see M. standing in the crowd, I had not expected him to meet me. As I approached I noticed he was unshaven. He took my hand and said gently: 'Sit down here on this seat. Everything is all right. Nobody is hurt.'

'*Hurt!*' I said, and my heart missed a beat. 'Why, has something terrible happened?'

He told me that in the night there had been a great fire at Clonfert. He and Alexander and two French people we had with us and the horses and dogs were all safe, but most of the house and furniture and pictures had been destroyed. Madeleine, our French cook, had run up to her room on the second floor to fetch something when she was supposed to be sitting out on the lawn, safe. Cut off by the flames, she had had to jump into a blanket held by M. and Alexander. She was bruised but no bones were broken. During the time it took to persuade her to jump the dining-room ceiling fell in; had it not been for her, M. and Alexander could easily have got the pictures out. My bedroom was the very centre of the furnace, nothing remained. All that was found among the cinders on the ground floor beneath were the blackened springs from the mattress of my four-post bed; a pretty bed with slender carved mahogany posts and a canopy of blue taffeta. The dining-room also was completely burnt; it was full of pictures of M.'s forebears, and it had a charming French table of about 1840 inlaid with roses and ribbons, all destroyed.

It had happened in the middle of a bitter December night. M. sent the car to telephone for help, but by the time the fire brigades from Ballinasloe and Birr got to Clonfert it was too late; the damage was done. The firemen were brave and efficient but what saved the west end of the house, the drawing-room and the library, was that the wind changed. The fire began in the chimney of the maids' sitting-room where peat and wood were burnt winter and summer. An old beam in the chimney, dried no doubt by our central heating, had smouldered and finally blazed up, and the whole chimney was found to be coated with a deposit of inflammable tar-like substance, said to be the result of mixing peat and wood on the hearth.

At the back of the house there was a farm; Mrs. Blake Kelly was wakened by the persistent neighing and whinnying of her horses. Reluctant to stir out of bed, for it was bitterly cold, she finally got up, looked out of the window and saw the blaze. She called her son: 'The palace is on fire!' He ran round to the front of the house, he knew where Alexander slept and threw pebbles at his window until he woke up. But for the horses and their terror of flames there might have been a tragedy.

To make matters worse great floods rose so that the Dublin road became impassable and Clonfert was cut off. A few days later when I was able to go and I saw the blackened ruin I felt not only sad but guilty. It seemed as if we had come to a centuries-old house that had slumbered peacefully near the bog for ages until we pulled it about, put in heating, dried it unnaturally, and now it was ruined. A curious thing happened: when I heard about the fire, and for many days afterwards, my hands trembled so that I could hardly hold a pen to write a letter.

A month before, in November, hearing that Michel Mohrt, the French writer, was giving a lecture tour in Ireland and that he was to lecture at Galway I invited him to stay with us.

When soon afterwards back in Paris he heard about what had happened he wrote his sympathy and compared our disaster to the fire in *The Spoils of Poynton*. Fortunately for us it was not quite so bad as that. Quantities of our possessions were saved. The losses I minded most were a drawerful of letters including all M.'s letters to me from Brixton, three studies in sepia ink that Tchelichew had done of me and the boys which he gave me at the time when he painted us, a drawing by Lamb of Jonathan aged one year, photographs of M. and the children, the irreplaceable things with which one surrounds oneself. For years afterwards it happened from time to time that I was looking for something or other and suddenly remembered it had been in one of the rooms at Clonfert and was turned to dust and ashes.

We had been expecting Ingrid and Jonathan and their children for Christmas at Clonfert. Andrew and Debo immediately offered to lend us Lismore, a boon which not only saved our Christmas but much more besides for Lismore is one of the loveliest places on earth. The family gathered together; Max had been at school in Germany at the time of the fire, I was afraid he might be terribly sad, but he found the horses at Lismore and loved hunting with the West Waterford.

We had promised to have a Christmas Tree party for the children at Clonfert, in the end it had to be in the village school. The priest helped us to arrange it. At that time some of the people were very poor and there were not many toys for the children. Ingrid and I bought dozens of toys in Cork and we drove over for the feast in the school. Jonathan was Father Christmas. It was fun, but so much less lovely than it would have been in the house. On the long wet drive back to Lismore I became desperately sad. It was as if we were turning our backs on a place where we had received so much kindness and friendship and where perhaps our presence could, even though very slightly, have served to help a poor and neglected neighbourhood. Since those days there has been a transformation. The bog is not only a place to hunt over on foot, peat is cut and processed into fuel and it has given work to hundreds of men; a certain prosperity has resulted.

About fifteen years after the fire James Pope-Hennessy was writing his life of Anthony Trollope and he took rooms in Banagher, the town on the Shannon where Trollope was postmaster as a young man. One day James was asked whether he would care to see the house 'where the Mosleys lived'. He said he would and he was driven over to Clonfert. He told me the ruin seemed incredibly old. Big trees were growing out of it so that it was smothered in greenery. He said it was a ruin in a jungle, and one felt it might have been there for hundreds of years. Myself, I have not got the heart to go back. As I have said, I sometimes think if we had never seen Clonfert the nice old house might be there to this day, standing among the beeches between the ancient cathedral and the bog.

While we were at Lismore that Christmas Ikey Bell came to see us and told us about a house for sale a few miles up the Blackwater near Fermoy. We bought it at once, and what was left of our belongings came from Clonfert. Ileclash is a sunny, cheerful house standing on the cliff above the river. From my room there was a spectacular view of the Blackwater winding its way between cliff and water meadows towards Lismore and the sea. We were not far upstream from legendary Careysville where all the salmon that come up the river congregate together so that the fishing there is famous the world over. M. sometimes caught a salmon on our own little stretch of river. Our cook wrote to Max: 'Your Dad brought a salmon into the kitchen. He was as pleased as if it had been an elephant.'

At Ileclash Max hunted with various packs, but much the most fun was the Avondhu hunted by our neighbour Paddy Flynn. They often got back very late, once it was hours after darkness had fallen. Somebody had seen a fox and the two of them had let the hounds out of the van where they were ready to go home to the kennels and had hunted until it was pitch dark. Such a thing would never happen in England, or perhaps anywhere in the world but Ireland. It is a paradise for sport because the people are young in heart, quite without fear and always ready for a lark.

Ileclash had none of the loneliness and solitude of Clonfert. Within walking distance there was Fermoy and Lismore was not far away. In the winter Andrew was there for the fishing and sometimes at the end of the day he blew in with a salmon, or I went over for dinner and billiard fives. In April Debo arrived, but by then we were usually on the move back to France. M. could never bear to miss the week he loved best in all the year, when Paris is ablaze with the chestnuts in full bloom. He came to Ireland much less than I did, he travelled about Europe. The only place where he never touched politics was in France; a matter of courtesy, since we were guests living in the country for much of the year.

As time went on we went to Ireland more rarely; the boys when they grew up could no longer spend weeks on end at Ileclash. In 1963 we sold it, and henceforward our only home was the Temple. Pam had left Tullamaine a few years before, but Desmond lives in Ireland at Leixlip near Dublin. He founded the Irish Georgian Society in order to try and save eighteenth-century country houses and the streets and squares of Dublin from 'development'. When Castletown was threatened with development (the modern word for destruction) Desmond bought it and made it a museum of the Irish eighteenth century. The book he wrote with Desmond Ryan called *Houses and Castles in Ireland* is a beautiful book; it has sold in enormous quantities, principally in America, and all the profits it makes go to the Society.

It was when we were first at Ileclash that Jerry Lehane came. He and Emily Reilly got married, and they and their son John have been with us in Ireland and England and France ever since. Theirs has been a wonderful contribution to more than twenty happy years.

23

Venice and Paris

WHEN WE FIRST came to live in France the bitter divisions caused by war and occupation were very much part of the scene. There were a few determined neutrals, but nearly everybody was in one of the two camps. Dozens of our friends had been in prison, either put there by the Germans or else by the Gaullists. One clever writer and honest man, Alfred Fabre-Luce, was imprisoned by both. Abominable things had been done, but towards foreigners at least the old French virtue of live-and-let-live was the rule. Stanislas de La Rochefoucauld who with his wife Yvonne were old friends of ours had a theory that prison left its unmistakable mark on a person: 'But one can't see it on *your* face,' he told me. I was only half pleased by this.

In any event, whether marked or not, one thing is certain: as a foreigner and a visitor both in France and in Ireland a precious sense of freedom was something I felt thankful for. Claudel says: 'On parle de la liberté, mais pour la comprendre il faut avoir été captive.' Freedom from fear of the policeman's knock is, I think, one of Churchill's and Roosevelt's four freedoms. I cannot truthfully say I felt fear, but I have heard the policeman's knock, and once is enough. Freedom in Britain is being restricted in every sphere; people are hemmed in by rules and regulations generously added to year by year. New laws, rules and regulations are at present England's biggest growth industry; but so long as you know, for example, that it is against the law to advertise for a Scotch cook you may keep out of prison.

From 1950 on, we went to Venice nearly every summer where Paris friends abounded; they gathered round Daisy at Palazzo Polignac and Charlie Beistegui at Palazzo Labia. I loved dining at the Labia and then walking the whole way back to S. Marco; there is nothing more heavenly than Venice on a summer night, the reflections, the shadows and unexpected vistas. It is beautiful when the sun shines and the bacino S. Marco is blue and sparkling; it is beautiful in the rain. Once, caught in a terrific thunderstorm when the sky opened and the rain deluged, I took cover upstairs at the far end of the Piazza. After a while every gutter and spout on St. Mark's poured forth water so that the whole church was veiled in water. It looked as though it had just that moment risen from the sea which was running off its elaborate domes and the white lace-like stone decorating the façade, an illusion one could almost believe in because since the Piazza was ankle-deep in rain there was not a soul in sight. A collection of shells and precious stones and coral, St. Mark's could have grown beneath the waves.

It is curious to consider the Venetian glass blowers who walk each morning through their incomparable city, and leaving the sounds of the sea and the bells behind them spend their days in dark cavernous rooms with fiery furnaces making objects so frightfully ugly that each year one imagines one has seen the very worst they can be capable of, only to be surprised the following summer by yet more hideous examples of their inventiveness. Wonderful skill, handed down for generations, and presumably a demand for their wares, combine to produce clowns with baggy trousers and red noses, Prince Charming candlesticks and glass baskets full of dainty blossoms. A glass blower will make a shining golden bowl and then quickly spoil it by sticking hot glass flowers on it before it has hardened. As a child, Max loved watching the glass blowing and sometimes I went with him into the hot den.

All over Venice there is greenery; plants and creepers grow from every crevice and hang in festoons, boxes of petunias and geraniums and pots of oleanders fill the windows and balconies, and in some of the campos there are plane trees and feathery acacias. In the Piazza there is not a leaf or a flower, only stones and sky, for there is no water either except when a spring tide or a storm floods over it. In summer it throbs with heat, in autumn a bright clean light is shed from a Tiepolo blue sky, in winter it is shrouded in mist. At night there is a hard, steady light and black shadows cast by the moon. Every season, every hour of day and night discloses new beauties to a lover of Venice.

One summer the Lopezs gave a party on their yacht. Daisy
Fellowes and her guests, David Herbert and Jamie Caffery,
were on board *Sister Anne*, also moored near the *Dogana*, and
we all went across to *Gaviotta* together and installed ourselves
at a table on deck. There was an elaborate supper, what Emilio
Terry used to call 'des purées d'orchidées'. Daisy was rather
cross for some reason; she refused dish after dish and asked for
'a little bit of gruyère cheese'. As she had doubtless guessed,
there was no gruyère cheese on the boat. David said under his
breath: 'I'm not going to swim the canal to get her cheese.'
Perhaps she heard; in any case she decided to return to *Sister
Anne*, taking her guests with her. No sooner had she gone
below to her cabin a few moments later than they were on their
way back to *Gaviotta* and the party. M. and Elisabeth Chav-
chavadze were leaning over the rail encouraging them when
Daisy's face appeared at her porthole. She was visibly dis-
pleased. Elisabeth said to M., 'Whenever I see Daisy in that
mood I'm so frightened my mouth goes dry.'

Daisy played the same trick on us, with more success, at a
Temple luncheon party. Refusing wine, she asked for Coca-
cola, rightly guessing we should have none. The Duke of
Windsor insisted on telephoning his house for a bottle of it;
I went with him to show him the telephone and heard him say:
'Hallo! Hier ist der Herzog,' to his gardener. The Coca-cola
appeared in a trice. The Duke spoke little French, and he therefore got an Alsatian gardener to whom he could talk in German.
He said he remembered as a child the older members of the
royal family waited until the English courtiers were no longer
in the room, and then comfortably relapsed into German.

Just as addicted to teasing as Nancy, Daisy's teases often
took the form of carefully planned practical jokes. She invited
Elsa Maxwell, an old American who looked like a toad and
who organized parties for café society, to dine at Les Zoraïdes.
Miss Maxwell was at the Hotel de Paris at Monte Carlo.
'Princess Grace will pick you up and bring you,' said Daisy.
Much gratified by this, Elsa Maxwell was hovering near the
steps of the hotel when on the stroke of eighty-thirty a Rolls
Royce drew up. She hurried forward and made a deep curtsy.
As she rose from the ground she saw that the occupant of the
car was Grace Radziwill. Daisy's jokes were always designed

in such a way that they could be due to pure chance. 'Oh!' she would say, 'I never thought of that!' and she gave her little tinkling laugh.

For many years before the war Daisy was 'the best-dressed woman in the world', and she was accustomed to being the most elegant and admired person at any Paris party. Her aunt, Princesse Edmond de Polignac, was giving a musical soirée and decided she would wear all her jewels, tiara, necklaces, bracelets, on the front of her dress so that from throat to waist she was covered in glittering gems. When Princesse Natty de Lucinge arrived she exclaimed: 'Oh! princesse, que c'est merveilleux, vos diamants!'

'Oui,' said Princesse Winnie; 'oui, je crois que ça doit faire un certain effet, car Daisy en arrivant tout à l'heure m'a dit: Oh, ma tante! Que c'est joli, ce tulle!' and Daisy had pointed to a wisp of tulle round her aunt's neck. Princess Natty told this to Jean de Baglion years later. She never allowed me to say, 'Daisy is a saint.' '*No*,' she used to say, '*not* a saint.'

An old friend who came to Paris from time to time was Pavel Tchelichew. During the war he had lived in America, and his English was now as rapid and inaccurate as formerly his French had been. He told me that the voluminous correspondence between him and Edith Sitwell was put away in a safe to be opened and published in the year 2000. When he asked about Jonathan and Desmond and I told him they were married with infants of their own: 'These babies!' said Pavlic, '*they* will read the letters!'

He died in Rome but his ashes were brought to Paris, the city which, like so many painters, he looked upon as his spiritual home. There was an Orthodox service at Père Lachaise conducted by a young red-bearded pope, and Sauguet gave the oraison funèbre. Every individual in the little crowd had dearly loved Pavlic, he was brilliant, original, with more than a touch of genius.

For six years during the fifties we had a monthly magazine, *The European*, which I edited. It was not a financial success and it never had a wide circulation, but it seemed worth while at the time that there should be at least one review in England devoted to the European idea, the idea, as M. had put it in 1948, of 'Europe a Nation'. When we started it in 1953 the Conservatives were back in office. Churchill, in opposition, had made one or two pro-Europe speeches, and although Anthony Eden was hostile to the whole concept there had been some reason in 1951 to hope that now Labour had been defeated a move would be made in the right direction. In 1950 a volume of Churchill's speeches had come out, edited by Randolph, with the encouraging title *Europe Unite*. Now that he was once more prime minister he immediately abandoned the idea, just when it had become evident that our former Empire having melted away, and as the French were being driven out of their overseas colonies one by one, while Italy and Germany had already lost theirs, the intelligent thing to do was for Europe to unite. The alternative was permanently to accept the ignoble role of pensioners of the United States. Although as leader of the Opposition Churchill had also welcomed the idea of a European army, no sooner was he back in office than, in Walter Hallstein's words, he 'obstinately opposed the European Defence Community and the European Political Community'. Professor Hallstein is doubtless correct when he says that until the middle fifties Britain hoped to go on playing its old role of balance of power politics; it 'still did not recognize its inability to play a world role in view of its declining military and economic strength'.* Suez was the turning point, when the anti-European Eden was prime minister. His disappearance from the scene came too late; what would have been welcomed by France and Germany in 1951 was no longer so. The Treaty of Rome was signed in 1957 and the European Community was formed without Britain, a tragic mistake on the part of our country. In 1961 when Mr. Macmillan applied to join he ran into the veto of General de Gaulle, and Britain was finally admitted only in 1971; the result of British shortsightedness and Gaullist intransigence had been that the idea of Europe was hampered for a generation.

In *The European* M. wrote political notes every month in which he constantly stressed the importance to Britain of joining the Community.

I collected articles, and if we were short of copy I wrote myself. I wrote a Diary, and reviewed political memoirs, mostly

* Walter Hallstein, *Europe in the making.*

by old friends or old enemies. In September 1953 I printed a letter from Muv:

Sir,

I wrote the following letter to the *Scottish Sunday Express* after reading a paragraph in their issue of 28 June 1953 under the title 'Politics and Personalities' by Cross Bencher.

To the Editor of the *Scottish Sunday Express*

Sir,

I could not believe my eyes when I read the assertion of Cross Bencher concerning the outbreak of war in 1939: 'Britain was determined to fight. And the British would have been a wiser people if they had decided instead to let Germany and Russia fight it out. Isolationism . . . was the best policy.'

These were the very words and the very sentiments which landed a thousand loyal British subjects in prison for the duration of the war. I am waiting to see what happens to Cross Bencher! Nothing, of course, as everyone now agrees with these ideas, too late, alas!

Yours faithfully,

S. Redesdale

My letter was not printed, and the usual courtesy of an acknowledgement from the Editor was also omitted. I am not really surprised, as it is not popular to revive memories of the time when Habeas Corpus and Magna Carta were no longer in use in England and the years when imprisonment without trial was quite usual. I must say it is interesting to find these opinions on the war, which were formerly considered so wicked, published without comment in the *Sunday Express*, so much are they now taken for granted.

Yours faithfully,

Sydney Redesdale

Inch Kenneth, Gribun, Isle of Mull

My mother received a letter from a Mr. E. J. Robertson, from the Chairman's Office of the *Daily Express*; he said he had seen her letter in *The European*, and that after a 'most thorough enquiry personally conducted by the Editor' they had been unable to find any trace of her letter to the *Scottish Sunday Express*.

9

About our imprisonment without trial M. wrote: 'Lord Chatham opposed the war against America in violent language; Charles James Fox opposed the war with France, and most of the Whig leaders hurried to Paris to dine with Napoleon during the brief peace of Amiens. No-one thought of arresting them, or suggesting that they might help the enemy. We were still living in the tradition of the great Elizabeth, who appointed a Catholic to command her fleet against Catholic Spain. Dago values were not yet in command of England.'

On the whole I enjoyed doing *The European*, though due to my natural laziness I was also quite pleased when after six years M. decided to give it up. Even with a monthly magazine there is the constantly present worry of the inexorable passing of time, the feeling that 'it's later than you think'. We depended on the post, since I was usually in France or Ireland and sometimes even further afield. Unless I could see the galleys I knew there would be misprints to disfigure a whole issue. Twenty years ago the posts within Europe were dependable; if it was sometimes difficult in those days it would not be possible now to dream of editing a review from afar.

In 1959 *The European* ceased publication. One year before, the Americans had released Ezra Pound, who ever since the war had been locked up in a lunatic asylum; the Americans and Russians hit upon identical treatment for their dissident poets. During the war Pound, who was a credit crank and thought usury the source of all evil, broadcast from Italy, his home for many years. According to our ideas it was inadmissable to broadcast from any country except your own in time of war, and Ezra Pound's diatribes against usury, even though they were nothing to do with war, became a hostile act as soon as America was a belligerent. When the American army reached Pisa Ezra Pound was imprisoned in a wire cage, and subsequently in a lunatic asylum in the United States. The spitefulness of the American revenge was almost biblical in its ferocity. After twelve terrible years Pound went straight back to Italy, where he lived happily for the remainder of his life.

The world of letters owes a debt to Dominique de Roux for *Les Cahiers de l'Herne*, his idea and his creation. The volumes about Céline, for example, contain testimonies and descriptions connected with the life and work of the novelist which would have been lost but for *l'Herne*. Considering how difficult and obscure Ezra Pound's poetry is even for the English it was very bold to publish two *Cahiers* about Pound in French, but all over Europe he is venerated and admired, so that curiosity about him knows no frontiers. In Alan Neame's words: 'If any poet incarnates the vicissitudes of the century it is the author of the Cantos.' Over the years, we published some of the Pisan Cantos in *The European* with imaginative and fanciful notes by Alan Neame. As our magazine declared itself to be an 'open forum' contributors did not necessarily agree with M.'s political ideas, though all of them were for united Europe. On the literary side the most amusing and interesting articles came from John Haylock, Alan Neame and Desmond Stewart. They sometimes came to Orsay, and whether or not the results of our editorial conferences entertained our readers we certainly amused each other.

Dominique de Roux induced Ezra Pound to come to Paris, where he had lived for years before he settled in Italy, to visit old haunts and to sit to the German sculptor Arno Breker. We dined with them. I was put next to the poet; he spoke not one word. This was disconcerting to begin with, but he seemed perfectly contented and sat looking nobly benign while general conversation washed over him. 'Does he never speak?' I asked Dominique. 'Non non, ah non. Jamais,' was the reply.

Cyril Connolly who went to see him in Italy later on, hoping I suppose to interview him, was met with the same total silence. He made the best of it, announcing that when he left Ezra Pound after two days he found he missed and regretted the silence of the sage.

The political side of *The European* has lost its actuality, but it is a reminder of M.'s farsightedness. The literary and critical pages of the magazine contain nuggets of gold among the inevitable dross.

We were careful about libel, which in England can be an expensive luxury, and we published a story by Hugo Charteris without realizing how rash this was. Hugo was a dangerous writer in the sense that he always took real people for his characters, generally his best friends or near relations, and described them in a brilliantly accurate way so that no doubt as to their identity remained. He then attributed to them every crime in the calendar, holding them up to hatred, ridicule or contempt, sometimes to all three. Shortly after Hugo's story appeared in *The European* we happened to meet Boofy Gore who said: 'I'm Looty Cook.' Looty Cook was the name of one of the characters in the story. Boofy Gore and Hugo had both worked on the *Daily Mail* and he said the story was not fiction at all but simply a report of an incident that happened in the newspaper office. 'I don't mind,' he added kindly. Strangely enough, as far as I know, Hugo was never sued for libel, but some of his novels remained unpublished as a result of the threats of his victims.

We printed his Looty Cook story in the early days of Hugo's career as a novelist; later on I should have been apprehensive of even the most seemingly harmless tale if it came from his pen. All novelists draw their characters more or less from nature and thus all novelists are bound to use people they know for models. But whereas most of them digest and transmute, Hugo spewed his up whole and then proceeded to decorate them with extraordinarily unpleasant additions, criminal pasts and so forth. He quite expected his victims to be upset and I know of at least one case where he asked: 'Did you mind?'

'Not a bit,' said the victim.

'*Oh!* You *must* have,' said Hugo.

Just occasionally Nancy put a person or an episode into a novel with great truthfulness, an example being Basil in *Don't Tell Alfred* and his activities as courier for a travel agency. When Alexander was about eighteen he earned his keep one summer holidays by taking English tourists to Spain and bringing them back again. Each time, as there were a few hours to spare in Paris, he went to rue Monsieur to ask for a bath. He described his work, 'packing in the meat' as he called it, to Nancy in picturesque detail. 'May I come with you to the Gare d'Austerlitz?' she asked one day.

'Oh no, don't come,' he said, and then seeing her disappointment, 'well, all right, but you mustn't seem to belong to *me*.'

In the taxi he put on his armband and at the station he herded the flock while Nancy stood quietly shrieking a little way off.

She was puzzled by the wonderful stamina displayed by the tourists. 'Why *do* they do it?' she asked one day. According to

Alexander they were crammed into carriages like so many black holes of Calcutta, perishing of heat and thirst.

'Oh, different reasons. For some of them it's sex.'

'*Sex?* In the black holes of Calcutta?'

'Oh no, when they get there. The girls often pick up men at the customs.'

'*What?* On those dirty old tables then?'

'Oh, Aunt Nancy, of *course* not. On their day off,' he explained. In *Don't Tell Alfred* Nancy imagined the rest; the scene at the station 'packing in the meat' was authentic.

Osbert Sitwell in his autobiography laughs at his mother's friends, the Fun Brigade, because they fled at the sight of any author for fear he might take them and put them in a book. Of course they were perfectly right, it can happen and it frequently does.

24

Inch Kenneth and London

FROM FRANCE AND from Ireland we made frequent journeys to England. Every year I went up to Scotland to visit Muv and often to Northumberland to visit Farve. The journey to Inch Kenneth was grim; it was impossible to get up there in a day from Paris. I elected to spend a night in Glasgow; the great attraction there was the picture gallery with the Burrell collection. Next morning there was a train to Oban which caught the boat to Mull. At Salen Muv's ancient shabby car would be waiting; there was a drive of eleven miles across Mull and then a mile of sea to Inch Kenneth in her boat, the *Puffin*. One arrived half dead to a wonderful welcome and a delicious Scotch tea.

As Muv grew older one of us took her up to Scotland when she left London every April. Once she and I arrived at Oban on a stormy day and when we disembarked at Salen pier there was no car; this meant that it had been too rough for her boatman to be able to cross from Inch Kenneth to Mull. With our mountains of luggage we went to the inn, but it was full. We sat on plastic chairs in the bar, tired out. Muv was completely unmoved but the thought that we should be sitting there for the rest of the afternoon, and then for the long unnaturally light evening, and then all night long, and possibly for several days until the weather changed, sent my heart into my boots. It was all I could do to conceal my despair. There was no question of going back to Oban, Muv would never have dreamed of such a thing and in any case there was no boat until the following day. The rumour soon went round the village that Muv was marooned, and a saintly old person appeared with an offer of putting us up for the night. I slept badly; it was the uncertainty that was so depressing. There was no particular reason why the storm should abate. Late on the following day the old motor appeared. We had only been twenty-four hours at Salen but it had seemed more like a fortnight.

We crossed to Inch Kenneth on a grey and choppy sea. Clambering from the dinghy into the motor boat, both of them dancing on the waves, was not easy for Muv, aged eighty, but as we settled into the stern of the *Puffin* wrapped in oilskins against the driving rain she shouted to me above the horrible noisy wind: 'Fun, isn't it?' I shouted back: '*Great* fun.'

I never quite understood the love my mother felt for her island. It was inconvenient to the last degree. There was no telephone, and if the sea was rough there was no post. She spent a good part of each day looking through field glasses to see if any people should chance to appear on the opposite shore at Gribun, or whether a black spot had been fixed on her garage which meant there was a telegram for the island. When, on calm days, the boat went over to fetch the mail excitement mounted. Ages seemed to go by, even after the boat came back, until the little sack was given to Muv to open. If it contained nothing but bills the disappointment was dreadful. When I was going to the island Debo started writing a week in advance, and wrote every day, so that I could be sure of a letter from the little sack; I did the same for her. It sometimes seemed as if the post which linked her to life and to the mainland was far and away Muv's greatest pleasure, a close second being the wireless news and the newspapers.

It was difficult not to wonder whether the trouble and annoyance of the long journey were worth while if at the end of it one was to live for letters and news which were so much more readily available almost anywhere else. However, I kept these impious thoughts to myself, and the island had compensations in its lonely beauty. If Muv saw through her binoculars that there was a picnic party on Mull, or better still if a yacht appeared in the sound, she sent her boatman to fetch whoever it might be and then gave them a terrific tea. She said during the time it took for the boat to make the journey her cook had time to make fresh scones. There again, such a haphazard choice of guests was, to me, a strange taste. It must have been the gambler in Muv which made her positively enjoy the unpredictable journeys and the luck of the draw at her tea parties.

She was a great reader of biographies, diaries and the like, her library books were posted to and from London. Sometimes a book she had looked forward to proved to be a dud but there was no chance of changing it for another, the long process of posting had to take its weary course. Everything on the island was more difficult than elsewhere, including farming. When the bull was needed he had to swim over from Mull, the rope on the ring in his nose made fast to the motor boat. Several men had to be found to push him into the sea which he entered with the greatest reluctance. One year when I was there Muv had acquired a bull of her own. He roamed the island at will and one met him face to face round the corner of a rock on one of the beaches.

'*Dangerous*, Dana? Oh, I don't think so. He's a dear old fellow,' said Muv vaguely.

As to the garden, although it was in a sheltered spot it was not sheltered from really violent storms. She took me that way after my arrival one year and the whole thing was pitch black, salt spray having killed all her vegetables and flowers in a single night. She laughed so much at the look on my face that we had to sit on the garden bench surveying the desolate scene for several minutes while she recovered her composure.

Children adored the island. My boys when they were small, and then my grandchildren, looked forward to their visits the whole year. The boatman took them trawling at night, they collected shells, Muv read aloud to them, and they loved the adventure of the journey.

Visiting Farve was much easier. He sent to Newcastle and seemed pleased to see one. After dinner he said: 'Dina, shall we have un petit brin de feu?' and he got his keys and opened his safe and took out a firelighter. Nothing else was kept in the safe. It was a relic of the old days when one of us might go to his cupboard for a firelighter to make the damp logs burn in our cold Asthall schoolroom. At Redesdale there were no children to take his firelighters but the idea that they might vanish was ingrained. Farve's safe would have been a grave disappointment to a clever burglar.

He, like Muv, listened to the news on the wireless, or at any rate both in their remote dwellings turned it on, very loudly because of their deafness; whether they actually listened I never could quite make out, it may have been a habit acquired during the war and they let the sound wash over them.

Unlike Muv, he was not in the least interested in any of us or our various activities. He once invited Alexander, aged twelve, to stay; he met him at Newcastle. They had never set eyes on one another before and I asked when he got back: 'How did you know Farve?'

'I looked at all the old people on the platform, and I saw one noble old gentleman, and I knew it must be him.' Farve was rather pleased by this polite description.

In March 1958 M. and I were in London. Muv and Debo decided to go to Redesdale for Farve's eightieth birthday, he had not been too well that winter. In the night I woke and suddenly knew that I must go with them. Early next morning I went to King's Cross and ran along the train until I found them in their carriage. We stayed not at the cottage but at the Redesdale Arms, a comfortable nearby inn. I shall never forget the expression on Farve's face when Muv appeared at his bedside, and his smile of pure delight. All their differences forgotten, they seemed to have gone back twenty years to happy days before the tragedies. She sat with him for hours, Debo and I going in and out. After a couple of days Muv and Debo travelled on to Scotland and I returned to London. They had hardly arrived when they were wired for to go to Farve; a few days later he died.

When Farve was in his early forties, at Asthall soon after the first war, Tom predicted that he would mellow with age. 'Oh yes, Farve, you will. *Everyone* mellows with age,' he said confidently. He was proved right. The mellowing happened gradually and in many ways I regretted it. There were no more rages, but there were no more wildly funny jokes either. He was quieter, less eccentric, sadder too no doubt. He had already lost his hold on life. All his pleasures, shooting, fishing, playing poker with men friends, were finished and done with. His only son was dead. For most people there are still spectator sports in old age, of which the most passionately interesting is the continuing serial story of politics and world affairs. From this Farve seemed totally detached. Books he had never indulged in; he never cared for gardening. The future must have looked to him empty. When he died I mourned the Farve of long ago; what I could hardly bear to contemplate was that one day Muv too would disappear.

On the island she was so well and happy and so pleased with

her surroundings which combined her two loves, Scotland and the sea, that such thoughts never came into my head. It was in the winter, when she lived at Rutland Gate Mews, that she began to seem old, and once when she had been staying with us at the Temple and I took her to the airport, as I watched from the barrier while she slowly disappeared from view down a long corridor I had a premonition that this would be her last visit to France and I was blinded with tears.

In 1960 we took a flat in London where we spent three winters. This enabled me to see her almost every day; she often came to us and I went to her for tea and scrabble. Her Parkinson's disease got gradually worse. Her poor hand tapping on the table and her dachshund's tail thumping on the floor were a sort of percussion chorus which made her laugh. Often we met at Harrods bank; on one of the comfortable Harrods sofas Debo and I sat either side of Muv shouting scandals to amuse her, she was so deaf that the whole bank partook of our secrets.

Max was now at Christ Church and when he was just twenty he married Jean Taylor, a lovely, clever and sweet person; she was only nineteen. Like Jonathan, Max was a married undergraduate.

In 1962 the communists made a great effort once again to prevent M. from speaking; they organized violence and there was fighting at M.'s meetings, often shown on television, though needless to say nothing else was reported, not a word of his speeches for example. For many years his meetings, indoor and outdoor, had been perfectly orderly; now, obviously, word had gone forth that they were to be attacked. The government immediately capitulated; on orders from the Home Office the moment there was any attempt to disrupt a meeting the police closed it. Under the Public Order Act M. had not the right to keep order at outdoor meetings, and since the police gave way at once to the disorderly, outdoor meetings came to an end. This happened when public meetings were in any case being replaced by television, but M. was banned from television. Over and over again he consented to give interviews before the cameras, invited to do so by Malcolm Muggeridge, Daniel Farson and others, but when the time came for the films to be screened they were always banned. From 1968 on, a fairer administration gave M. a number of opportunities to state his opinions on television.

A neighbour of ours at our London flat was Lady Hoskins, the widow of a General, who lived on the ground floor. She became fond of Max, and once as he was leaving the house on his way to his father's meeting, during this period of violence, she waylaid him in the hall.

'Max!' she said, 'Please take this!' and she held out her late husband's sword which usually decorated the wall of her drawing-room.

'Oh no, Lady Hoskins, thank you very much, but you see I should be arrested at once if I was carrying that sword,' said Max.

Telling me about it afterwards he added: 'The old dear didn't realize it was an offensive weapon.'

At one outdoor meeting M. was set upon by communists as he was walking to the platform. It was at Ridley Road in East London, where he and other speakers had held innumerable meetings both before and since the war and where he was on the best of terms with the local population. The police were holding back his supporters some way off which gave the reds a chance to hurl M. to the ground. There were shouts of 'Put the boot in', but M. held one of his assailants in such a way that though they were rolling on the ground he was able to use him as a shield to ward off the blows and kicks of the rest of the cowardly gang. Max flung himself upon his father's attackers; moments later the police arrived and arrested him along with the gang; they were all put in a black maria. M. resumed his walk to the improvised platform, but the police closed the meeting thus once again giving in to violence and preventing free speech.

Max was bailed out, and next morning I went to the police court to hear him defend himself. A senior police officer cross-examined him; he suggested that Max had gone to the meeting hoping for a fight. Max replied that he had gone hoping to hear his father speak. 'But you *expected* a fight, didn't you?' asked the policeman. 'No, and nor presumably did you, or you would surely have disposed your men more effectively,' was Max's reply. He went on to ask whether it was suggested that he should have stood idly by while his father was being kicked by a gang of roughs. 'It was not only my right, but my duty to go to his aid,' he said (*Daily Telegraph* 2/8/62). He was acquitted.

Apparently this, for M., very dangerous situation had arisen because television crews were waiting and the police thought that if pictures were taken of M. arriving surrounded by cheering supporters it would look too favourable; they therefore arranged that he should walk to the platform alone, between police buses. Max had driven there with him. The communists were given their golden opportunity, and but for M's. presence of mind he would have been badly hurt, or worse. They were not local people but had been sent from afar.

At about this time a short letter appeared in *The Times* signed by Victor Gollancz and Frank Pakenham. They said that much as they deplored all that M. stood for they also deplored the violence being used against him.

I wrote to Frank asking what it was that M. stood for that he deplored. Was it united Europe? was it his economic policy? Frank wrote back saying he had imagined when he saw my letter that I was going to thank him for writing to *The Times*, and then all he got was a rocket. In fact, I loved him for having written, but the ritual disapproval of 'everything' M. advocates has always seemed to me one of the great nonsenses and hypocrisies of the post-war years.

In 1959 there had been a general election. M. was asked to stand in North Kensington. It was a constituency in which several streets had recently been taken over by West Indians. At that time any number could enter the country, and as the West Indies were suffering from slump thousands crossed the Atlantic and settled in England. M. thought the whole idea wrong from start to finish. He advocated helping the West Indies in a number of ways and sending the West Indians home to decent conditions. In 1959 it would have been possible to reverse the decision taken by the government to import unskilled labour. Britain should have insisted upon 'Dominion status' for itself. If great empty countries like Canada and Australia restricted immigration, how much more so should crowded Britain? Since we had been reduced by the war to a relatively weak position in the world we depended for survival upon skill, brains and inventiveness; among the fifty-five million inhabitants there were plenty of unskilled workers without importing more. Furthermore it was only necessary to glance at the United States to see what an intractable problem race relations could become.

M. fought the election on his whole programme of united Europe and economic reform, as well as the question of immigration. Only a small part of the constituency was affected by the arrival of the West Indians; unfortunately the remainder took the then popular liberal line. If M. had been elected England might not be in the unfortunate position it is as I write these words: the sick man of Europe. At every stage of our decline he has put forward a constructive policy; had he been in Parliament his voice could not have been ignored.

Canvassing for him in North Kensington I had a good look at the appalling housing in parts of the constituency. The blacks had made this slum far worse simply by overcrowding. A man called Rachman organized a profitable racket and squeezed more and more people into the disgusting houses. Highly disagreeable as the situation was for any white person unable to move to some other district—and there were many such, and their life had become a sort of hell of noise and filth and misery—I also felt sorry for the blacks. They hated the climate, and they cannot have relished the interest they aroused in clergymen and assorted do-gooders, the kind of people anyone normal, whatever his colour, would be careful to avoid. If they could find no work they went to collect the dole and the sight of them in the queue, drawing out pounds shillings and pence, as money was called in those days, further irritated their white neighbours, who could easily think of ways they would prefer that their rates and taxes should be spent and did not hesitate to tell them so.

All in all, it would be difficult to parallel in its wide assortment of evils and annoyances great and small the insouciant gesture of the Tories when they opened wide the doors to black immigration.

As the numbers multiplied the people immediately affected became angry, but they had nobody in the House of Commons to speak on their behalf. Far from it; they were scolded by politicians and clergy for not welcoming the change in their neighbourhoods; many a letter was penned in the quiet of a cathedral close telling them how fortunate they were to have so many black people living among them, bringing steel bands to liven up the streets and so forth. As they remained unconvinced the politicians were gradually obliged to change their tune, but as usual it was far too late and the damage was done. A flourishing race-relations industry prospered, while lazy employers admitted that it was 'marginally cheaper' to employ black labour than it would have been to install new machinery in their factories, thus ensuring that much of British industry remained old fashioned and soon became obsolete. The slums, through overcrowding, are worse than ever before; dirty, untidy, noisy as well as insanitary and inconvenient. The bad housing in our big cities has to be seen to be believed; it is a quite unnecessary blot upon Britain which neither the Conservative party nor the Labour party has ever tackled in a serious way. Hardly a week goes by but some incident, a statistic concerning juvenile crime among blacks, or the preponderance of unemployed blacks, is published giving rise to calls from the busy race-relations industry for ever more legislation.

In the sixties when Labour was back in office, R. H. S. Crossman, a minister in the Labour government, wrote in his diary: 'if the Conservatives were to launch a strong anti-coloured-immigration line, they might really start winning votes.' He wrote further that George Wigg told him: 'it has been quite clear that immigration can be the greatest vote-loser for the Labour party' if it was seen that Labour was 'permitting a flood of immigrants to come and blight the central areas in all our cities'. This was unfair, because it was not Labour but the Conservatives who had opened the flood-gates, but they had realized before the Labour leaders how unpopular this policy was, and therefore they were looked upon by the electorate as the party more likely to halt coloured immigration. Since, however, the central areas of many cities were already what Lord Wigg called 'blighted', a competition in vote-catching was fairly meaningless so far as this particular problem went. It is just one more example of short-sighted stupidity in the rulers our unfortunate country has burdened itself with. It sometimes seems as if they must sit down together and deliberately try to devise a policy which is certain to make things harder for everybody. One would be inclined to believe this were it not that we know by experience that nothing is thought out; the politicians are blown hither and thither by pure chance.

M. had always insisted that the immigrants must be decently treated once they are in the country; nevertheless he was violently attacked by politicians and press, as was said of him in another context, 'simply and solely because he was right.' What he was saying in the fifties, when it was easy to do something about it, nearly everyone is saying in the seventies. As usual he was right, but he was right too soon. If this problem is ever to be solved it will have to be in a European context, because if their countries of origin are to be induced to receive the immigrants back the inducement will have to be the only one that counts: economic and financial.

In the autumn of 1968 M.'s autobiography, *My Life*, was published. The BBC gave him the whole of its Panorama programme, and it was seen by a record audience. The interviewer was James Mossman, and he was asked at the beginning by Robin Day whether he had found M. rather different from what he expected. 'Startlingly different,' said Mossman.

Reviews of *My Life* were notable for the fact that all the clever or remarkable men paid tribute to M.'s brilliance and character; only a few scribblers and hacks did their best to denigrate. Notable opponents, with peculiarly English generosity, praised the book. A. J. P. Taylor wrote that M. is 'A superb political thinker, the best of our age.' Malcolm Muggeridge said he was: 'The only living Englishman who could perfectly well have been either Conservative or Labour prime minister,' and Sir Colin Coote: 'He displays yet another talent, for it is the best-written volume of memoirs emanating from my generation.' Lord Longford wrote: 'In the field of ideas he was a creative force,' and Colin Welch: 'We are confronted by a man of powerful will and bold intelligence, self-disciplined, by no means lacking in shrewdness or even humour, a spell-binding speaker, a truly formidable figure,' while Christopher Sykes spoke of 'memorable and important pieces of writing.'

I was pleased with the reception of *My Life*, for I had been urging M. for years to write down his memories.

25

The Windsors

A FEW MILES along the valley from Orsay in what was then the village of Gif the painter Drian had an old mill which he wanted to sell. Nancy longed to buy it. She loved the idea of a garden with a stream running through it. At the same time she thought she might be lonely and cut off from her friends, all of whom strongly advised her to stay where she was at rue Monsieur.

The Moulin de la Tuilerie was finally bought by the Windsors, who made a lovely flower garden in the English style and a luxurious Hollywood-like dwelling, every barn and outhouse as well as the mill itself filled with bedrooms and bathrooms and dining-rooms of various sizes to fit parties large and small. They were kind neighbours to us and we had happy times at the mill for many years until they decided to sell it. When they first came over to the Temple the Duchess of Windsor said: 'Yes, it's very pretty here, but where do you *live?*'

I loved the Duke and have seldom met his like for charm. He was always ready to laugh and be amused and then his rather sad and anxious expression changed and his face lit up in a most engaging way. He had the almost miraculous memory that royal personages so cleverly cultivate and which everyone finds flattering. A favourite topic he could seldom indulge in, because so many of their guests were American or French or Spanish or German, was English families. He remembered people's sisters and cousins and aunts. He would say: 'Now let me see. Lady so and so was Lord so and so's *great aunt*. Recto?' He pronounced lady almost, though not quite, lidy.

He remembered Grandfather. 'When we were little kids at Sandrin-ham we looked forward to Lord Redesdale's visit. He always gave us a little presy.'

'Did he really? What sort of little presy?' I asked.

'Oh, a *sovereign*. He used to give us each a gold *sovereign*,'
said the Duke. I loved the way he pronounced Sandringham as
if it were two words; he did the same for Devonshire. 'Is that
the Duchess of Devon *Shire?*' he asked M. one day when Debo
was at the Temple. His accent, formerly tinged with cockney,
had acquired more than a touch of American and it made
everything he said twice as amusing.

The food at the mill and at the Windsors' Paris house in the
Bois de Boulogne was the perfection of perfection. The Duchess
had an extraordinary talent in that department though both she
and the Duke had the appetites of canaries and scarcely touched
the delicious creations of their brilliant cook. Her clothes too
were lovely, I never saw her in an ugly dress. This exquisite
taste did not extend to the choice of furniture, pictures and
house decoration. Their houses were comfortable and rich but
not beautiful, except on occasion the dining-room table could
be lovely with its silver and Dresden china.

One Sunday we were lunching at the mill and one of the
papers was full of Carrington and her love affairs with extracts
from some book, either Michael Holroyd's *Lytton Strachey* or
more likely Carrington's own letters edited by David Garnett.
There was a huge photograph of her on the front of the magazine section. 'She wasn't really quite like that,' I said to someone; the Duchess heard.

'Did you *know* her?' she asked.

'Yes.'

'David! David!' she called to the Duke across the room.
'Diana *knew* Carrington!'

Casting my mind back to Ham Spray I thought how amused
and surprised Lytton and Carrington would have been by this
unexpected scene long years after they had died.

At Mona Bismarck's Paris Christmas dinner parties I was
always put next to the Duke. One year when there were two
tables, M. was at the other table next to the Duchess. Half way
through dinner she looked round to see how the Duke was
getting on; seeing we were laughing she said to M., 'It's all
right. They're talking about those *old people*.' She meant the
English, and no doubt she had guessed rightly.

In Mona's library there hangs a large eighteenth-century
portrait of two children in long dresses one of whom is beating

a drum. Recognizing it as Le Pesne from Nancy's picture book I told the Duke: 'That little child with the drum is Frederick the Great.'

He was interested and turned to Mona. 'Did Eddie inherit that from the old Fürst?'

'No, sir,' said Mona truthfully. 'He got it from Jansen.'

The Windsors always had a bad press. The newspapers were determined to emphasize the emptiness of his life in order to point the obvious moral. He on the other hand was equally determined to prove that the world had been well lost for love, and in addition to his boundless admiration and affection for the Duchess, too consistent and too deep to have been anything but genuine, this attitude which originated I suppose in defiance became so much part of him that if deception there was he certainly completely deceived himself. I always had the feeling that here was somebody with superlative gifts, not of intellect but of sympathy and instinctive understanding of the human predicament, who had lost his chance to use the gifts. True, the loss was his own doing but it was nevertheless a sad waste.

His insistence upon the title of Royal Highness for the Duchess was not simply an affair of good manners on his part. He thought it was her right, and Walter Monckton told me that in his opinion if the Duke had brought an action in the English courts, he would have won it, but this of course was something he would never do. The argument was that Queen Victoria had decreed that the children of the monarch and their wives should be royal highnesses. Although he himself had abdicated the Duke was indubitably the son of a monarch and a royal highness, and the Duchess was his wife according to the law of the land and thus she was a royal highness too.

It was sad when the Windsors gave up the mill, because the garden there was his joy. The sale hung fire for ages and sometimes they went down for a few hours and wandered about like lost souls. Various things had been moved out and everything was different; these visits depressed them. In Gif itself, not far from the mill, unbelievably ugly blocks of flats mushroomed. Their precursor was a relatively harmless petrol station, hated by the Duke. It had a row of flag poles in front of it which he called 'those ghăstly măsts'. Far more *ghăstly* were the multicoloured flats, among the worst in the Ile de France which has endured more than its share of horrors in the buildings of recent years.

Their parties were always enjoyable and never dull; this was the Duke's doing, and the Duchess was an excellent hostess. When his health began to fail his courage was exemplary. One suffered because he tried so hard to talk at dinner; sometimes a whisper came out, sometimes a bark. The last evening I ever saw him, when the time came to say goodbye he was nowhere to be found. He was out on the drive talking to Jerry. We dined there ten days later and he was too unwell to come down. Not long afterwards he died. He was a kind friend to M. and me and we mourned him deeply. Looking back, I like to think of him as he was at the mill, for example at a big luncheon party when we took Kitty Mersey, who was with us at the Temple, over to Gif. Kitty and I sat on either side of him which was, I suppose, quite wrong as there were several French ladies present. He and Kitty name-dropped to each other for hours; he had quite an orgy that day of talking about *those old people*, a game at which she was far more adept than I could ever be.

Some may have been surprised that when he lay in state at Windsor no less than sixty thousand men and women made the journey to pay their last respects. It was thirty-six years since he had left England, and as I have said he never had a good press. But he had never been forgotten, and spiteful books by censorious ladies and faithless friends will not succeed in demolishing this unusually sweet and lovable man.

26

The Antagonists

TWO FAMOUS MEN whom I chanced to know fairly well were Churchill and Hitler. I knew them in a superficial way, simply as an occasional guest, and never for example worked with either of them. But they interested me greatly, and I observed them as closely as I could when I had the opportunity.

Modern war is so devastating in the suffering it brings that it should be the first aim of every politician to avoid it. Neither Hitler nor Churchill, whatever they may have said on the subject, really believed that war was the ultimate evil. They were fascinated by problems of strategy, by weapons, by tactics, in short, by warfare. They admired the qualities it calls forth in men more than they deprecated the appalling cost in disaster they give rise to. Courage, endurance, loyalty and other virtues are displayed in their most spectacular way in wartime, but the other face of war is destruction, injustice and vicious revenge.

Whether a conference and a decision to hold plebiscites in disputed areas—'self-determination'—would permanently have defused the European crisis in 1939 can never be certain because it was never tried. Churchill's was the most powerful voice in England in favour of war. M., who for years past had pressed for re-armament, wanted peace with strength. Since those days, our continent has never ceased to be an armed camp; there has never been peace. Britain is no longer a world power, and the 1939 situation will never recur for us. I am just as much opposed to interventionist wars against communist states now as I was to intervention against national socialist Germany in 1939. As to 'evil things', they have proliferated in Europe, and will continue to do so wherever communism rules.

Hitler and Churchill had more in common with one another than perhaps either would have been prepared to admit. To begin with, love of country, a deep and romantic love, was strong in them both. They were word-spinners, speakers, talkers, charmers of their fellow men with the spoken word, self-intoxicated by their own oratory. They worked at night; they liked to sit up until the small hours, talking, thinking as their own words stimulated ideas, getting up late in the morning. They were fearless, physically and morally brave, bold and imaginative, ambitious and incorruptible. Both were brilliantly clever, neither had the advantage of an university education. Churchill was first and foremost a writer, Hitler a speaker, but both dealt in words. Both were soldiers as young men and politicians for the rest of their lives. Both liked their cronies and being surrounded by old familiar faces, and sitting a long time over dinner telling tales of days gone by.

Churchill was, I believe, loved by those who worked for him in his household; so was Hitler, as witness the book of reminiscences by his chauffeur, Kempka, written and published at a time when it was unpopular, even dangerous, to defend his memory in any way at all.

Both men were leaders. It has often been told how Churchill encouraged with his speeches the will to resist and the will to fight of his countrymen. Hitler did the same. General de Gaulle wrote:

'L'Allemagne, séduite au plus profond d'elle-même, suivit son Führer d'un élan. Jusqu'à la fin, elle lui fut soumise, le servant de plus d'efforts qu'aucun peuple, jamais, n'en offrit à aucun chef . . .'

Churchill was fifteen years older than Hitler and he lived almost twenty years after Hitler's death, so that he had thirty-five more years on earth, the last of them hardly worth living, I imagine. Nobody could have loved their respective countries more than these two men, and each firmly believed he was leading to greatness and glory. In the event, both countries were diminished and weakened, the victor and the vanquished, a result for which each blamed the other. Both of them were ruthless; yet gentle and kind in private life. Both rather liked the company of women but seem to have had monogamous natures. Both strove for power, and liked it when they got it.

Both were builders, each according to the means at his disposal. Churchill built a wall at Chartwell, Hitler built halls, and palaces, and had grandiose projects to build more. I remember when he came back from a visit to Rome he could talk only of Michelangelo, whom he considered Europe's greatest architect. Some of Hitler's buildings were destroyed during the war; any that were left intact were blown up after the war, for reasons best known to the dynamiters. I never understood why, because if they were as meretricious as they were supposed to be, surely they should have been preserved as an object lesson? Chartwell and its wall, on the other hand, is a place of pilgrimage for tourists.

Neither of them liked modern art, nor left-wing intellectuals, about whom they had strikingly similar things to say. Neither was partial to the goody-goodies. Randolph told me that his father, during his years as prime minister, refused to read the lesson in the church at Chequers, as most prime ministers apparently do; had there been a church on the Obersalzberg I have no doubt that Hitler would have refused to do whatever the Catholic equivalent of reading the lesson may be. Hypocrisy was not among their failings.

Of course there were many differences too. Churchill was a bon vivant, Hitler was not. Hitler loved music, Churchill preferred six-pack bezique for relaxation. If some stage production appealed to them they went to its performance over and over again: Hitler to *The Merry Widow*, for example, Churchill to a brilliantly realistic play, *St. Helena*, about Napoleon's imprisonment on the windy island.

Probably the supreme moment in Hitler's life was when he drove into the old Ostmark at the time of the Anschluss; to Braunau where he was born, to Linz where he had been at school, to Vienna where, as a very young man, a 'failure', he had dreamed of a great German Reich which, by his efforts, had now become reality. Everywhere he was greeted by crowds of cheering people throwing flowers in his path. It must have been a pinnacle, far surpassing his conquests during the first years of the war.

Churchill's moment of triumph was flawed. At the time of victory he already knew well that the victory was hollow. The conferences at Teheran and Yalta had made it abundantly clear to him that having defeated Germany he had helped to bring communism into the heart of Europe, and that President

Roosevelt, every bit as much as Stalin himself, was bent upon the destruction of the British Empire. There is a famous photograph of the three of them sitting together at Yalta of which de Gaulle remarked: 'Two farmyard pigs and a wild boar'; the wild boar was Stalin. Churchill already knew that England was too weak to be heeded, let alone to resist its all-powerful allies. The title he gave his book about the end of the war tells it all: *Triumph and Tragedy*.

Hitler died by his own hand in the agony of total defeat, and with him died a few of the people who had loved him best. Churchill lived on for endless twilight years. He too was surrounded by people who loved him. Who knows what his thoughts may have been as he sat gazing absently into space? During the war he had enjoyed himself, perhaps too obviously. Photographs of him in the papers, wreathed in smiles, accompanied by one or two lovely daughters in assorted uniforms, may slightly have irritated his fellow countrymen as the war dragged on. Be that as it may, when in 1945 they had the opportunity to do so they voted him out of office.

Probably the protagonists of these exceptional men will disagree with the analogies I have drawn. Soon after the war I met an old Australian lady who told me she admired Hitler. 'You knew him,' she said, 'is it true that he had beautiful hands?' I replied that his hands were white and shapely, and I added: 'Strangely enough, they were very like Churchill's.'

'Oh no,' she cried, 'I can't believe that! I'm sure Churchill has got ugly hands.' (In point of fact his were the finer.)

This is typical of many people who reject truth in even the most trivial matters if it conflicts with a prejudice. It applies not only to enthusiasts but to some who should know better, including university dons who write 'history'. They are so carried away by their likes and dislikes that they leave the path of truth. It is all of a piece with literary critics who cannot bring themselves to praise a book, even a novel, written by a political opponent. This intellectual dishonesty makes the critics themselves look foolish. I cannot remotely imagine pretending not to admire or enjoy Aragon's novel *La Semaine Sainte*, for example, or Sartre's play *Le Diable et le bon Dieu*, or his brilliant book *Les Mots*, simply because I do not share the political opinions of these gifted writers. Left-wing critics are now getting to work on Solzhenitsyn, who has committed the sin of saying that communist dictatorship has proved more brutal than dictatorships of the Right. Because of this they are beginning to say that Solzhenitsyn is not much of a writer after all. He will not suffer from this; he shines, as a man and as a writer, light years above and beyond such people.

I have not mentioned a hobby shared by these great antagonists: both were amateur artists. Their pictures make large sums in the salerooms, but this is doubtless not unconnected with their fame in other spheres.

Schiller says: 'Verwandt sind sich alle starke Seele'—all strong spirits are related. Churchill and Hitler were strong spirits, and they were related, and perhaps each contained within himself a seed of destruction, something which is by no means an inevitable ingredient of a 'starke Seele'. General de Gaulle wrote about Hitler's death words which may be true:

'Pour le sombre grandeur de son combat et de sa mémoire, il avait choisi de ne jamais hésiter, transiger ou reculer. Le Titan qui s'efforce de soulever le monde ne saurait fléchir ni s'adoucir. Mais, vaincu et écrasé, peut-être redevient-il un homme, juste le temps d'une larme secrète, au moment ou tout fini.'

If so, the tear will have been for Germany; not for himself.

Among the fulsome eulogies which accompanied Mao Tsetung to his grave a discordant note was struck by a writer who pointed out that not only had Mao fallen upon the peaceful neighbouring country of Tibet and destroyed it, with its ancient culture, utterly; he had also killed many millions of his countrymen for the crime of not being communists. Yet the Chairman's foreign visitors, leading politicians in their own countries and not particularly gullible, found a man of immense charm and gentleness. Is it a mystifying paradox? In my view, it is not.

27

A Vale of Tears

MY GRANDMOTHER DIED when I was twenty-one, and her funeral at Batsford was the first I ever attended. Her coffin was carried by her four surviving sons. The service astonished and shocked me, with its emphasis not only on sorrow but on misery. How could the glorious world, filled with varied beauties both natural and man-made, with the pleasures of all the senses, not to mention the joys of friendship and love, how could all this be described as nothing but a vale of tears? It seemed like sacrilege to me then, and wholly unsuitable for Grandmother, whose long life had been so happy, and who was good and beloved. Now that I am old I see that the vale of tears and my youthful vision of a perfect world exist side by side, the shade and the light. Both happiness and unhappiness are transitory, and therefore the secret of life is to treasure every moment of good luck and to bear the other with what fortitude one may.

In the spring of 1963 we sold our Irish house, and henceforward the Temple was our only dwelling. We had spent most of the winter in London, and I thought Muv seemed very frail; so much so that we made a half-hearted attempt to stop her going to the island, and Pam tried to persuade her to spend the summer with her in Gloucestershire, but she was determined to go up to Scotland. Madeau Stewart volunteered to look after her on the journey, and hardly had they arrived than telegrams flew to us all to say that Muv was ill.

Nancy, Pam, Debo and I hurried up from various directions as quickly as we could. I flew from Paris to Glasgow and there I caught a bus to Oban. I had no heart for the picture gallery, and although I knew I should be stuck in Oban overnight it seemed desirable to get there because nearer to my objective. It was not quite eight when I got to the hotel. I was given a room, but no dinner, and I was told there were no restaurants in Oban where one could eat after seven.

Unlike the French, the Scotch will have no truck with any notion about a customer being always right; so wrong, in fact, is the customer that they almost succeed in making him feel guilty as well as hungry. Very grudgingly, a cheese sandwich was produced. I was much too sad and anxious to be cross, and sat in the cheerless lounge where it was to be broad daylight for many a long hour trying to telephone for news. The post office lady at Gribun said my mother was no worse.

Next day I arrived at teatime; it was her birthday, the tenth of May; she was eighty-three. She was obviously very ill. She had her four daughters, Madeau Stewart, two nurses and her devoted island people, the boatman and his family, her cook and maid, with her. Two of my grandchildren, Patrick and Marina Guinness, were also there when I arrived, with Nanny Fitzgerald. The children, aged five and six, were beautiful and kind. When taken in to see Muv they spoke loudly enough for her to hear, telling her how they had spent their day. She loved them. One evening I said to Patrick: 'Perhaps better not go in to see Granny Muv tonight, she's very poor,' and he replied in the pretty Irish voice he had when he was a small child: 'Is it poor she is? She must have been a wealthy young lady once, for she has everything so nice here.'

I repeated his words to Muv, it was one of the last times I saw her laugh, and as the sad days went by she said from time to time: 'I'm not a very wealthy young lady today.'

The children went back to Ireland, and Desmond came to the island to say goodbye. Dr. Flora Macdonald came over from Mull except when it was too rough, but there was little she could do. Parkinson's disease had my mother in its grip, she talked with difficulty and could hardly swallow. If one said: 'How do you feel?' she answered: 'I feel like death,' and she wished to die. We helped her to the window to see her Shetland pony foal, Easter Bonnet, who was destined to become a champion. She could no longer read, or even scrabble.

A very saintly man, Mr. Ogilvie Forbes, came and stayed on the island to help us. He understood the boats. One day he took us across the water to a tiny uninhabited island to see the birds' nests. When we jumped ashore a cloud of squawking, shrieking sea-birds, every imaginable species of gull and duck, flew into the air and hovered anxiously and noisily about while we picked our way among innumerable nests, thick on the ground. The moment when all the birds flew up in the air put me in mind of when Faust's old coat gets a shake and the insects and moths fly out all chattering together.

We took it in turns to sit with Muv, she liked to have one of us there and the one she liked best was Pam, calm and practical. Then she fell into the sleep they call coma. When she died, Mr. Ogilvie-Forbes got a piper who played a lament as she made her last journey over the sea to Mull in the *Puffin*. She was buried near Farve at Swinbrook. We were in the vale of tears, and I felt suddenly twenty years older.

My mother's loyalty to us was wonderful. She was devoted to M., and he to her. When she was in London, even after she became old and frail, she insisted on going to his meetings. Once in Kensington Town Hall some well-wisher had put tear gas in the heating system; the audience coughed and spluttered and tears poured from our eyes. Muv was undaunted. While the politicians ran the country downhill, she recognized in M. the combination of intelligence and character which could have halted our further decline, despite the war which had proved so costly to Britain. She never forgave the politicians who had imprisoned M. and his patriotic followers during the war; she was outraged when they instituted imprisonment without trial, something previously reserved for Ireland and our colonies, in England itself.

Her intelligence, common sense and uncompromising honesty were out of the ordinary, but it is her love, and her laughter, that make her irreplaceable. Not only did my four sons mourn her but also my grandchildren. Their great-grandmother and her fascinating island had been part of their lives as long as they could remember; for them too it was the end of a chapter.

During the *événements* in Paris in May 1968, in what was to prove her last illness-free spring, Nancy and I talked several times a day on the telephone. The troubles had blown up in a storm when the political sky had seemed cloudless. The automatic telephone was one of the few things which still worked, despite the general strike. Trains and buses were at a standstill, there was no post, no newspapers, the petrol pumps were dry. At the height of the crisis, Nancy rang me up to say: 'The General has left Paris and nobody knows where he is!' De Gaulle had flown, without even telling his prime minister, Georges Pompidou, where he was going. The moment I heard this piece of news, it came to me in a flash that he must have gone to Germany, where the army was stationed. I said: 'I expect he's gone to see the generals,' and this proved to be the case. As my guesses are often wrong, I cannot resist boasting that just for once I guessed right. After this things gradually went back to normal, the student's barricades were cleared off the streets of the quartier latin, there was a large all-round increase in wages, and at the elections a big swing to the right; but for de Gaulle it was the beginning of the end.

Nancy's long and painful illness lasted nearly five years; it began towards the end of 1968. She had moved from the rue Monsieur to a house she bought in Versailles; a house associated in my mind with suffering and misery. Nancy herself liked it, and she loved its little garden. Ever since she had lodged in Versailles while writing *Pompadour* and *The Sun King* she had been in love with the place, and made up her mind to live there. She let the garden rip, saying it was a *champ fleuri*, and so it was in May and June. During the other months it looked rather neglected and tussocky, until in the winter the uncut grass turned yellow and grey. Like Lady Evelyn Guinness forty years earlier, she preferred it so.

Early in 1969 Nancy came up to Paris, and as we often did we spent the day together. Before going back to Versailles she suggested, as it was a mild afternoon, we might sit for a while in the gardens of the Palais Royal.

She said quietly: 'I've got very bad news about Mark. He's dying.' Mark Ogilvie-Grant was unique in Nancy's life; probably he was to her what my brother Tom had been to me. They wrote to one another constantly, and she stayed with him in Athens almost every summer. She used to say: 'Mark locks me into the house at night while he goes out Jekylling and Hyding,' and Mark laughed indulgently. Now she was deeply sad. He had been unwell of late, and had gone to London for medical tests. Cancer of the œsophagus was diagnosed; he had an operation and died about a week later. Mark's death was a cruel blow to

Nancy, already feeling none too well herself, and henceforward nothing seemed to go quite right for her.

Her last book, *Frederick the Great*, she finished when she was already ill. She bravely travelled to east Berlin and Dresden accompanied by Pam and Mr. and Mrs. Richard Law, in order to see Potsdam, Sans Souci, the Neues Palais, and as many places as possible built by or associated with the Prussian king. She had hoped to go to Silesia, but was not well enough. I followed their journey with anxiety, wondering how Nancy would stand the effort involved. She and Pam wrote often, from cheque-point Charlie (Pam's inspired spelling) onward. Despite bouts of pain Nancy enjoyed everything, including (according to her) delicious food, vegetables and above all potatoes 'tasting like they did when one was a child'. Apparently this was because they were not grown in artificial manure, and the official in charge of the party told her that before long there would be plenty of fertilizers to make the potatoes taste of nothing; he was quite cross about the fuss the sisters made of the delicious 'D.D.R.' potatoes.

In one of Frederick's castles Nancy became friendly with the learned curator, who spoke French. She promised her a copy of the book, and as soon as it was published she put it in the post. It came back unopened; the curator was not allowed to receive a book from the west.

As Nancy knew no German I translated what was necessary, Frederick-William's letters to his son, and the replies, for example, and as a reward (and perhaps also because we had both been so amused by Carlyle's *Frederick*) she dedicated the book to me. 'It's not only the best book I've ever written, it's the best book I've ever read,' she said.

Reading was her solace during those horrible years of illness. Everyone sent her books, knowing how she dreaded a bookless day; Heywood Hill's, Hamish Hamilton, friends and relations and writers, but she was not always pleased. 'I can't think what's come over the shop,' she used to say. (Heywood Hill was always 'the shop'.) 'How can they imagine I'm going to read *this*?' and into the poubelle went the offerings. The truth was we were all at our wit's end. In order to satisfy, the book had to interest or amuse, it must not be too dry, or entail too much effort, yet the silly and trivial exasperated her. Trollope was a stand-by, for luckily she had read hardly any of his novels before, but she preferred something to make her laugh aloud. The first volume of Malcolm Muggeridge's 'Chronicle of Wasted Time', *The Green Stick*, entranced her. 'It's dazzling,' she said; and she loved *Girls will be Girls* by Arthur Marshall. The only magazine she enjoyed was *Private Eye*; it made her laugh, though as she seldom read a newspaper one had to explain the background of some of the jokes. Other magazines from England and America lay in heaps, unopened.

During those terrible years I realized that laughter can, up to a point, chase away pain. Often when I arrived to sit with her she would be lying in misery, and after a while she could sit up and be as funny and brilliant as ever. My theory was that this had a physiological reason: the blood ran faster and the pain diminished. This is probably nonsense, medically speaking; but what do doctors know about pain? (Or care, one might add. It sometimes seems to be the last thing that worries them.)

Yet except for a few great friends and her sisters, Nancy dreaded the company that might have cheered her. She feared the onset of her pain, and that she would be obliged to send people away when they had made the effort to come down to Versailles. This made me regret the rue Monsieur.

The pain (it was an ache, a cramp, in her back and her leg, and was thought to be rheumatism, or something to do with her spine) generally came on in the morning, and it was then that she wrote innumerable letters to sisters and friends. Upon receipt of these letters, a pathetic mixture of jokes and despair, the friends would write to me. Surely, they would say, something could be done to help her? The truth was that, until very late in the day when it was discovered that she was suffering from a rare form of cancer, all the things we did and all the miseries she submitted to simply made her worse. The diagnosis, when it came, was too late to save her.

Almost the worst of the miseries of those years were endured in the Rothschild hospital in Paris, where she had painful tests. There were no private rooms and she was obliged to share a double room; during her stay she had three different roommates; unluckily they went from bad to worse, and the last of the three did unmentionable things which drove Nancy into the depths of depression. I am not at all sure that, if one cannot be alone, a ward is not preferable to sharing a room with one insensitive and stupid person. When the day of deliverance came I fetched her in an ambulance, which tore along the road to Versailles at top speed ringing its alarm non-stop, a thrilling race which she very much enjoyed. M. and I interviewed the hospital doctors. The tests had shown nothing at all, so that the whole uncomfortable sojourn had been useless. The pain went on as before.

The same uselessness applied also to the quacks and the real doctors she consulted, the former recommended by friends as healing wonder-workers. We spent our lives in waiting-rooms, nervously looking at *Match* or *Elle* and hoping against hope for the cure that never came. Although these outings combined the maximum of boredom for us both with exhaustion for Nancy, I believe they were worth while. It was important to be able to hope, and to be trying to find the cure which eluded her. Strangely enough, both the quacks and the doctors shared the same formula. When she telephoned after a week or so to tell them there had been no improvement in her condition since the new treatment, and that the pain plagued her as before, they always had the same answer.

'Ah! You must give it time! At least three weeks!' After twenty-two days she would say sadly: 'The three weeks are up.'

I went away to Venice each summer, and Debo, Kitty Mersey, Pam, Cynthia Gladwyn, Billa Harrod or Dig Yorke came over from England in turns to be with her, also Decca from America. I must have told Nancy in a letter that, arrived in Venice, I had slept the clock round, for she wrote back: 'Why were you so tired? You haven't been doing much, have you?' She had no notion of the anxieties, the telephonings, the conferences with doctors, the emotional wear and tear of being a helpless on-looker while she suffered. It is a terrible thing to see a person close to one gripped in incurable disease.

Occasionally I felt almost sorry for the doctors, upon whom she could not resist pouring out witty sarcasms. Bedside manner is more important than healthy people realize, and attempts at a sort of hearty familiarity mixed with an implied: 'Don't worry, leave it all to me. I know best' attitude infuriates a clever though medically ignorant patient who is getting steadily, and visibly, worse day by day. To one of her doctors she wrote: 'If I were as bad at writing books as you are at curing people I should starve.'

During several months when she was in a London hospital Pam and Debo took over. Once when I visited her there she asked me to get her an alarm clock. She wanted to set it so as to be sure not to miss a wireless programme: *'All gas and gaiters.'* No visitor, nurse or doctor was allowed into Nancy's room when *'All gas and gaiters'* was on the air.

She came back to France to die. When spring came we moved her bed to the window so that she could see her *champ fleuri*, at its very prettiest with moon daisies, buttercups and poppies under the apple blossom.

Nancy's illness taught me many things, of which the gloomiest is that the theory that doctors have mastered pain is rubbish. 'With these marvellous new drugs, nobody need suffer now,' people say. Nancy had all the marvellous drugs, in ever-increasing quantities, and until she entered the final coma and life was slipping away, she suffered. As with my mother's last illness, when it was obvious that she could not recover and her miseries became too great to be borne, the bitter moment came when I found myself wishing she could die; her own reiterated wish. The unfairness of it overwhelmed me; why should she die when she enjoyed life so much, and gave pleasure to millions with her books? I felt, like Simone de Beauvoir and her sister when their mother died (*'Une mort très douce'*), that were it not for the fact that it happens to every one of us soon or late, the 'injustice' of it would be beyond bearing.

She died on the last day of June, 1973, and we took her ashes to Swinbrook, where the little church was full of friends and relations, many of them the very same as had come to Unity's funeral twenty-five years before. The liturgy is, miraculously, unchanged. It is a marvel that somebody has not improved upon 'the twinkling of an eye', substituting 'one-tenth of a second' in place of the beautiful, imaginative words. And the vale of tears? Yes, up to a point, Nancy's life had its share of tears. But in her books, and for her friends, she invented wonderful laughter, and the longer I live the more I value this gift. It is a sign of sharp intelligence, and it gives endless pleasure.

Nancy's biographer was her old, much-loved friend Harold Acton. He sat at a great table in a disused room at Chatsworth,

it was smothered in her letters: to Muv, to Mark, to Alvilde
Lees-Milne, Mrs. Hammersley and many more. He wrote *Nancy
Mitford: A Memoir*, using these letters in such a way that one
hears her voice all through his book. Pam and Debo and I went
in and out, disturbing him, my sisters accompanied by enormous
dogs whose wagging tails swept the letters off the table and
on to the floor. Harold worked for long hours, and renewed
himself among the beauties in which Chatsworth abounds:
pictures, books, gardens and the wintry park with its huge and
aged oaks. He took his choice of letters back to Florence, and
soon his book was ready.

28

Laughter and the Love of Friends

AT THE END of a long life it seems to me true that Belloc's 'laughter and the love of friends' are indeed among the things that have made it worth living; friends, and relations. Although I believe in Wahlverwandtschaft, elective affinity or the relationship of choice, which has given me a supremely happy marriage, I treasure my sisters, children, step-children and grandchildren, and the amusement of shared jokes with clever descendants. Tolstoy says happy families are all alike. Ours is a happy family, but it should never be forgotten that luck can change overnight. It can happen to anyone, as it happened to Balzac's Curé de Tours, that a seemingly perfect and well-regulated life quite suddenly begins to unravel and disintegrate. Therefore a wise person will cherish every moment of contentment, amusement or ecstasy as it comes.

I have written pages here about Nancy and Unity and almost nothing about my other sisters, but since they are such an important part of my life I must try to sketch them in, however superficially. Pam's kindness to M. and me at various dire moments in the past I have already described. There is nothing she would not do for a sister; she is boundlessly staunch and generous. Pam is a real country person, like Farve. Like him, she prefers animals to people, and woods and fields to any town. She lives in a charming house in Gloucestershire with a Beatrix Potter view, not one ugly thing in sight. Her food is perfection. She has got an un-rivalled memory for the food of long ago, and can describe a dinner eaten in 1930 as though it were yesterday. Her descriptions are idiosyncratic: 'Nard, isn't hare soup the richest, loveliest soup you ever laid hands on?'

When Muv was dying, and throughout Nancy's illness, Pam was the one they longed for—so kind, so practical, so calm.

'I assure you I hardly ever open a book. Of life, though, my experience has been very wide.' The words are Zuleika Dobson's, and Zuleika has a good deal in common with my sister Debo. When the hero of Max Beerhohm's novel says to Zuleika: 'Yet you often talk as though you had read rather much. Your way of speech has what is called a literary flavour,' Zuleika replies: 'Ah, that is an unfortunate trick which I caught from a writer, a Mr. Beerbohm, who once sat next to me at a dinner somewhere.' A great many writers have at one time or another sat next to Debo at dinner, and most of them have become her bosom friends. At least one, Patrick Leigh-Fermor, has suspected her of being a secret reader. If one asks Debo: 'Have you read so-and-so?' the answer is an angry and impatient: 'Of *course* not.' Myself, I incline to the view that, just as some people pretend to have read what they have not, so Debo pretends not to have read what she has. Is it possible to be so clever, so funny, so original and so well-informed without, just occasionally, opening a book? (She admits to reading poetry.) Possibly it is; but as to Zuleika's 'literary flavour', Nancy's books are a positive catalogue of jokes and turns of phrase invented by Debo; next to Farve, she is the most important source, and her sayings are scattered through all Nancy's post-war novels. Debo's letters, scribbled in the train, at the hairdresser or between times at an agricultural show, are fantastic in their flights of fancy and their funniness; her descriptions of people and of scenes sharply in focus.

Of my sons I shall not speak; they are too close. Jonathan and Ingrid were divorced; I forbore to cavil, remembering my own youth. Both have married again, both are happy and pleased. The last of my boys to marry was Alexander; he married Charlotte Marten who, like me, comes of a big country family; she is the loveliest and cleverest girl one could ever imagine.

Next to loved relations and friends, the greatest luck is to live in beautiful surroundings. The little Temple with its classical perfection of design gives unending pleasure. Since the war I have arranged more than a dozen houses and flats, some quite big, others very small. Each time when at the end of my labours I have shown the results to M., he has said, like Seismos in *Faust*:

Und hätt'st du nicht gerüttelt und geschüttelt,
Wie wäre diese Welt so schön?

(And had it not been for your upheavals, how could this world
have become so beautiful?) He always liked the results of my
'upheavals', but it never stopped him selling and moving on,
each time for excellent reasons connected with his politics, all
he minds about. The exception has been the Temple, where
we have lived on and off for twenty-six years and where, if
such a thing were possible, I should like to live for ever and
ever.

We have seen the trees and hedges we planted there grow,
framing the house and hiding a garden full of flowers and
shrubs and roses and honeysuckle, delicious scents and bright
colours reflected in water. Here I work all summer, regretting
my gardening ignorance and often referring to my bible: *The
Small Garden* by Brigadier C. E. Lucas Phillips.

When we first lived at Orsay we used to take a short cut
from the Paris road across fields to get to the Temple, bumping
over the grass. One autumn evening I was driving with Debo
and out of the mist loomed a camel; he put his great head to
the car window and had a look at us. He belonged to a circus;
next day he was gone. Now municipal playing fields, wide
motor-roads and groups of villas have appeared where the circus
animals used to be turned out to graze. Acre upon acre of
market gardens and strawberry beds, cultivated for thousands
of years, have been destroyed and coated with concrete for the
innumerable commuters to Paris. Fortunately for us, the Temple
is in a valley with a little vista of trees and water. Had there
been a 'view' it would have been spoilt by now, but it has
remained, a small oasis in a suburban desert.

When the summer ends and it is cold and wet, Paris is only
half an hour away. Seen from a distance, for example from the
terrace in the park at St. Cloud, it is easy to get the impression
that Paris has been completely ruined since the war. Julien
Green noted truly in one of his books that the view from St.
Cloud could just as well be of Detroit. Yet despite the disastrous concrete towers ringing the city and planted in a
haphazard way within it here and there (the most incongruous
are at Montparnasse and the Halle aux vins) when one is

walking in the centre of Paris one sees little that is ugly; more often than not the towers are masked by the familiar old streets and squares. Many vistas on the other hand have been spoilt, and it is shocking to look up the Champs Elysées from the Carrousel and to see above the Arc de Triomphe, where there should be only sky, the absurd new skyscrapers of the Defénse. Fortunately President Giscard d'Estaing has forbidden any more towers to be built; it is a case of better late than never.

Paris is still a lovely city; there are still traces of a *douceur de vivre* not found elsewhere. More people have witty things to say; more people are perfectionists; there are hundreds of brilliant cooks, dozens of gifted dressmakers, any number of clever, meticulous artisans. One day, ordering curtains from my tapissier, he showed me two kinds of curtain rings from which to choose; they looked identical, but on close examination one was solid and expensive while the other was lightweight and cheap. The tapissier picked up the cheap ring, and saying angrily: 'Voilà ce que je pense des anneaux creux!' he flung it into the dusty and cobwebby recesses of his old shop. The second rate is ruthlessly discarded.

A sad change in the streets of Paris of recent years is that the priests have abandoned their soutanes and now dress 'en clergyman' in grey flannels, while the beautiful habits of the nuns, each, as Marthe Bibesco once pointed out, in the fashion of the century when their order was founded, are no longer worn. Inside the churches a stern puritanism is the order of the day.

When I awake in Paris my spirits rise; there is an exhilarating lightness in the atmosphere. There is a feeling that something agreeable is about to happen, and very often it does. The legend that the French are inhospitable to strangers is completely untrue. Nobody could love their friends more than I do, but with a few exceptions who have come into this account of my life I shall not mention the living. A catalogue of their delightful virtues would quickly pall; they know very well they are doted upon and appreciated by me, and none more so than our Paris friends.

I am glad I saw Paris before the skyscrapers were built, and that I knew the Ile de France before the demographic explosion and the motor car together transformed it into a maze of

motor-roads and built-up areas. I regret places I could have
seen before the war and did not. I wish I had visited Jerusalem
before it was ruined by blocks of flats, I wish I had been to
India, to Indochina; my advice to the young is hurry! Go to
Dordogne before the grand panorama is all dotted with villas,
go to Greece. I am happy to have lived in the English country
as Laurie Lee describes it in *Cider with Rosie*; and even to
have known poor old Hyde Park before the Knightsbridge
barracks were pulled down to make way for the obscenity
which has wrecked the place; and to have seen Dresden before
it was bombed.

Malraux once wrote: 'Le musée est, après tout, ici bas, ce
qui donne la meilleure idée de l'homme.' Unfortunately this
is becoming daily more true, as man destroys the sublime
works of his ancestors out of doors while death duties, threat
of thieves and high insurance premiums gradually banish
pictures from the walls of private houses, including those which
are open to the public. Having seen how the galleries in
Washington and New York show their treasures, I no longer
mind so much when European art crosses the Atlantic. Com-
mercialism and crowds are more destructive than bombs, and
since we live in a barbarous age I count myself lucky to have
been to Stonehenge as it was when Hardy wrote *Tess of the
d'Urbervilles*, and that I saw Paestum as Goethe saw it.

Another lucky chance; I heard all Wagner's operas many
times before it became the fashion to dress them up in a
ridiculous way. Even Flagstad singing Isolde would have been
slightly diminished had one been obliged to look at a row of old
coats hanging on a line, or whatever the latest innovation may
be. Only Wagner attracts these oddities. With my musical
friend Geoffrey Gilmour I have heard many marvels at the
Paris Opera, *Don Carlos*, for example, and *Turandot*, perfectly
sung and with splendid decor by the brilliant Jacques Dupont,
in recent years. The vogue for spoiling Wagner's operas will
surely pass.

I am also glad I had the good fortune to know various men
and women whose fame reverberates down the years; painters,
writers, politicians, and can measure what is written about
them against my own experience. History is not necessarily
either objective or true, depending as it does so largely on the

prejudices of the historian. Probably this does not greatly matter, but once the fact is recognized it encourages scepticism about received ideas.

Index

Muggeridge, Malcolm, 258, 263;
 *Chronicles of Wasted Time, The Green
 Stick*, 278
Murasaki, Lady, 1; *The Tale of Genji*
Mussolini, Benito, 48, 151

Napoleon, 210, 250
Neame, Alan, 251
Nelson, Mrs., 200
Ney, Marshall, 111
Nicolson, Hon. Sir Harold, 72
Nietzsche, 2, 87
Noailles, Vicomte de, 234
Noailles, Vicomtesse de, 125
Norman, Lady Florence, 13
Norman, Ronald, 13
Norman, Sibell, Mark and Mary, 13, 39
Nuffield, Viscount, 166

Odom, Mr., 162
Ogilvie-Forbes, Mr., 274, 275
Ogilvie-Grant, Mark, 100, 101, 276
Ogilvy, Lady Clementine *see* Lady
 Redesdale
O'Neill, Hon. Mary (Mrs. Gascoigne),
 46
Ormsby-Gore William, 2nd Lord
 Harlech, 95
Orosdi, Mme, 50
Osmond, Dorothy, 70
Oxford and Asquith, Margot Countess
 of, 103

Painter, George, 53
Pakenham, Frank, 7th Earl of Long-
 ford, 137, 260, 263
Palewski, Gaston, 232
Parsons, Hon. Desmond, 112
Philby, Kim, 219
Philip II, 221
Philipps, Rosamond (Rosamond
 Lehmann), 83
Philipps, Wogan, 2nd Lord Milford,
 83
Phillips, Brigadier C. E. Lucas, *The
 Small Garden*, 284
Polignac, Princesse Edmond de, 247
Pine-Coffin, Mrs., 54
Pompidou, President, 276
Pope-Hennessy, James, 242
Pound, Ezra, 250; *The Pisan Cantos*,
 251
Price, Miss, 30

Private Eye, 278
Proust, Marcel, 53; *A la recherche du
 temps perdu*, 113; *La bible d'Amiens*,
 50 fn.

Quandt, Harald, 141, 208

Racine, 190, 211
Radziwill, Princess (*née* Dorothy
 Deacon), 110
Radziwill, Princess Stanislas (Grace),
 246
Ramsay, Captain Archibald Maule-,
 169, 177
Ravensdale, Baroness, 160
Redesdale, 1st Lord (Grandfather), 1,
 2, 4, 11, 12; *Memories*, 1; *Further
 Memories*, 14, 18, 26, 27, 264, 265;
 Tales of Old Japan, 1
Redesdale, 2nd Lord, 'Farve', 6–11,
 13–16, 20–27, 32–44, 56, 68, 89,
 132, 139, 144, 145, 215, 256, 257
Redesdale, Clementine Lady, 'Grand-
 mother', 1–4, 12, 16, 38, 77, 78, 273
Redesdale, Sydney, Lady, 'Muv', 6, 8,
 10–20, 22–31, 44, 47, 53, 54, 59, 60,
 78, 83, 103, 144, 154, 162–167, 170,
 171, 180, 184, 189, 191, 196–201,
 204–207, 215–217, 219, 237, 249,
 254–258, 273, –275
Reilly, Emily (Mrs. Jerry Lehane), 243
Reinhardt, Max, 91
Rennell, Lady, 132
Ribbentrop, Joachim von, 182, 183
Rilke, 87
Ritson, Lady Kitty, 2, 27
Roberts, 'Khaki', K. C., 184
Robertson, E. J., 249
Rodd, Hon. Peter, 100
Romilly, Esmond, 136, 143, 144, 207
Roosevelt, President, 205, 219
Rosse, 6th Earl of, 68
Rothschild, 3rd Lord, 91, 92
Roux, Comte Dominique de, 250, 251
Rubinstein, Ida, 105
Rudel, Hans-Ulrich, *Stuka Pilot*, 212
Russell, Bertrand, 3rd Earl, 4, 55
Ryder, Iris, 198

Sade, Marquis de, 120
Sandys, Mrs. Duncan *see* Churchill,
 Diana
San Faustino, Princess di, 92, 111